IMMIGRANTS AND ELECTORAL POLITICS

IMMIGRANTS AND ELECTORAL POLITICS

Nonprofit Organizing in a Time
of Demographic Change

Heath Brown

CORNELL UNIVERSITY PRESS   ITHACA AND LONDON

First published 2016 by Cornell University Press
First printing, Cornell Paperbacks, 2016

Printed in the United States of America

Library of Congress Cataloging-in-Publication Data

Names: Brown, Heath A., author.
Title: Immigrants and electoral politics : nonprofit organizing in a
    time of demographic change / Heath Brown.
Description: Ithaca : Cornell University Press, 2016. | Includes bibliographical
    references and index.
Identifiers: LCCN 2016018127 | ISBN 9781501704833 (cloth : alk. paper) |
    ISBN 9781501704840 (pbk. : alk. paper)
Subjects: LCSH: Immigrants—Political activity—United States. |
    Immigrants—Services for—United States. | Elections—United States. |
    Nonprofit organizations—Political activity—United States. | Community
    organization—United States. | Political participation—United States. |
    United States—Emigration and immigration—Political aspects.
Classification: LCC JV6477 .B76 2016 | DDC 324.9730086/912—dc23
LC record available at https://lccn.loc.gov/2016018127

Cornell University Press strives to use environmentally responsible suppliers and materials to the fullest extent possible in the publishing of its books. Such materials include vegetable-based, low-VOC inks and acid-free papers that are recycled, totally chlorine-free, or partly composed of nonwood fibers. For further information, visit our website at www.cornellpress.cornell.edu.

Cloth printing   10 9 8 7 6 5 4 3 2 1
Paperback printing   10 9 8 7 6 5 4 3 2 1

Contents

Acknowledgments

I began writing this book at Seton Hall University and ended it at John Jay College of Criminal Justice, City University of New York. Both institutions, especially the Department of Public Affairs at Seton Hall and the Department of Public Management at John Jay, are to thank for the support and resources they provided to help with various aspects of the project. At Seton Hall, I also received great assistance from several graduate students: Jarrod Crockett, Noah Ginter, Maria Keen, and Alex Rodas. Michael Soupios provided excellent technical assistance with fielding the survey.

So many leaders of immigrant-serving nonprofits shared their time and expertise with me. In particular, Wayne Ho pointed me in several excellent directions and supported the research. Sections of the book were presented at the annual meetings of the American Political Science Association, the Northeastern Political Science Association, and the Midwest Political Science Association, as well as at a workshop hosted by the CUNY Murphy Institute. I have to thank colleagues involved in these events and who reviewed early drafts, including Jeffrey Berry, Michael Fortner, Kristin Goss, Marie Gottschalk, Darren Halpin, Sean Harvey, Thomas Holyoke, Jane Junn, Roseanne Mirabella, Sangay Mishra, Bonnie Oglensky, Jesse Rhodes, Steven Smith, Dara Strolovitch, and Dennis Young. The Scholars Strategy Network, especially Theda Skocpol and Avi Green, helped to share some of the early analysis. Sections of the book also appeared in *Nonprofit World*, *Nonprofit Quarterly*, *Social Science Computer Review*, *Nonprofit Policy Forum*, and the *Journal of Civil Society*.

Michael McGandy traveled with me from start to finish of the manuscript, and I greatly appreciate his editorial patience and persistence, as well as the assistance of the rest of the team at Cornell.

As always, the coffee shops where I wrote this book, especially Steeplechase, Clinton Bakery, and Li'l Jays, deserve great thanks.

Finally, my family and all our immigrant stories informed and supported the book. My wife and editor, Kate Storey, made sure this book ended up in print, and I thank her for that and so much more.

POLITICAL VARIETY AND ELECTORAL EFFICACY OF IMMIGRANT NONPROFIT ORGANIZATIONS

Seated in a circle with Chinese-speaking volunteers, Julia Chung, the civic engagement associate from the MinKwon Center for Community Action, trains the group in the art and science of phone-banking.

During the two-and-a-half-hour session at the cramped New York City office of the Chinese-American Planning Council (CPC), Chung prepares the five volunteers to call hundreds of Chinese Americans, most living in the surrounding blocks in Flushing, Queens. She explains to the volunteers, a mix of Mandarin and Cantonese speakers, that the purpose of the calls they are about to make is to ask the community "what they care about most, if they have voted, and if they've run into any voting problems."[1] In part because they are less likely to vote, Asian Americans, especially those with limited English-language abilities, have been ignored in city and state politics. Chung knows that to overcome this problem, MinKwon must better understand the community's problems. She urges the volunteers not to take no for an answer and not to get discouraged when they get rejected by a voter.

After the group does some practicing, taking turns pretending to be a voter on the other end of the conversation, it's time to make the calls. There are no extra phones for the volunteers to use, no elaborate call center on site, so Chung directs them to take their seats at the desks of CPC's employees who have gone home for the day.

When the voters begin answering the calls, Chung sees her volunteers light up. "A lot of the phone-banking is done by our youth, so we have a student that is super shy—a wallflower—then we see them pick up the phone and talk to voters in Korean or Chinese, they are so comfortable, so comfortable that we are amazed," Chung says. And for the prospective voter at the other end of the line, hearing a native language builds trust and confidence. For recent Asian American immigrants—new to the country and its politics—finding a local organization they can trust means a lot. Chung explains, "MinKwon and CPC are huge names in the Chinese community, and [the voters] say 'I trust you and your organization and I know that you are a legitimate organization.'"

It's the enthusiasm of community volunteers, with the help of sophisticated technology and resources from a national philanthropic foundation, that keeps MinKwon going. Money from grants allows the small organization to pay for access to Catalist/VAN, a voter information database, which then enables the volunteers to target phone calls to Chinese-speaking residents and later go door to door mobilizing for last-minute voter turnout.[2] For a nonprofit organization with a limited budget, assistance from the community and foundations permits a significant role in electoral politics.

And the various tactics work. In 2012, MinKwon registered sixty thousand voters in New York City, and Queens elected its first Asian American woman member of Congress.

This book is about understanding how and why nonprofit organizations that represent immigrants participate in electoral politics. Asian American immigrants in New York are not atypical. Immigrants across the country tend to register and vote at low rates, thereby limiting the political power of many immigrant communities. Organizations can help to boost electoral participation through mobilization, but we do not have a clear understanding of what affects the patterns of nonprofit electoral activity. Some nonprofits, like MinKwon, adopt multifaceted political strategies, including registering new voters, holding candidate forums, and phone-banking to increase immigrant voter turnout. Other nonprofits opt to barely participate at all in electoral politics, preferring to advance the immigrant community by providing exclusively social services. In the book, I examine why these patterns of nonprofit political participation emerge in order to show how this relates to new threats to immigrants, on the one hand, and immigrant integration into U.S. society, on the other. To be sure, immigrants have been under political attack in the United States, and nonprofits can serve as a defense against the potential harm done by anti-immigrant activists. Many nonprofits, though, lack resources and fear the repercussions of venturing into politics. To investigate these issues, I interviewed dozens of nonprofit leaders and surveyed hundreds of organizations. These organizations operate in traditional centers of immigration, such as New York City, Detroit, and Chicago, as well as new gateways for immigrants across the South. To capture the breadth of the immigrant experience, I selected organizations operating in six states: Florida,

Illinois, Michigan, New Jersey, New York, and North Carolina. The stories that emerge from my research include incredible successes in mobilizing immigrant communities, such as MinKwon's registration of sixty thousand voters in New York, but also efforts to suppress nonprofit voter mobilization in Florida, and the organizational response to hate crimes directed at immigrants in Illinois.

Two Key Cases

Immigrant-serving nonprofit organizations operate in vastly different political environments and serve a variety of immigrant communities. Some parts of the country have long traditions of immigration and immigrants participating at the highest levels of politics, while others have shunned immigrants and imposed barriers on full participation in state and local politics. These variations relate to the strategies and tactics organizations employ. For example, Arab Americans began settling in Dearborn, Michigan, and working in the auto industry in the early twentieth century. They were primarily from Lebanon and Iraq, many were Christians, and some were ethnic Chaldeans, not Arabs. In their early history in Dearborn, Arab American immigrants had many needs, but there was a dearth of nonprofit organizations providing social services. In the early 1970s, a group of Arab American activists came together to form the Arab Community Center for Economic and Social Services (ACCESS) to help fill the void.[3] ACCESS aimed to provide employment, health care, and language services. Helen Samhan, a board member of the prominent Arab American Institute, described how ACCESS "built an empire of institutions that all relate to some form of human service: a job center, citizenship training, a medical center, a health center."[4]

Within a few years, ACCESS expanded from primarily direct social services to advocacy and later cultural-institution building in the form of the Arab American National Museum (Rignall 1997). As ACCESS grew more prominent in the community, Helen Atwell, one of the founders of the organization, threw her hat into the electoral ring in 1972, becoming the first Arab American city council candidate in the city's history. While she lost her race, others followed her and won elective office. ACCESS quickly grew as a source of political representation for the community, in addition to being a prominent social service resource. The Dearborn Arab American community also gained economic prowess and increasingly could help fund the growth of ACCESS—today with a staff nearing three hundred—and the creation of other organizations, including new national advocacy organizations like the Arab American Institute and later the National Network for Arab American Communities. ACCESS has been at the center of the emerging Arab American community in Michigan, and it has used this position in the local community to create a national voice and political identity for Arab Americans. In part because of the evolution of ACCESS, the community has built a strong presence in local, state, and national politics. And when the September 11, 2001, attacks happened, ACCESS worked closely with national philanthropies, such as the Ford Foundation, to respond to new threats to the community and win grants to fund its portfolio of electoral tactics. Over the last forty years, ACCESS has transformed from a mainly service-oriented nonprofit to one that uses a wide array of electoral tactics and more closely resembles an interest group.

In other parts of the country, immigrant-serving nonprofits have grown in influence not by expanding services as ACCESS did, but rather by contracting in scope to focus primarily on neighborhood issues. For example, New Immigrant Community Empowerment (NICE) was founded in the late 1990s by an attorney, Brian Pu-Folkes, in response to anti-immigrant violence in Queens, New York.[5] NICE campaigned across every borough in New York City to fight against the nativism, bigotry, and racism directed at immigrants. NICE established a mission to serve immigrant interests across a broad range of ethnicities, but at its founding, unlike ACCESS, NICE had a political focus, providing few social services to immigrants. When I met with the executive director, Valeria Treves, in her office in Queens, she described the early history as "grass-top" focused.[6]

Several years later, as funding for its political advocacy work diminished during the mid-2000s, the organization shifted to providing more direct social services. Treves recounted to me: "Our office was located near where the day laborers met," and, with no public facilities available, many began using the organization's conveniently located restroom. From this humble service to the community, NICE began providing legal and employment services directly to the growing undocumented population. "We realized that providing multiethnic, multi-language services was not feasible," Treves said. NICE soon shifted its mission and goals—employing a grassroots approach—to enhance the political and economic power of first-generation, largely undocumented workers from Latin America residing in the Queens neighborhood of Jackson Heights. Today, with a tiny full-time staff, NICE provides a host of individual services related to back pay for wages, workplace safety, and employment protection.

Following this shift in focus, NICE did not abandon politics altogether. Instead it adopted a particular electoral strategy that builds on the unique characteristics and identity of the community it represents. Because many of them are in the country without legal permission, few of NICE's constituents are legally permitted to gain citizenship, let alone obtain voting rights, yet all are capable of expressing a political voice. Using the VAN database, NICE organizes those in the community to go door to door ("door knocking") in a small segment of blocks in Queens. NICE volunteers target already registered voters and encourage them to vote, but NICE steers clear of trying to register new voters. Treves explained that, because many are not legally permitted to register, the community wanted this more limited strategy, and that anything else would be deemed inauthentic. Without authenticity, immigrant-serving nonprofits may lose that close connection to the community and the trust constituents place in organizations to best represent their interests. Over its history, NICE shifted from a broad-based, citywide political advocate to an organization that primarily provides social services to Hispanic American immigrants living in the neighborhood, along with a narrow electoral strategy.

These two nonprofit organizations, ACCESS and NICE, demonstrate some of the diverse ways immigrants receive services, representation, and collectively express a political identity. But why did each develop such different ways to participate in electoral politics? And why don't more immigrant organizations participate in elections in general? In order to move beyond individual cases and anecdotes, scholars develop theories to explain broad patterns of politics. In the case of explaining how and why immigrant organizations choose to participate or not participate in politics, however, there are relatively few solid theories. Much of the scholarship on immigrant politics has focused on immigrants as individuals. From that research (summarized in chapter 1), we know immigrants in the United States vote at lower levels than other groups, and that there is variation across each immigrant community in voting patterns. Immigrants are also less likely to engage in other political activities—what researchers often call "political incorporation"—such as protesting, running for office, and lobbying government. So we know a lot about immigrants as individuals, but we know only a little bit about the organizations that serve immigrants. (The edited volume by Ramakrishnan and Bloemraad [2008] is an exception to this tradition.) For example, we know that a larger percentage of Hispanic Americans turn out to vote compared to Asian Americans. We do not know whether the organizations that represent Hispanic and Asian Americans also differ in electoral participation.

Additionally, because most immigrants have limited representation within the world of Washington, DC, lobbying, interest group scholars have not contributed much to our understanding of immigrant-serving nonprofit organizations. Most immigrants are represented, if at all, by nonprofit organizations, which political scientists have also tended to downplay as political actors (Pekkanen and Smith 2014). This gap in political research has limited our understanding of the institutional dimension of immigrant politics and has made it difficult to fully appreciate the operations and electoral activities of nonprofit organizations. For example, we do not know whether the same factors that lead interest groups to participate in elections also lead nonprofit organizations to participate. And we do not know whether interest groups and nonprofit organizations use the same tactics and strategies. My aim is to build upon the organizational cases presented earlier to help solve the puzzle of nonprofit political participation, show the factors that lead immigrant-serving nonprofits to participate in electoral politics, and also the factors that lead to particular electoral strategies.

Throughout the book, I examine the strategies of politically active organizations, such as the MinKwon Center, ACCESS, and NICE, and also cases where immigrant-serving organizations are not fully engaged in elections and immigrants have few organizations representing their political interests. Undocumented workers reside in neighborhoods in every state, yet few have their economic and civil rights protected as they are by NICE in Jackson Heights (Bernhardt et al. 2009). And over a decade after the September 11 attacks, Arab Americans citizens still serve as convenient political targets, often with too few organizational resources to adequately defend their civil liberties in the legal and political process. In this book, I investigate these situations and the ways that nonprofit organizations provide an outlet for the political and electoral interests of immigrants, as well as situations where nonprofits remain at the sidelines of electoral politics, unwilling to participate in even the most limited electoral strategy.

Motivations and Key Research Questions

Using the 2012 election as an example, this book focuses more broadly on how nonprofit organizations, some acting explicitly as interest groups, others more implicitly so, fight for immigrants in presidential elections, statewide races, and local campaigns. The press and political pundits were right to frame the reelection of Barack Obama as president as a harbinger of the growing power of Hispanic and Asian American voters, but the media often overlook the variety of immigrant nonprofit organizations that have been working hard to energize these voters for decades. In order to deepen the understanding of immigrant politics, I seek to answer the following research questions in the book: (1) Which contexts shape how nonprofit organizations represent immigrants? (2) What drives some immigrant-serving nonprofits to engage in complex and technologically sophisticated electoral strategies and others to opt out of even the most basic electoral action? And, (3) Once an immigrant-serving nonprofit decides to participate in electoral politics, what factors relate to its choice of electoral strategy and electoral venue? This book answers these questions and shows that electoral representation differs by immigrant community, and that the particular political context faced by immigrants drives nonprofit electoral strategy. As the reelection of Obama demonstrated, the strategies have electoral efficacy and political importance.

The answers to these questions are particularly important because they explain more than merely the unique aspects of the 2012 election. First, immigration has for much of U.S. history been a salient and controversial political issue and will likely continue to be into the future, including in the 2016 campaign. Every two and four years there are hundreds of individual races in which immigration and immigrants are central to voters' decisions and to voting outcomes. In some parts of the country, Hispanic and Asian American immigrants are sought after as the critical votes in closely contested races, and in other parts of the country, such as Florida and Tennessee, they have been implicitly targeted for suppression through a variety of means to limit voter participation.[7] Immigration itself has been a heated policy debate in recent races as a potential linchpin for innovation and high-skilled job growth, and in other cases immigration has been the basis to compete over who would construct the biggest border fence.

Second, these questions matter because evidence shows that unlike most of the *ineffective* mobilization done by national political parties, when local organizations mobilize immigrant voters, turnout can increase significantly (García Bedolla and Michelson 2012; LeRoux and Krawczyk 2013). Despite the potential benefit of get-out-the-vote (GOTV) work, local organizations have always struggled to fund operations, leaving little room for new electoral activities and the potential gains from community-led mobilization. Some organizations rely on the support of philanthropic foundations that have for a century attempted to better assimilate and integrate immigrants into U.S. society. In chapter 2, I show how foundation grants force organizations to balance their unique missions to provide diverse social services with a growing sense of political empowerment to affect local, state, and national policy making.

Third, these are significant questions because local and state context varies considerably. Immigrants reside in greatly different communities, some rich with immigrants and others with very few. In chapter 3, I show how very different local political campaigns—exemplified by six different cases—relate to immigrant voters, immigrant candidates, and immigrant-serving nonprofit organizations. The local context, whether city or county politics, is especially important for immigrants because most immigrant communities are too small to dent the national political scene. It is more likely in the near term that immigrants can be better represented in municipal affairs if organizations provide an effective voice in local elections.

Fourth, these are important questions to answer because the particular civic characteristics and political attitudes of immigrants shape the nonprofits that serve them. Since their legal and political status is intrinsically connected to their identity, when it comes to the issue of voting, immigrants differ too greatly from other social groups—such as the elderly, the disabled, or environmentalists—to treat immigrant-serving organizations in the same way we do other types of organizations. Immigrant-serving nonprofits mirror many of the political characteristics of their community. For example, when I spoke with a leader from the Korean American Community Center of Princeton (KCCP), he explained that "during an election year . . . different leaders will come asking for our vote," but because the older generation does not prioritize politics, "[politics] isn't what we do."[8] KCCP and other immigrant organizations reflect the complexity of the general immigrant experience, but also the particular immigrant community in which they are based. For this reason, it is not always clear why one immigrant-serving nonprofit opts to represent the community in electoral politics and another opts not to.

Fifth, and perhaps most important, the answers to these questions matter to the health and vitality of the democracy. Organizations can act as a voice for immigrants, particularly those who lack voting rights because of their legal status. Since relatively few elected officials are immigrants, organizations can play a valuable representative function for immigrants. It is thus crucial to understand the political role played by immigrant-serving nonprofits, particularly in regard to elections.

My aim in writing this book is to use aspects of the 2012 election in order to answer these questions and better understand immigrant politics through the lens of the organizations that serve them.

Who Represents Immigrants?

Certain immigrant communities are represented by the well-known national organizations that are invited into the Republican and Democratic Parties' selection of a presidential candidate, yet many immigrants and immigrant-serving nonprofit groups are routinely forgotten during presidential campaigns. Major political parties expend few resources and give little attention to informing and mobilizing the majority of immigrants. Parties listen to immigrant organizations even less during election time. The explanation for this pervasive negligence in electoral politics can be found in the complex position of the American immigrant. Immigrants residing in the United States, today as in the past, face the problem of political duality. Their lives are shared between nationalities and ethnicities, divided between religions and languages, and split between citizenships.

Before we go much further, it is worth defining two tricky terms that are at the center of this book: immigrant, and immigrant-serving nonprofit organization. First, what it means to be an immigrant differs greatly according to whether you impose a strictly legal definition or whether you use the various conventional notions. Legally, immigration status determines a set of rights given to certain individuals living in the United States. By legal definition, immigrants are those who were born in another country and later relocated to the United States *with the legal permission of the government*—a stipulation that separates them from others. Within that category of immigrant, we can also separate those who have become *naturalized* U.S. citizens—that is, those who have completed the steps to gain nearly full constitutional rights—from those who are called *aliens*, meaning the person is legally permitted to reside in the country on a permanent basis (legal permanent resident, or LPR). LPRs are given only certain rights, like the right to employment, but not others, such as the right to vote. There are two other categories to consider: *nonimmigrant* residents, such as students or tourists, who are given temporary permission to live in the country based on the stipulations of a visa, and those who are called *undocumented aliens* or *illegal aliens*, meaning the person is residing in the country without legal permission. Nonimmigrant residents are given a small number of rights, but usually prohibited from employment rights, while undocumented aliens have almost no rights—legal, employment, or political.

These legal definitions of what it means to be an immigrant are critical to public policy debates and the lives of those living in each category, and are different from the common usage of the term "immigrant." In everyday conversation, if your parents grew up in another country but you were born in the United States, you might refer to yourself as an immigrant and identify your family as an immigrant family. In common usage, being an immigrant often has less to do with legality than with this idea of *identity*. To be an immigrant means something about identifying with another country. For this reason, people use the term "first-generation immigrant" and "second-generation immigrant" to indicate that, while someone may have been born in the United States, that person's identity is shaped by life elsewhere and a culture distinct from that of the place where the person now resides. In this way, being an immigrant has a generational dimension to it and can last decades after a family's arrival in the country. Conversely, while the legal definition renders someone who has not been granted the legal permission to reside in the United States a nonimmigrant, many undocumented residents would self-identify as an immigrant. The person may share much with legal immigrants, including language, culture, and strong ties to those living in another country. In this way, being an immigrant means feeling like a newcomer or cultural outsider, whether or not the U.S. government agrees.

Finally, what it means to be an immigrant often relates strongly to racial and ethnic identity, and the intersections or *intersectionality* of identities (Crenshaw 1991). Immigrants can have roots in any country outside the United States, yet for much of U.S. history, there have been prejudices about who belonged and who did not, including questions of race, religion, and language. The country's history with the Atlantic slave trade and the long legacy of slavery makes the relationship of immigration and ethnicity fraught with racism. Through the 1800s, newcomers from Ireland were treated with great scorn and prejudice because of ethnic and religious differences. What it means to be an immigrant has always had a lot to do with integration into mainstream society, and that has usually included a very narrow view of what means to be white. In the early 1900s, much of integration had to do with language, so Italian American immigrants who did not learn English were shunned and treated as foreigners. Language remains an important part of what it means to be an immigrant, as do race and ethnicity. Today, because most immigrants from Western Europe are quickly and easily integrated into U.S. society, the activism of the organizations that serve them is less critical to explore, and not a concern of this book. For many others, those living at the intersection of numerous contentious identities, and sometimes in the United States for decades, they remain attached to an immigrant identity, because racial, ethnic, and even language prejudice continues to position their community as outsiders.

Which Organizations Represent Immigrants?

In this book, I accept that the term "immigrant" takes on many different meanings and is inherently complicated. For some immigrants, the organizations they join serve as a way to confront these complications, maintain an identity, and integrate into new neighborhoods. I loosely define an *immigrant-serving nonprofit* as a formal organization that pursues some activity primarily as a service to immigrants, whether the organization (like NICE) does so for mainly undocumented immigrants, or (like ACCESS) for mainly second-generation immigrants, or for any other community that is strongly linked to an immigrant identity. In reality, most organizations that are at the center of this book serve an array of immigrant types, and therefore it would be unwise to try to divide up immigrant-serving organizations in ways that were not true to the varied immigrant identities that they pursue.

Immigrant-serving nonprofit organizations, including community-based organizations, civic groups and hometown associations, and a variety of other nonprofits, provide a mechanism for integration, for building social capital, and a means to maintain old ties (de Graauw 2008; Ramakrishnan and Viramontes 2010; Bloemraad and de Graauw 2011). These groups, many incorporated by the Internal Revenue Service as 501(c)(3) nonprofit organizations, deliver social services, naturalization assistance, and cultural activities. There are immigrant organizations that focus on protecting the rights of business owners and professionals, pushing for lower taxes, and promoting commercial activity. These organizations advance the *economic interests* of immigrants. Other organizations, like NICE, represent immigrant workers, many of whom perform the most physically taxing and often unsafe activities, and are vulnerable to withheld pay and given limited protections for their health and welfare. These immigrant-serving organizations protect immigrant rights and *labor interests*. Some groups even offer ways for immigrants—many not yet permitted the franchise—to participate in the politics of their new home. There are immigrant-serving organizations that have operated since the early 1900s, with deep and established roots in the community, that also maintain connections to the institutions of government and politics. Other organizations are brand-new, formed in the last decade, with small staffs, limited resources, and little accumulated political capital, yet still push for a say in local rule-making and public-spending decisions. These organizations, including ACCESS and the MinKwon Center, represent the *political interests* of immigrants. Immigrant-serving nonprofits pursue these economic, labor, and political interests, sometimes individually and sometimes at the same time. One of the arguments of this book is that we cannot merely look at those organizations labeled as "advocacy" or "political" organizations to represent immigrants. A variety of nonprofit organizations represent immigrants, many with a primary mission to serve educational, housing, and nutritional needs, but some also see politics and elections as compatible with an identity to best serve the community.

Old and new, rich and poor, each type of organization operates in a complex political arena, and each organization can represent immigrants to political candidates on issues critical to the community. I am also focused on formal *nonprofit* immigrant-serving organizations, meaning those organizations that operate to serve immigrants but not as a way to generate private profits. While there are for-profit organizations that benefit immigrants, ad hoc groups that serve immigrant interests, informal organizations that have not institutionalized operations, and other nonprofits that share services with immigrants and other segments of the population, I focus this book narrowly on immigrant-serving nonprofit organizations.[9] It is these nonprofit organizations that operate for the general good of immigrants that I will examine separately from those others types of organizations.

Immigrant-serving nonprofits operate in communities across the country and range in number, mission, and size. Immigrants who make up a small portion of their state or locality may not be able to support an active array of organizations. They may then be forced to rely on pan-immigrant organizations and share representation with other immigrant communities, even if their needs differ and interests conflict. Other newcomers, with no local immigrant-serving nonprofits catering to their needs, may be left out of politics entirely, detached from participating in the civic life of their new home. The local context in which immigrants reside sets political parameters and shapes the institutional representation they receive.

Once settled, a cluster of immigrants, in fashion akin to Robert Dahl's framing of local politics in his seminal *Who Governs* (1961), may slowly grow to a voting bloc courted by elected officials and then further to a political community with enough clout to run its own candidates. In the past, though, this process was instigated by local political machines that saw advantages in incorporating Irish, Italian, and German immigrants in their electoral strategies (Hochschild and Mollenkopf 2010; Golway 2014). As local parties lost interest in newer groups of immigrants, and parties eventually waned in influence, the political advancement of immigrants became increasingly abetted by nonprofits able to link immigrants together in common cause and provide them with the opportunities for pooling resources, assimilation, and acculturation (Andersen 2010; Su 2012). The movement from minor to major player in local, state, and national politics has nearly always been accompanied by organized and effective institutions. Yet it is important to remember that even with organizations in place, institutional barriers external to a community, including structural racism and xenophobia, will always make full political integration difficult for anyone viewed as an outsider—including many nonimmigrants with roots in the country that go back to the founding. This book sets out to understand immigrants and immigration through these organizations and institutions, the situations in which they engage in electoral politics, and the consequences of an organization's decision to opt out of politics.

Developing a Theoretical Model

Based on these loose definitions and pulling from various strands of previous research, I construct a theoretical model to explain the patterns of immigrant-serving nonprofit participation in elections. A theoretical model is an argument about which factors explain a particular political activity. A good theoretical model helps us move from specific cases, such as those at the start of the chapter, to understanding cases in general. For the situation of immigrant-serving nonprofits, I begin with the assumption that each organization wants to improve the lives or advance the interests of the immigrant community it serves. Some immigrant-serving nonprofits, like NICE, in Queens, improve the lives of immigrants through primarily nonpolitical activities. On the other hand, another set of immigrant-serving nonprofits, including ACCESS in Michigan, does so by acting as a political interest group and pursuing political action. One of the most important factors that explains why ACCESS is highly involved in electoral politics and NICE is relatively less involved is the political identity of the community each serves. ACCESS and NICE reflect, respectively, the different political identities of second-generation Arab Americans in Dearborn and first-generation Hispanic Americans in New York City with corresponding political activities.

My theoretical model—which I call "reflective electoral representation"—draws on lessons gleaned from scholarship on nontraditional interest groups. For example, as Jeffrey Berry has long argued, because nonprofit organizations often serve those in dire need, their political activities should be taken more seriously and be better understood. Berry and Arons (2003) found that very few nonprofits participate in politics or elections. Most remain politically inactive: cash-strapped, fearful of prohibitive governmental regulations, and uncertain about the appropriateness of political action. So one argument why many immigrant organizations, in particular, do not engage in politics may be the same argument as to why nonprofits, in general, do not engage: politics is just too expensive and sometimes against the law. This theory, though, does not do a very good job of explaining why ACCESS has been so involved in politics, since it is a nonprofit organization and faces the same regulations and resource constraints as other nonprofits.

Building on Berry's argument that the political aspects of nonprofits need to be examined, I look to explanations from interest group scholars for additional guidance. An interest group is simply an organization that operates to advance *primarily* political interests, such as the American Bus Association, which represents the political interests of private bus owners. For example, Matt Grossmann (2012) argued that the political behavior of individuals in a social group—women, the elderly, youth—spurs interest groups to form. Thus, when the political attitudes of a social group are ambivalent about politics, few organizations will form, and when political attitudes are strident and focused on political action, numerous organizations will form. He called this theory "behavioral pluralism." Behavioral pluralism explains why some communities, such as business owners, have a rich array of interest groups representing their interests in Washington, DC, while others, such as college students, are represented by barely a handful of interest groups. Perhaps behavioral pluralism explains why certain immigrant communities, like the Arab American community in Michigan, are served by numerous advocacy organizations, while other immigrant communities are served by very few.

Grossmann's theory of behavioral pluralism explains a lot about the formation of interest groups, but it does not directly address the various ways nonprofit organizations, in general, form and develop a political identity. Because I pay much more attention to a wider range of nonprofit organizations, many that are not explicitly political, I look to other scholars to extend Grossmann's theory and apply it more generally to immigrant-serving nonprofits. For example, Darren Halpin (2014) found that newly formed organizations spend a lot of time thinking about identity. Halpin argued that the founders of an organization ask basic questions such as "What is our broad mission and purpose?" and "How should we engage in policy?" To answer these questions, Halpin contended, leaders are guided by those they serve, including community members, activists, and financial donors. The community makes judgments about the authenticity of an organization and responds accordingly with lavish support, ambivalence, or outright rejection. For these reasons, an organization orients its identity (often articulated most clearly in the mission statement) to what the community does or does not want. As organizational scholars Dennis Gioia and colleagues (2010) wrote: "Organizational identity is progressively, even continuously, negotiated by organization members—via their interactions with each other and with external stakeholders" (p. 35).

It seems reasonable that these theories about organizations, particularly identity and authenticity, are also fresh on the minds of the leaders of immigrant-serving nonprofit organizations and those in the immigrant community. NICE in New York City figured out its largely undocumented immigrant members would be uncomfortable if asked to conduct a voter registration drive; so NICE adopted an identity to focus on other activities. ACCESS, on the other hand, heard the community calling for political representation, so the organization changed its mission to include a wider array of political activities. Much like a traditional interest group that fails to reflect the identity of members, an immigrant-serving nonprofit may lose the trust of its community if the organization's identity is deemed inauthentic or if the organization pursues tactics deemed inappropriate. But for a nonprofit organization, in contrast to an interest group, this sometimes means eschewing politics altogether and opting for an organizational identity and strategies that leave elections to others. By studying the full range of immigrant-serving nonprofit organizations, I demonstrate how this process of reflection happens in a variety of circumstances.

Reflective Electoral Representation

Drawing on these strands of the interest group and organizational studies literature, I offer my theory of *reflective electoral representation*. I argue that immigrant-serving nonprofits are imbued with many of the characteristics of those they serve. They reflect the complexity of the American immigrant experience, but also the characteristics of the particular immigrant community in which they are based. Immigrant-serving nonprofits are different from other types of nonprofits especially when it comes to political advocacy related to elections, because citizenship, voting rights, and political voice are so integral to what it means to be an immigrant. Unlike organizations focused exclusively on health, education, or homelessness, for example, immigrant-serving nonprofits serve those for whom voting rights (or the lack of those rights) is the glue that binds (or divides) the community. Voting is not simply a way that immigrants express a political opinion; voting and civic participation are integral to the identity of immigrants, and thus it is particularly important to understand the relationship between immigrant-serving nonprofit organizations and various aspects of electoral politics.

I conceptualize an immigrant-serving nonprofit organization adapting and evolving its identity to best reflect the community. An organization may start as a purely service-oriented nonprofit, as ACCESS was originally, providing housing or education services to local immigrants. But as it operates, leaders may recognize a changing context and new ways to authentically represent the community in the political arena. Organizational leaders ask themselves questions such as, Does the community want us to do more? Does the community want us to participate in electoral politics? The answer to these questions will be a reflection of the political characteristics of the immigrants they serve and changes in the size or composition of the immigrant community. As such, if the answers are yes, the organization may decide to develop an electoral strategy and employ electoral tactics such as registering and mobilizing immigrant voters. The organization then will begin to transition into more of an interest group. As figure I.1. shows, the organization will change from a service-oriented nonprofit to a hybrid organization, still pursuing a social mission, but with an increasingly prominent

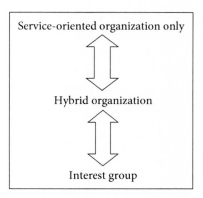

FIGURE I.1. Dynamic nature of organizational identity formation

political dimension. Later, the organization may again ask, Can we do more to authentically represent the community? If the answer is again yes, that organization, much as ACCESS did, may continue to evolve, taking on additional electoral tactics, potentially creating a new political division or entirely separate 501(c)(4) political organization. The organization would now possess an identity that is much closer to an interest group. Of course, organizational transition may occur in multiple directions: an organization that has taken an electoral strategy in the past may grow frustrated with politics and later shed or limit its political identity, similar to how NICE changed. Also, certain organizations may start as hybrid organizations or as interest groups and later add or subtract electoral tactics. My explanation here simply argues that organizational identity has a reflective and dynamic quality, and movement along this continuum does occur.

From Identity to Electoral Strategy

Thus far, the theory of reflective electoral representation suggests that nonprofits may evolve an organizational identity and increasingly take on some of the characteristics of an interest group. But in order to maintain authenticity, as an organization shifts its identity, it still must adopt electoral strategies and tactics that are compatible with the identity of the community. It also has to respond, as interest groups do, to the larger political context in which it operates. When nonprofits adopt the identity of a hybrid organization or interest group, we then can look to other theories from public policy scholars for guidance about what strategies they might employ. For example, if an organization has already decided to get involved in elections, which factors dictate its electoral strategies and where it will place the focus of its electoral work? Scholars of interest groups have developed arguments to answer this question (Schattschneider 1960; Elazar 1966; Baumgartner and Jones 1993). Drawing on these theories, I show that state political culture and dramatic focusing events drive immigrant-serving nonprofit organizations toward using tactics in certain electoral venues and away from these tactics in others—what I call *electoral venue choice* in chapter 6.

To be clear, as Berry showed, nonprofits are not free to do whatever they please. The choice to participate in an election reflects the identity of the community, but it is also made in the context of the larger political and legal environment in which the nonprofit operates. Federal and state regulations by and large allow 501(c)(3) nonprofits to participate in elections and politics, as long as (1) the organization does not dedicate a large portion of expenditures to legally defined lobbying, (2) the electoral work is nonpartisan in nature, and (3) the nonprofit does not endorse candidates for office. So I was not surprised by the answers I received when I surveyed nonprofit leaders. One responded, "Our agency is a not-for-profit organization; we are not allowed to do political activities," and another, "Other than contacting legislatures about questions our clients have or reporting on how state money is spent, we keep a low profile."

Other organizations, however, select from legally permitted options. The following list presents a range of electoral tactics available to all nonprofit organizations, including those serving immigrants. These tactics are drawn in part from recommendations made by Nonprofit Vote—an organization started in order to support nonprofits that engage voters:

Monitoring campaign news
Translating electoral information into foreign languages
Using newsletter, website, or social media to share election information such
    as the last day to register or dates of early voting
Providing voter registration forms to clients during direct services
Registering internal nonprofit staff to vote
Placing voter information in lobby or office common space
Designating staff or volunteers as election point people
Holding a voter registration drive at a community event
Conducting in-person or phone-based get-out-the-vote (GOTV) drives
Organizing candidate forums
Joining an electoral coalition with other organizations
Submitting policy recommendations to candidates
Endorsing ballot initiatives or state constitutional amendments
Writing opinion editorials for local newspapers on election issues

Monitoring news about candidates and campaigns, translating electoral information into native languages, and providing information to constituents on an organizational website, for example, are all legally permissible tactics that can be employed without significant effort or considerable public attention. Additionally, as MinKwon did in New York City, an organization might send volunteers door to door asking newly naturalized citizens to register to vote, make phone calls in two or three different languages from a call center using sophisticated databases of voter information, or hold a candidate forum and invite the community to ask those seeking its votes important questions about immigrant issues.

In chapter 4, I provide a more detailed explanation of these tactics and the various strategies they imply. The basic argument of the book is that tactics are not chosen randomly; rather they are associated with particular electoral strategies, and some organizations are more likely than others to use certain strategies.

In this book, I support my two-part theory, the first part focused on nonprofit identity and the second focused on political context, with extensive interviews and new survey data. I draw on data from surveys of immigrant-serving non-profits in six states that were chosen to reflect a variety of political cultures and immigrant demographics: Florida, Illinois, Michigan, New Jersey, New York, and North Carolina. By selecting states that vary by culture and demographics, the analysis can be generalized to immigrant-serving nonprofits in other states and a wider array of circumstances. For example, organizations in New York represent the interests of immigrants living in a city with a long and complex history of immigration. Conversely, organizations in North Carolina represent immigrants with a much shorter history in the country, yet a rapidly growing presence in the state. Many immigrants in North Carolina are undocumented and face difficult legal circumstances, while in Michigan most immigrants are second-generation, and relatively few were born outside the United States. In Illinois and New Jersey there are large Indian American communities, whereas in Florida the Asian American immigrant community is quite small while the Cuban and Jamaican American communities are large. This state geographic and demographic variation strengthens what can be taken away from the analysis. The statistical evidence in the book shows that the two factors of organizational identity and political power explain much about immigrant-serving nonprofit electoral strategy, controlling for other factors such as organizational age and resources, as well as campaign factors such as the competitiveness of the election.

Chapter Outline

The following chapters are organized to marry the political sphere with the organizational sphere as a way to show the interrelationships between immigrants, nonprofits, and electoral politics. I first present three contexts (demographic, organizational, and campaign) in which nonprofits adopt electoral strategies, before I elaborate my theoretical model and then test the theory with original data. My aim is to avoid the habit of placing organizational decision making into a vacuum, devoid of many of the historic and contemporary contexts that actually shape decision making.

Chapter 1, "The Precarious Position of Immigrants," explores the demographic shifts that took place between 2000 and 2012, which saw the composition of immigrants in the United States change greatly. Despite growing in number over the last three decades, immigrants have participated in politics at lower levels than other U.S. citizens. This chapter examines the gap in immigrant voting with the help of important findings from political behavior and political sociology research. This literature shows how varied immigrant politics are in the

United States and also suggests why nonprofit engagement in elections should draw more attention.

Chapter 2, "Foundations and Funding," places immigrant organizations into the complex, quasi-federated web of funding and grants. Immigrant-serving nonprofit organizations work at the grass roots, providing direct services to individuals. Operating high above are multibillion-dollar private philanthropic foundations that have for over a century been interested in how the country has assimilated immigrants. Since the early 2000s, major foundations have moved immigrant and voting issues to the top of their agendas and provided millions of dollars of grant funding to organizations connected with or serving the interests of immigrants. At the same time, other foundations have supported policy efforts initiated by the Tea Party movement to restrict voting rights and advocate a very different view of immigration reform. The chapter describes these two competing political trends and also asks theoretical questions about what these spikes in funding mean for the autonomous identity of nonprofits and the representation of immigrants.

Chapter 3, "You Don't Vote, You Don't Count," examines 2012 primary contests and general election campaigns in many parts of the country, in the wake of controversial 2010 congressional redistricting. In some cases, immigrants were the subject matter of these campaigns; in others, immigrants were the actual candidates. In all cases, immigrant-serving nonprofit organizations adjusted their strategies to different political situations. The chapter explores specific races and the development of voter ID laws that threatened to undermine nonprofit voter mobilization of immigrants in many states. The chapter uses these races to demonstrate six important themes that run throughout the rest of the book. It also examines national immigrant-serving organizations and their use of campaign donations in the 2012 election.

Chapter 4, "A Model of Immigrant-Serving Engagement," articulates a new model of electoral engagement for immigrant-serving nonprofits. In the political and financial landscape leading up to the 2012 election, nonprofits faced opportunities and barriers to engaging in electoral politics. I use the reflective electoral representation theory to identify several factors associated with the level of nonprofit engagement in electioneering, and the electoral venue choice theory to argue that a different set of political factors will be involved in which venue (local, state, or national) an immigrant-serving nonprofit focuses its work.

Chapter 5, "From Mission to Electoral Strategy," explains the survey methodology used to field the original questionnaire to eleven hundred nonprofit organizations in the six states. I then analyze the data collected from survey respondents with a particular focus on the first part of the theory of immigrant-serving nonprofit engagement. The evidence shows that aspects of mission, organizational resources, and policy relate to which electoral tactics an immigrant-serving non-profit makes use of. Most significantly, the new law to tighten voting procedures in Florida reduced the likelihood that organizations in that state held voter registration drives.

Chapter 6, "Choosing Where to Focus," extends the analysis from the previous chapter to the second dimension of advocacy and election: venue choice. The chapter presents an analysis of the factors related to an immigrant-serving non-profit engaging in elections primarily at the national, state, or local level. It shows that when dramatic local events occur, such as a hate crime, nonprofits tend to focus their work at that level rather than at the state or national level; but when the size of the local immigrant community is large, the group will focus more on the state or national level.

The concluding chapter, "Boldly Representing Immigrants in Tough Times," circles back to the political sphere and examines what actually happened on Election Day. How did first- and second-generation immigrant candidates (Grace Meng, Ted Cruz, and Tammy Duckworth) fare? What can we say about immigrant voting behaviors in light of what we now know about immigrant-serving nonprofit behavior? Further, given these patterns, what can nonprofits do in the future to better incorporate electoral work into their missions? And, finally, what do the findings suggest for the presidential election in 2016 and beyond? The final chapter looks ahead to future elections and recommends that immigrant-serving nonprofits consider seven issues when they decide to engage in an election: technology, staffing, institutionalization, continuous strategy, coalitions, new gateways, and authenticity.

1

THE PRECARIOUS POSITION
OF IMMIGRANTS

Part of what makes elections important to the study of immigrant-serving non-profits is that elections have historically spurred organizational formation and the use of innovative electoral tactics. New organizations and tactics have always been inextricably linked to the demographic characteristics of the time period. In the mid-1800s, organizations across New York tempted Irish immigrants to the polls with lavish picnics and the promise of representation in city politics (Golway 2014). Irish American immigrants soon gained influence over local elections and later political power in New York City government.

During recent elections, new nonprofit organizations emerged that relied on an innovative array of tactics to reach first- and second-generation immigrant voters. A good example is the nonprofit Voto Latino. Founded in advance of the 2004 election and active in 2008, Voto Latino began major mobilization work in 2010, during the decennial census. An accurate count of the people every ten years is constitutionally mandated, but this is exceedingly difficult within communities that have high numbers of non-English speakers, many of whom are dubious about completing government documents, or responding to federal officials knocking on their door. Undercounting of certain groups in the census can result in a variety of negative outcomes for those groups, including weaker political representation and fewer government services. Maria Teresa Kumar, CEO and president of Voto Latino, summarized her group's strategy to address these concerns: "Our mission was to have the census be appealing, sexy, and hip"—not an easy accomplishment for a younger demographic, as Kumar noted: "Of the twenty million eligible Latino voters, roughly half are under forty."[1] Voto Latino targeted this bubble of youth voters—many eligible to vote for the very first time in 2012—to be certain they were counted, registered, and energized.

Kumar and her Washington-based staff knew certain important attributes of this demographic: they are active users of technology; they typically do not speak Spanish as their primary language; and major political parties rarely communicate with them. Kumar said: "Latinos were the fastest adopters of smart phones . . . but nobody was talking to them and appreciating their Americaness," so major political parties were missing out on an opportunity to rally their support. "[Political parties] do a great job of communicating with their parents, but not the booming generation," she said. In 2008, younger Latinos (ages eighteen to thirty-five), both U.S. born and naturalized, were less likely to be interested in the election than older Latinos (age thirty-six and above) (Sandoval 2010). Voto Latino understood the particular identity of the audience it served and aimed to change this political pattern.

Voto Latino hired staff and built partnerships with local organizations that maintained close ties to each community in thirteen states. It purchased the necessary outreach technology for its local affiliates and gave them access to national databases of voters and local residents. With these data, the organization's staff could share messages about the census with local youth. And Voto Latino capitalized on the wide marketing and use of T-Mobile smart phones to pull in young voters.[2] Hispanic Americans were also the quickest to abandon land lines and adopt exclusively cell phone technology—49 percent of them, according to a survey by the Pew Center (Christian et al. 2010). If a young Hispanic American citizen "pledged" to complete the census form and shared this information with friends online, Voto Latino provided that person with twenty free downloads from iTunes.

The organization also recognized that social media mattered to these youth voters, but not in the way one might expect. According to Kumar, Latino youth "are very finicky about the authenticity of the voice you use to communicate with them." At the time, Facebook was the technology of their parents, but since "Latino youth were already speaking in 140 characters," to reach them you had to use Tumblr and Twitter, and use English. Voto Latino formed partnerships with Hispanic American celebrities like Rosario Dawson, Pitbull, and America Ferrera. It challenged the singer and *American Idol* judge Demi Lovato with "trending"—a phrase used within social-media platforms to promote the popularity of a word, phrase, or message—one of the key messages of the census campaign. She succeeded in less than an hour, meaning that this message to participate in the census immediately reached millions of young Latino voters and other users of Twitter.

Voto Latino was formed based on the recognition of a demographic trend, what that trend could mean to the election, but, most importantly, what the

particularities of the trend meant for strategy. Voto Latino adopted an organizational form or *identity* that mirrored the particular demographic and political
characteristics of its constituents. Young Hispanic American citizens could be
reached with technology in a way that they could not be in the past, and that
older Hispanic Americans still could not be. Social media permitted Voto Latino
to contact huge numbers of first-time Hispanic American voters in an efficient
and effective way, but only if it did so using the language and style those voters preferred (Wells 2015). Voto Latino had to pursue an *authentic* strategy, not
one grafted onto the organization by constituents outside its target community.
And by working through local organizations, rather than creating an entire infrastructure of local affiliates, Voto Latino could mobilize its community for the
census and then build on those successes and its infrastructure to rally for the
2012 election. Immigrant-serving nonprofit organizations are not merely mobilizing voters on the days leading up to an election. Electoral tactics commence
years in advance with the foundation of representational politics: accurate counting of the population.

Voto Latino was not alone in recognizing the impact of demographic changes
at the national, state, and local levels. Other nonprofit organizations saw how
the changing nature of immigration and the immigrant experience could re-
shape U.S. politics, but only if these new immigrants could be counted on to
register and then vote. Thus, demographic change is the first context into which
immigrant-serving nonprofit organizations must fit. In this chapter, I show first
how these demographic trends revealed by the 2010 census relate to research on
immigrant political participation, and, second, how political institutions, especially nonprofit organizations, have advanced and sometimes slowed immigrant
voting. This helps reveal some of the gaps in the literature on immigrant politics
and where the empirical analysis later in the book will advance the larger study
of immigrants.

The Changing Place of Immigrants

In 1950 there were 152 million American citizens. Over the next decade approximately 250,000 legal immigrants entered the country each year, most from Italy,
Germany, and Canada. Since then, following federal immigration policy changes
in the 1960s that removed restrictive country quotas, immigration expanded
considerably, along with what we know about the racial and ethnic diversity of
the country. By 1980, Mexico replaced various European countries as the largest
source of foreign-born living in the United States. At that time, around fourteen
million Americans were of Hispanic origin, and fewer than four million were

Asian or Pacific Islander (two categories that are often grouped together in the term Asian Pacific Islander American, or APIA). In the 2000s, fewer than a million new legal immigrants entered the country each year, with Latin America as the largest source. The 2010 decennial U.S. Census showed that there were 50 million Hispanic Americans residing in the United States, or 16 percent of the total 308 million U.S. population, an increase of 3 percentage points from 2000 (Ennis, Ríos-Vargas, and Albert 2011).[3]

Most Hispanic Americans in 2010 lived in three states: California, Texas, and Florida; but the recent census also showed dramatic increases in other states. The Hispanic American population in states across the South (Alabama, Mississippi, Arkansas, Tennessee, Kentucky, Maryland, and South Carolina) doubled from 2000 to 2010. And some of the fastest-growing cities in the country (Lincoln, California; Surprise, Arizona; and Frisco, Texas) were all centers of Hispanic American growth.

By 2012, the makeup of the Hispanic American population was also in flux (Lopez and Dockterman 2011). Mexican Americans made up the largest subgroup within the U.S. Hispanic population: 63 percent of the total, and a 50 percent increase since 2000. However, recent Mexican American immigration slowed compared to other groups. The number of Salvadoran Americans more than doubled (152 percent growth) between 2000 and 2010, as did the Guatemalan American population (180 percent growth). These two ethnic groups alone made up nearly two-thirds of the Hispanic American population in the Washington, DC, area. Popular notions of immigration often fail to appreciate the change and diversity of recent U.S. trends. The common perception that almost all immigration is from Mexico overlooks the spike in immigration from other Central and Latin American countries. These oversights are not surprising, but they distort an understanding of the politics of immigrants, since it is likely that the political values and beliefs of Mexican, Guatemalan, and Salvadoran immigrants differ in important ways. The nonprofits that represent each of these communities will adopt organizational identities and missions that mirror these differences.

The 2010 census data also showed the growth of other non-Hispanic immigrant groups, though the census questionnaire uses a question about "race" ("Asian Indian," "Chinese," "Samoan," etc.) rather than "origin" to make this classification.[4] Asian Americans were, in actuality, the fastest-growing racial/ethnic minority in the United States between 2000 and 2010. According to the census, the Asian American population in the United States grew almost 50 percent, nearly four times the rate of growth of the population overall. Much like Hispanic American change, growth in the Asian American population also occurred in new places. Of the Asian American population living in the country, the percent living in the South increased by 3 percentage points, from 19.1 percent to

22.1 percent. In Nevada (116 percent increase), Arizona (94.6 percent increase), and Georgia (82.9 percent increase), the Asian American population ballooned. And Asian Americans represented 15 percent of the total state population in California and nearly 10 percent in New York and New Jersey. Houston, Chicago, and Los Angeles together totaled over two million Asian American residents. And within the Asian American community, much as in the Hispanic American community, there is growing diversity: for example, the Hmong make up the largest Asian American group in Minnesota; Vietnamese Americans the largest such group in Louisiana; and Filipino Americans the largest in Nevada. The variation within the Asian American community also relates to linguistic, cultural, and religious diversity, along with a spectrum of nonprofit organizations that adopt very different integration strategies from city to city and state to state.

Demographics of the Six States

Because of the richness and diversity of their immigrant experiences, but also to make the analysis manageable, this book focuses on six key states: New York, New Jersey, Michigan, Florida, Illinois, and North Carolina. Each of these states has experienced interesting demographic changes related to immigration and immigrants. The demographic characteristics of each state in 2012 related strongly to the array of nonprofit organizations and the particular politics of immigration. In choosing to focus on these six states, I generalize carefully about immigration and immigrant experiences in the country overall. Moreover, the large immigration into western states, particularly Arizona, Texas, and California, has been studied extensively by other researchers (See Eastman 2012; Gleeson 2012; Mireles 2013). Rather than replicate that research, my decision to focus on these six states outside the western United States allows for a different immigrant experience to be told.

The immigrant communities in these six states vary widely. First, in terms of ethnic diversity, New York (41.7 percent nonwhite or Hispanic) and New Jersey (40.7 percent nonwhite or Hispanic) had the largest percentages of nonwhite or Hispanic residents, with the percentages in both states greater than in the United States overall (36.6 percent nonwhite or Hispanic). More interesting than this are the differences within the nonwhite population. In Florida, nearly a quarter (22.9 percent) of the population is Hispanic/Latino, whereas the corresponding figure was less than 10 percent in Michigan (4.5 percent) and North Carolina (8.6 percent). Conversely, there were tiny percentages of Asians in Florida (2.4 percent) and North Carolina (2.2 percent), while New Jersey (8.5 percent) and New York (7.4 percent) were much higher than the figure for the nation overall (4.8 percent).

Second, these immigrant communities differ in terms of whether they are predominantly first or second generation. If we compare the Hispanic population in each state, the majority of those residents were foreign-born naturalized citizens, or first-generation Hispanic Americans, in Florida (51.6 percent) and North Carolina (54.9 percent). In Michigan, on the other hand, where the size of the population is similar to that of North Carolina, a small fraction (9.9 percent) were foreign-born, meaning most Hispanic Americans in Michigan are second or third generation. For the percentage of foreign-born Asians, Illinois, Michigan, New York, and New Jersey resemble the national figure (31.6 percent), but Florida (10.9 percent) and North Carolina (19.9 percent) had Asian American populations that were more heavily second and third generation, rather than first.

Third, New York and New Jersey stand out in terms of the relatively large portion, approximately a quarter of the state population, of those foreign-born. However, North Carolina ranks as the number one state in the country for the increase (+273 percent) in foreign-born immigrant population between 1990 and 2010. Owing to the large size of the existing foreign-born immigrant population, New York actually ranks second-to-last in terms of growth.[5] Within the population of foreign-born, Michigan had the largest percentage that was born in Europe (24.1 percent). Florida, on the other hand, had a foreign-born population almost exclusively (75 percent) from Latin America. Michigan, which had a small foreign-born population overall (7.1 percent), had a near majority (46.1 percent) of that group from Asia (included in this figure is the large immigration into the state from the countries in the Middle East). New York, New Jersey, and North Carolina resemble each other in that they all had around half their foreign-born residents from Latin America and between a quarter and a third from Asia.

Fourth, if you examine one level deeper, to specific countries of origin, these differences become even more pronounced. Illinois, for example, had the third most foreign-born residents from Mexico (720,106), behind only California and Texas, which each had more than two million. The states with the most foreign-born from China (including Hong Kong) were New York (second most), New Jersey (sixth most), and Illinois (seventh most). New Jersey had the second most foreign-born from India (206,100), followed by New York and Illinois, at fourth and fifth most. Florida had by far the largest Cuban-born population, with nearly 80 percent of the Cuban-born population of the entire country, while Michigan had the second most from Lebanon.

These demographic patterns show that the six states are all rich in ethnic diversity and immigrants, and that the characteristics of these communities differ greatly. Some states have long-standing, entrenched communities dominated by second- and third-generation citizens. Others are awash in recent immigrants, naturalized after arriving in the United States as children or adults. Some states have seen immigration primarily from Asia, while others have had a large influx from Latin America. If one delves deeper, even starker contrasts emerge within each of these broad regional labels. As mentioned above, Mexican Americans are the largest source of recent immigrants in much of the South, but in New York, Dominican Americans arrived in large numbers generations ago, and remain, in large numbers, as second- and third-generation New Yorkers.

As the introductory chapter of this book demonstrated, the differences are more than merely numbers; they relate to common identity, politics, and organizing. A community that is dominated by second- and third-generation citizens, such as the Arab American community in Michigan, will have had the time to accumulate the financial and nonfinancial resources to build a political infrastructure and social-service nonprofits, such as ACCESS, to provide for a variety of needs. In other settings, where the immigrant community is newer, such as in Queens, New York, that infrastructure may not be fully assembled, and encouraging political participation may be more challenging for nonprofit organizations, such as NICE.

A Changing Political Map

The newness of immigration relates to political boundaries. As Voto Latino acknowledged, major demographic changes had a big impact on redistricting of congressional lines across the country. Based on population changes and interstate migration, states across the Southwest (Nevada, Utah, Arizona, Texas) and Southeast (Florida, Georgia, South Carolina) gained seats in the House of Representatives following the 2010 redistricting, whereas states in the Rustbelt (Illinois, Michigan, Ohio, Pennsylvania) and the Northeast (New York, New Jersey, Massachusetts) lost seats.[6] The increase in Hispanic Americans, in particular, resulted in the redrawing of congressional district boundaries to create thirty new Hispanic-majority districts in 2010, a sign that the population trends have begun to affect politics, and maybe that Voto Latino's efforts paid off. No majority Asian American districts were created in 2010, but, in certain parts of Queens, Asian Americans made up a plurality of voters, and Asian Americans were a large voting bloc in districts across Illinois, California, and Hawaii.

This evidence shows that the demographics of the country have been changing rapidly. Also, the increasingly Hispanic and Asian American populations live in states and local communities with shorter histories of immigration. Immigrants are no longer concentrated in a handful of northeastern cities and along the west coast. States across the South are now home to large populations of immigrants, but these states have had little experience with incorporating immigrants into political and civic society. For these reasons, immigrant-serving nonprofits face very different challenges to participating in electoral politics based on the size, composition, and other trends and characteristics of immigration in their locality.

The Political Plight of Immigrants

The demographic changes observed over the last several decades would suggest the emergence of politically powerful groups of first- and second-generation Americans located throughout the country and in the study's six states. One would expect the interests of immigrants to be reflected in party platforms, candidates seeking out the votes of immigrants, and numerous recent immigrants running and winning elected office. The record, unfortunately, is quite the opposite.

In all six of these states, the long history or recent growth in immigration has not translated to real legislative power or what scholars, such as Stella Rouse (2013), call "descriptive representation." Take, for example, the relationship between Hispanic American population and legislative representation. While Latinos make up 18 percent of the population in Florida, they make up only 9 percent of the legislature, and that is the closest relationship of the six states (Schmidt et al. 2013). New York is the next closest (16 percent of the population and 5 percent of the legislature), while 5 percent of North Carolina's population is Latino compared to less than 1 percent of the legislature. New Jersey, Illinois, and Michigan fall somewhere in between, and the levels of descriptive representation for Asian, Arab, and other immigrant groups are equally dismal.

One of the reasons for the weak descriptive representation at the state level is that immigrants have tended to participate in politics at low levels. Research on the political participation of immigrants and ethnic minorities shows that, measured with nearly every indicator and every methodology, immigrants participate below national averages, and low participation limits representation (Hajnal and Trounstine 2005). Though voting patterns have begun to change, the meager political participation suggests that immigrants have not always been fully integrated into the civic life of their new communities. Since the founding of the country, established populations have not always been welcoming to newcomers, and some policy makers have been particularly hostile. By remaining outside many of the conventional channels of political participation, immigrants may also sacrifice other nonpolitical benefits such as a socioeconomic network for jobs, finance, and cultural assimilation.

Integration and assimilation, though, can come with sometimes unacknowledged costs. Immigrants walk a tightrope between acceptance in their new homes and maintaining ties to the home country, region, or culture. For some, active political participation is not always a good thing (Junn 1999). Jane Junn wrote: "Modes of political participation such as voting or making a campaign contribution are implicitly acts in support of maintenance of a political system that may not be in the best interests . . . for people who benefit least from that system" (2012, 35). If higher levels of participation are associated with an immigrant community sacrificing authentic values and the freedom to maintain language and culture, then integration may run counter to the precepts of liberal democracy, and more participation may mean less. Assimilating, though often attached to many of the advantages provided by mainstream culture and institutions—access to college, jobs, and politics—may be too high a price to pay for some immigrant communities eager to maintain tradition and preserve a unique identity. These concerns about the loss of identity are often transmitted to and reflected by immigrant-serving organizations.

From other perspectives, organizing around immigrant identity poses different problems for a fully integrated society. Placing ethnicity ahead of U.S. citizenship may weaken the sense of commonality among immigrants and diminish the opportunity to be welcomed into the larger society. Critics decry "identity politics" as an effort to divide communities, rather than bring people together. For example, the conflict between too much or too little immigrant integration has been prominent in education policy. Advocates of bilingual education and a school curriculum rich in a diversity of ethnic perspectives have fought against those who advocate for a common curriculum based around a traditional canon (San Miguel 2013).

More involvement in politics—greater "political incorporation"—may also lead to positive and negative feedback loops (Hochschild and Mollenkopf 2009). Immigrants who mobilize and participate in politics may be greeted by elected officials eager for their support and solicitous of their votes: positive feedback. In other circumstances, greater involvement may lead to negative feedback: antipathy, resistance, and political retaliation. For example, increases in the foreign-born population of a state are associated with the passage of more anti-immigration state policies (Boushey and Luedtke 2011; Monogan 2013). Politics is a dynamic and unpredictable arena, one that immigrants and immigrant-serving nonprofits enter into without guarantees that outcomes will always be desirable. Immigrant-serving nonprofits walk this tightrope, often intending to genuinely represent the immigrant community, but sensitive to hostile claims that in doing so they are not promoting the common good.

Given this highly contentious political terrain, it is hardly a surprise that research shows immigrant citizens vote in relatively low numbers, though it is not easy to separate voting by ethnicity from immigrant status (Uhlaner, Cain, and Kiewiet 1989). For example, in the 1984 presidential election, non-Hispanic whites and African Americans registered and voted at similar levels, both around 80 percent, while Hispanics and Asian Americans registered at about 50 percent (53 percent and 55 percent, respectively) and voted at under 50 percent (44 percent and 48 percent, respectively). To be sure, not all Hispanics and Asian Americans are immigrants, but a larger portion of immigrants fall into these two broad census categories. For all other political indicators (contributing money to campaigns, working on campaigns, attending political rallies, and contacting officials), non-Hispanic whites were more active than Hispanic and Asian Americans.

Since the 1980s, the percentage of both Hispanic Americans and Asian Americans registered to vote and actually voting has crept upward but remained behind levels for white non-Hispanic Americans and African Americans (See figure 1.1). In 1992, nearly the same percentage of Asian Americans (27.3 percent) voted as

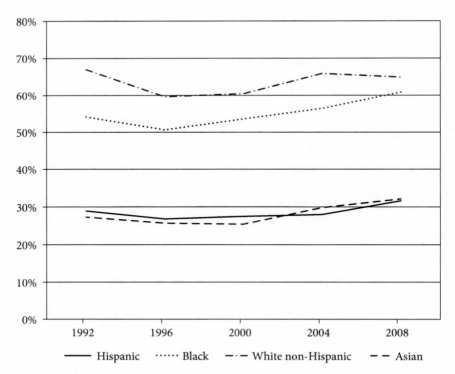

FIGURE 1.1. Percent voting of total U.S. voting-age population, by race and Hispanic origin, presidential elections, 1992–2008
Source: U.S. Census Bureau, Current Population Survey, November 2008.

Hispanic Americans (28.9 percent). By 2008, this figure had climbed to 32.1 percent for Asians and 31.6 percent for Hispanics.

It is also worth noting that there is considerable variation in voting patterns across the focal states of this study. While the non-Hispanic white voting in the off-year 2010 congressional elections remained about the same, for the other groups it varied greatly. Nearly 30 percent of Hispanic Americans in Florida and Michigan voted, while in Illinois, New Jersey, and North Carolina, fewer than 20 percent of Hispanic Americans voted (see figure 1.2). Similarly for Asian Americans in North Carolina, more than 20 percent voted; but in New York fewer than 10 percent did so. These differences reflect a variety of factors, including the peculiar local politics of each state, the variation in how each state permits voters to register to vote, but also the differences that exist within ethnic groups in terms of key socioeconomic indicators.

There are also differences within each immigrant community related to voting and political participation. For example, in the 1988 elections, foreign-born Hispanic Americans were less likely than native-born Hispanic Americans to vote and engage in other electoral activities (DeSipio 1996). However, in the

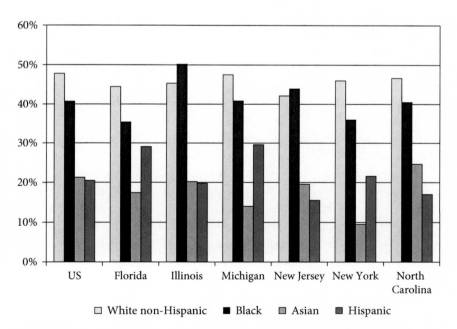

FIGURE 1.2.   Percent of the total U.S. population who voted, by race and Hispanic origin for select states, November 2010 election (population eighteen years and older, in thousands)
Source: U.S. Census Bureau.

2002 elections in California, foreign-born Hispanic Americans were more likely to vote than native-born Hispanic Americans, a difference attributed in part to voter mobilization targeted at immigrants (Barreto 2005). These generational differences sometimes hold for Asian Americans (Lien 2004), but in other cases researchers have found no higher levels of voting for first-generation Asian Americans versus second- and third-generation (Ramakrishnan and Espenshade 2001).

Addressing this discrepancy in voting for Asian Americans, in particular, has been confounded by popular conceptions, and government propaganda that goes back to the Cold War, of the community as a "model minority": a homogeneous and well-integrated ethnic group that thrives in economic, education, and other sectors with few systemic areas of concern (Cheng 2013). For example, a much criticized report from the Pew Research Center (2012) found a larger portion of Asian Americans (49 percent) hold college degrees, and that the median income of Asian Americans nationwide is over $15,000 more than that of the population overall ($66,000 versus $49,800). Critics of the "model minority" myth contend that these generalized findings mask deeper inequities and heterogeneity within the Asian American community (Lien 2001; Wong et al. 2011). For example, Vietnamese Americans have had a much lower college graduation rate (only 26 percent hold college degrees), a median income ($53,400) just slightly above the general public, and a poverty rate 2 percentage points worse than the general public (14.7 percent versus 12.8 percent for the U.S. population). For Filipino Americans, who have had higher levels of educational attainment on average than other immigrant groups, research shows that they face hurdles in postsecondary education success (Buenavista 2010), confront workplace discrimination, and suffer from poor health (de Castro, Gee, and Takeuchi 2008; Mossakowski 2007).

These interethnic differences also exist within Asian American political participation. Japanese Americans have been the most likely to vote (65 percent) and contribute to candidates (18 percent), but least likely to be a community activist (17 percent) (Wong et al. 2011). Conversely, Asian Indian Americans have been the least likely to vote (23 percent) but most likely to be involved in community activism (27 percent). Evidence of this sort led Lien (2001) to conclude that Asian Americans are "the most heterogeneous non-White ethnic community in the United States" (194). And the myth of the model minority has also hampered efforts to provide aid to Asian Americans in need, resulting, for example, in moves to restrict affirmative action for Asian Americans because of a perception that it was unnecessary. For a similar reason, the model minority myth may have also slowed the development of Asian American nonprofits charged with representing and advocating for policy solutions in the political and electoral realms.

Socialization and Ideology

As the myth of the model minority and evidence of interethnic generational differences suggest, the civic and political life of immigrants is complicated. Low voting turnout cannot be rationalized through simple aggregated explanations; the answers lie deeper. One factor that may explain a difference in immigrant voting patterns is that ideologies differ across generations, likely related to how and where immigrants are socialized into politics. For example, among Hispanic Americans, views about the role of government differ greatly between first and second generations (Taylor et al. 2012). A majority (64 percent) of those Hispanic Americans born outside the United States, first generation, believed that "government should promote traditional values," whereas a majority (53 percent) of those born in the United States believed that "government should not favor any particular set of values." Beliefs about government, and other related ideologies, may also relate to beliefs about voting and for whom one votes.

Generational issues also relate to language ability and English-language acquisition. Some, but not all, immigrants arrive in the United States with limited English proficiency, and some, but not all, substantially improve their English language abilities over their life. Second-language acquisition relates to the age at arrival and is also correlated with access to formal and informal education. Non-English-speaking Asian and Hispanic American immigrants are much less likely to vote; but for both ethnic groups, voting increases with education, income, and age (Cho 1999; Barreto and Muñoz 2003). These positive relationships are not simple effects; rather they are proxies of the complex socialization, civic learning, and political norming that occur as one ages in a new country and interacts with peers in places of work and formal education (Cho, Gimpel, and Wu 2006). Immigrants bring to their new home a foundation of political knowledge and socialization but then learn about American attitudes toward politics while navigating the legal process of naturalization or simply through integrating with neighbors, coworkers, and friends. An important question that I ponder in this book is the extent to which immigrant-serving nonprofit organizations mirror these deeply engrained political experiences and values of those they serve, or whether certain nonprofits initiate change through mobilization and political education. I return to this question throughout the remaining chapters of the book.

Part of the answer to these questions can be found by investigating the political development and institutions of other ethnic minority groups. For example, despite higher average levels of wealth and educational attainment, some groups, such as Asian Americans, have consistently voted at lower levels than African Americans (Wong, Lien, and Conway 2005). The explanation for this difference may be tied to the very different political histories of each group in the country. The civil rights movement of the 1950s and 1960s that mobilized large portions of the community to political activism still remains a central historical talisman for many African Americans (Schmidt et al. 2013). Evidence of the persistence of this solidarity can also be found in the political attitudes of African Americans. African Americans, and to a lesser extent Hispanic Americans, are much more likely to feel "very close" to their ethno-racial peers than are Asian Americans, who feel the lowest levels of solidarity with their own ethno-racial group (Masuoka and Junn 2013).

The civil rights movement also launched a host of political nonprofit organizations that became institutionalized over time, thereby cementing the mobilization of the community from election to election. Other ethnic minority groups, including new immigrant communities, have often lacked an analogous narrative of political struggle—either based in their country of origin or in their new home community—to galvanize collective action and the formation of associated nonprofit organizations. Asian American protest and political action have usually happened on a smaller and more localized scale, and historically within ethnic groups, rather than in a pan-Asian fashion. With some notable exceptions, organizations promoting a pan-Asian identity and common political agenda have much shorter histories than those promoting pan–Hispanic American or African American interests.

These differences in political history may also make it difficult to find common ground across community lines or to forge inter-immigrant unity. Faced with institutional barriers, including limits on common cause formed with well-established African American organizations, Afro-Caribbean immigrants in New York have struggled to find a political voice in city politics (Rogers 2006; Audebert 2009; Greer 2013). In other situations, aggressive political action may be seen as a threat to cultural beliefs about societal hierarchies and political norms (Ecklund and Park 2005; Buenavista 2010). These barriers to voting and political participation thus are both internal and external, some deeply embedded in the political identity of the immigrant community, others imposed by those outside the community.

But political participation is more than just voting, and in some circumstances an immigrant community may demonstrate its rich civic engagement in unconventional ways. For example, nearly half of Asian Americans (44 percent), compared to only a third of the overall population, "worked on some community problem," and most through a nonreligious civic organization (Pew Research Center 2012). Unlike voting, or registering to vote, other forms of political participation might not demand that an individual negotiate institutional rules that would expose language deficits or cultural insecurities. As mentioned earlier, some first-generation Americans lack sufficient English-language ability to read political information or even an electoral ballot. Second-generation immigrants, often the children, help transmit political information to first-generation parents in Asian American families (Wong 2006). There was similar children-to-parent mobilization to join the 2006 immigrant rights rallies held across the country (Bloemraad and Trost 2008). Despite research indicating that second-generation immigrants may vote at lower levels, children may provide needed political capital within the family and aid political socialization.

Political Institutions and Immigrants

To be sure, not every immigrant community suffers from low levels of political participation or political influence, and great advances in participation and power have been made since the 1960s (Schmidt et al. 2013). Scholars refer to "ethnic lobbies" or ethnic voting blocs and find that factors such as how unified the diaspora group is, the legitimacy of its claims, and cultural identity of the immigrant group in U.S. society relate to levels of political influence (Rubenzer 2008). Considerable and often controversial research has examined the Jewish American lobby in the United States and its specific influence on U.S.-Israel and broader U.S.–Middle East policy (Wald 2008). Scholars have studied the political influence of Cuban Americans, Indian Americans (Kurien 2001), Greek Americans (Karpathakis 1999), and Eastern European Americans (Garrett 1978), but in general researchers have focused on large, established immigrant groups or on pan-national movements. Many successful "ethnic lobbies" work closely with organizations based in a home country. These links provide institutional support and resources to those lobbying on behalf of international issues in the United States.

Immigrant groups that make up too small a percentage of the foreign-born population in the United States usually will not be able to mount a national-level lobbying campaign, which would depend on considerable financial resources. Despite gains in Washington representation for some ethnic groups, Strolovich (2006, 93) concluded that immigrants "have fewer resources and fewer of the organizational and political tools than do other interests such as business and professional associations." In addition, newer immigrant communities are often hesitant to be overly ambitious on the foreign-policy stage because of concerns about accusations of disloyalty and questions of uncertain patriotism. The strong negative backlash against Asian Americans in general, and Chinese Americans in particular, following allegations of illegal contributions to President Bill Clinton's 1996 campaign, still negatively influences the political attitudes of Asian Americans (Lee 2000). Investigations into these campaign finance violations

were strongly tinged with questions about the patriotism of Asian American donors. But others, such as Greek Americans, have successfully balanced the tension
between assimilation into U.S. society with activism in home-country politics
(Karpathakis 1999). It is possible to maintain ties and fully engage in politics in
a new home, but for some immigrant groups it is a balancing act and fraught
with great risks.

The success that Cuban Americans, Jewish Americans, and recently Indian
Americans have had in shaping national foreign policy has not occurred at random. These influential immigrant and ethnic groups have built an infrastructure
that links individuals and resources to the political process. The robustness of
their political influence has also been the result of demography. The geographic
concentration in key parts of the country—Cuban Americans in south Florida,
for example—can increase the dependence of elected officials on that group. As
political parties recognize that an immigrant group can sway an election, they
begin to pay attention and court the group's votes. The urban political machines
of the nineteenth century drew strength from the common cause they formed
with primarily Western European, English-speaking Irish, Scottish, and Welsh
immigrants. Political parties in New York, Philadelphia, and Boston worked to
naturalize these newcomers and provide patronage in exchange for loyalty at the
polls. Cognizant of this tradition, immigrant leaders have an incentive to band
together in common cause across ethnic boundaries, even if such unity may not
be an authentic representation of the diversity of identities, beliefs, and interests
that exist between ethnic communities (Beltran 2010).

Despite the obvious advantages to parties welcoming immigrant and ethnic
voters, recent evidence suggests that this occurs only sporadically (Stevens and
Bishin 2011). Political parties that had welcomed immigrants in the past rejected
later waves of immigrants from Eastern and Southern Europe, China, and Mexico (Su 2012). Partly as a result of this trend, but also a reason why it persists,
Hispanic and Asian Americans are now less likely to be affiliated with a political
party (Hajnal and Lee 2011). And in 2012, exit polling showed that fewer than
a third of Asian Americans nationwide were contacted by a political party or
organization about the election, and for some groups, such as Indian Americans,
the proportion was closer to a quarter (Pew Research Center 2012). Mainstream
political actors have largely ignored immigrants, focusing mobilization instead
on other voting blocs, even as party leaders rhetorically claim to welcome immigrants' support. In the aftermath of this breach, immigrants have had to fend
for themselves. As Weldon (2012) concluded: "Poor people and people who are
not citizens can and do organize social movements. Political parties, interest
groups, and electoral politics all fail to reach these segments of the population
who vote and organize less frequently than citizens in other groups" (170). In

recognizing this political vacuum, we can better understand why the work of immigrant-serving nonprofit organizations is so important.

Moreover, when immigration and immigrants become salient campaign issues, they are often subject to ethnic and racially tinged antagonism from hostile organizations. During the 2006 election, anti-immigration political advertisements evoked immigrants as "criminals," "illegals," and "threats" to the American way of life (McIlwain and Caliendo 2012). This framing of immigration by anti-immigrant organizations may have the effect of driving up hostility among nonimmigrants, but also serves to discourage and intimidate immigrants from participating in politics. (I return to this point in chapter 2 when I discuss the emerging role of Tea Party–affiliated organizations.)

Other factors act to counterbalance the lack of outreach from political parties and hostility from political advertising. The concentration of immigrants in a community or neighborhood seems to matter to immigrants engaging in politics. Arab, Hispanic, and Asian American voter turnout increases when potential voters reside in an area dense with others from their community (Cho, Gimpel, and Wu 2006). One of the benefits of living in an immigrant-rich neighborhood is that sufficient resources and common interest may coalesce so that nonprofit groups may form to help in the process of political engagement. In general, we know that joining an organization is associated with more political participation (Verba, Schlozman, and Brady 1995). We also know that when immigrants have community-based nonprofit groups in place that provide information on candidates, registration, and other factors that relate to voting, political participation increases. To varying extents, Hispanics and Asian Americans who belong to organizations are more likely to register to vote, cast a vote, and participate in other forms of politics (Wong 2006; Lee 2008; DeSipio 2002).

It seems clear that affiliating with an organization matters to political incorporation. In addition, what organizations actually do also matters to participation in politics. Nonprofit organizations have begun to learn from experiments that show which types of voter mobilization work and which do not work (LeRoux and Krawczyk 2013). For example, nonpartisan mobilization by organizations is less effective in turning out immigrant voters in general than when political parties make contact, though parties rarely contact many immigrants (Stevens and Bishin 2011). Indirect methods of voter mobilization and strategies that are formal and impersonal, such as mass mailings, tend to be ineffective (García Bedolla and Michelson 2012). However, when organizations incorporate a personalized approach, with language-sensitive canvassing, conversational phone-banking, and frequent follow-up phone calls, evidence shows that immigrant and ethnic minority voter turnout increases considerably. This intensely personal and authentic strategy worked so well that experiments show a 10 percentage point increase in voter turnout among Asian Americans who had pledged to vote and were given a follow-up call. Slowly, some of the mysteries of get-out-the-vote work have been uncovered, particularly as they relate to limited-English voters.

This evidence from a variety of disciplines and lines of scholarship suggests that organizations help to mediate between immigrants and politics. While traditional political institutions, such as the two major political parties, have recently ignored immigrants, other political institutions play a part in the political lives of immigrants. Organizational membership increases the likelihood of an individual participating in politics, and organizationally based mobilization also can increase the likelihood of immigrants participating in politics. For these reasons, the activities and operations of nonprofits that are dedicated to serving immigrants are important to study.

Immigrant-Serving Nonprofit Organizations

As the preceding suggests, scholars now know a good deal about immigrant voters and nonvoters. The failure of immigrants to engage in civic life in general and voting in particular is related to many factors, including language abilities and related language barriers to participation, variation in political socialization and political identity across immigrant communities, and the failure to benefit from associations with and mobilization by political and nonpolitical groups. Weak links to political networks may be the result of the lack of robust opportunities and limited political access. For example, nonprofit organizations operate in most communities, but their vibrancy varies with available resources. In some communities there are a limited number of nonprofits providing few services. Even in California, a state with a long history of immigration and many nonprofit organizations, in proportion to their share of the local population immigrants have been underrepresented in terms of the number of nonprofit organizations that serve their needs (Gleeson and Bloemraad 2012). And immigrant-serving nonprofit organizations in San Francisco are severely underfunded, in part because "immigrants are not seen as sufficiently legitimate interlocutors and civic partners" (de Graauw, Gleeson, and Bloemraad 2012, 2).

Despite the importance of immigrant-serving nonprofits and their seemingly critical relationship to higher levels of political engagement, what we know about the political dimensions of these organizations is rather limited. Historical accounts confirm the long record in some cities of the institutions that immigrants relied upon. For example, drawn to Chicago in the 1920s and 1930s by employment opportunities, Mexican Americans formed mutual aid societies, or *mutualistas*, to "ease the transition to life in the city and help resist nativism and bigotry"

(Innis-Jiménez 2013, 181). Organizations also formed in response to bigotry and anti-immigrant violence. The murder of Vincent Chin in Detroit, for example, created opportunities for interethnic solidarity and the formation of pan-Asian organizations (Zia 2001). And in Texas, Mexican American political organizations, such as the Texas Association of Mexican American Chambers of Commerce and American GI Forum, worked within Democratic Party politics to gain political power in the state in the 1950s and 1960s (Márquez 2014). These organizations lobbied for better jobs, civil rights, and protection from hate crimes.

In some communities, immigrant-serving nonprofits have filled the political gap not filled by political parties. The New Haven, Connecticut, described so famously by Robert Dahl (1961) is largely gone. As immigrants from Eastern Europe, Asia, and Mexico replaced the largely white immigration from Ireland, Italy, and Germany, immigrants were no longer seen as political assets. The Progressive Era reformers brought to an end the practice of political parties building urban machines on the backs of immigrants through the provision of jobs and social benefits in exchange for loyalty at the ballot box (Golway 2014; Su 2012). Today, not only are immigrants less likely to affiliate with a political party than in the past; political parties also do not play the same role in mobilizing immigrants during elections, nor in encouraging naturalization. Immigrant organizations have sought to fill this void with mixed results (Andersen 2010).

Immigrant-serving organizations also come in different forms. In New York City, for example, there are informal hometown associations, more formal but country/region-specific social service organizations, and large multiethnic social service providers (Cordero-Guzmán 2005). In addition to the level of formality and breadth of services, these groups differ by the source of funding, age, staff, and client base. These various organizations have had only limited success in establishing themselves a place in city politics, sometimes the result of conflicts that emerge between established political institutions such as African American organizations and Caribbean American newcomers, or between Dominican and Puerto Rican American organizations (Rogers 2006).

More to the point of advocacy and electioneering, immigrant-serving organizations interact in the political realm with other types of organizations. We know from Su (2012, 670) that as political machines lost interest in incorporating immigrants, "many [immigrants] found political outlets in labor unions, churches, and civic organizations." Labor unions, once deeply suspicious and hostile toward immigrants, have more recently come to support new immigrants and undocumented immigrants (Varsanyi 2006; Jacobson 2011; Gleeson 2012). As labor groups have shifted their stance, so too have their strategies moved toward grassroots efforts around which undocumented workers can be mobilized, such as rallies and get-out-the-vote campaigns. Labor unions, though, are not squarely focused on, nor have they always been sensitive to, the needs of immigrants. In California, for example, the United Farm Workers union struggled to organize the largely Hispanic American immigrant strawberry farmers because the union was viewed as technocratic and detached from local life (Mireles 2013). When immigrants rely on organizations that have a primary mission to serve the interests of nonimmigrants, even if those interests sometimes overlap, they will always have their full and authentic representation at risk. But when nonimmigrant organizations, such as labor unions, are open to newcomers, then immigrants can gain many of the benefits of these established institutions, including access to political socialization and political resources (Greer 2013).

Certain immigrant communities have quite active, politically oriented organizations. Dominican, Colombian, and Mexican Americans have a remarkably large and varied set of organizations involved in civic and political activities (Portes, Escobar, and Arana 2008). Benjamin Márquez's history of Texas politics (2014) documented the important role of Mexican American organizations in wresting control away from traditional holders of power in state politics. But many immigrant-serving nonprofits do not engage at all in politics. In the Washington, DC, metro area, for example, research shows that there are over five hundred immigrant-serving nonprofits, and their numbers are growing as a result of recent increases in immigration (de Leon et al. 2009). However, despite their proximity to the nation's capital, these immigrant organizations are not equally active in politics. Latino immigrants are much more likely to have organizations that participate in politics than are Asian and sub-Saharan African Americans, who as groups arguably lack the institutional histories and political contacts to easily lobby DC policy makers. While survey research finds that there are twice as many nonprofits serving Asian Americans compared to Hispanic Americans (273 compared to 132), a majority of the Asian American organizations were religious organizations, and only two (compared to six for Hispanic Americans) focus on politics. What this suggests is that the transition from purely service to hybrid political organization, described in the introductory chapter, happens disproportionately among different immigrant communities.

Some of these differences in the transition to participating in politics relate to who is being served; but as nonprofits, immigrant organizations in general are often limited by available resources and small budgets. Immigrant organizations are more likely to provide religious services or a multitude of social services, whereas mainstream organizations—those that primarily serve nonimmigrant populations—are more likely to provide education, sports, and health services. In terms of political advocacy, organizations serving immigrant groups in particular are "the most resource-poor, often depending on the time and monetary contributions of a handful of individuals" (Ramakrishnan and Viramontes 2010, and 2006, 76). Some immigrant organizations are informal and have not incorporated as 501(c)(3) nonprofits with the IRS. This limits the extent to which they can gather resources, as incorporation permits tax-deductible donations from supporters. Foundations (which I describe in detail in chapter 2) are also unlikely to provide grants to organizations that are not incorporated. In general, immigrant-serving organizations often lack the financial and political capital to participate in political decision making. Rather than pursue *mass* mobilization, many groups, such as NICE, in Queens, focus on *selective* mobilization, defined as "the strategic targeting of recruitment efforts to expend the least efforts to achieve the greatest effect" (Wong 2006, 9). Selective mobilization may be effective in some situations but will likely limit immigrant integration into politics if most organizations pursue this strategy to the exclusion of other broader ones.

What we know about immigrant-serving nonprofits has grown considerably and helps clarify that immigrants are served by a variety of types of nonprofits but that certain services are delivered inconsistently. Different immigrant communities are also served by nonprofits with varying missions and specialties. Politically oriented nonprofits in particular are some of the least well supported and are relatively rare, especially for immigrants outside the Hispanic American community. The patchwork of nonprofit organizations also helps explain why political and voter participation is so varied across immigrant communities and generations of immigrants. Immigrant mobilization, no longer a central focus of political parties, occurs intermittently, and rarely is driven by the techniques that are known to change voting behavior.

Unfortunately, we do not know the answer to many other important questions. When immigrant-serving nonprofits are politically oriented, which tactics do they use during election time? Do tactical choices differ by immigrant community or by other known organizational factors that relate to politics, such as resources? What then can we conclude about these differences in nonprofit tactical choice and strategy for how well various immigrants are represented during elections and in politics in general? The following chapters begin to answer these questions.

Conclusion

Voto Latino's emergence in 2012 was not a coincidence. The organization was formed and operates to this day based on a nuanced understanding of those it serves. By understanding the demographic changes within the Hispanic American community in the United States, Voto Latino has targeted a group underserved by many existing nonprofits and national political parties: young Hispanic

American voters. Importantly, much of the strategy the organization has adopted is directly aligned with what made this demographic group of first-time voters unique: their particular reliance on certain types of technology. Voto Latino understood the particular identity of the community it serves, an identity that is different from older Hispanic American voters and different from younger voters in general. The identity of Voto Latino reflects the unique characteristics and identity of younger Hispanic Americans.

From a macro perspective, trends in U.S. immigration and demographic change suggest other similar opportunities and challenges. Increasing numbers can bring political influence and result in improvements in social equity, often lacking in the past for immigrants. But these changes are contingent on full engagement in the political process, a particular problem for many immigrant groups that have tended to vote and participate in low numbers. It is then critical for organizations, both political and nonpolitical, to recognize the changing demographic context of the community in which they operate, to mobilize immigrants, and to provide a voice for their concerns in political decision making during, but not limited to, election season. Research, though, has provided only some answers to important questions about why many organizations opt not to participate, and the strategies and tactics of the organizations that do. Much of the research has focused on a few key states, mainly California and New York, and employed methods that either statistically analyze individual voting patterns or qualitatively analyze particular organizations or parts of the country. Without research on other states and localities, our understanding of immigrant-serving nonprofits remains incomplete. Without a more theoretically rooted and systematic way to analyze the strategies and tactics nonprofits use and what correlates with their use, it is difficult to reach generalizable conclusions. The next several chapters provide some additional answers: first by describing in more detail the local political campaign context and organizational context in which groups operated in 2012 (chapters 2 and 3); and then a theoretical model (chapter 4) and analysis of original data (chapters 5 and 6) drawn from a survey of immigrant-serving nonprofits in the six study states.

2

FOUNDATIONS AND FUNDING

Demographic change and patterns of immigrant political participation in the United States inform the context in which organizations act when making decisions about how best to represent the community in electoral politics. A second, historical context must also be considered.[1] Immigrant-serving nonprofits operate in an *organizational* context that stretches back two hundred years in the United States. This larger historical context can help show how various factors encourage and discourage immigrant-serving nonprofits from participating in politics. Philanthropists and social reformers have expressed an interest in immigrants since the turn of the nineteenth century, some aiming to assimilate newcomers, others to punish. A hundred years later, a similarly complex environment of support and opposition shapes the operations of immigrant-serving nonprofits, pushing some to become a type of interest group, and others to remain solely focused on providing social services.

Most recently, hundreds of millions of dollars were spent to support the nonpartisan activities of a web of thousands of organizations to register, educate, and mobilize voters, including eligible immigrant citizens. This spending fit into a ten-year project led by major philanthropic foundations to support a range of efforts to promote immigrant rights and integration through a variety of different types of nonprofit organizations. American politics have always been defined by the habit of pursuing social aims through partnerships between organizers and private funders. But the recent philanthropic interest and approach to immigrant issues has particular historical antecedents in Progressive Era beliefs about American society and assimilation. In the 2000s, the way foundations framed immigrant issues had evolved from earlier efforts, and the method used to give out funding grew increasingly complex as new types of organizations emerged to make philanthropy more efficient and effective. In order to understand where some immigrant-serving nonprofits derive funding and technical support, it is important to examine the array of interrelated organizations that care about immigrant issues. This chapter aims to do just that.

At the same time, and partly counteracting this philanthropic push, millions of dollars went to address alleged voter fraud through changes in election laws—moves perceived by many as a way to suppress the immigrant vote. Conservative funders also supported organizations tied to the Tea Party that pursued tighter immigration policies at the local, state, and national levels. Paradoxically, some of these policy objectives also hark back to the Progressive Era, when new restrictions on immigrant rights and voting first emerged. Thus, from the Left and the Right, immigrants, immigration, and the nature of voting provided the focus for intense interest in the 2012 election.

To appreciate these competing efforts, and how they relate to local nonprofit organizations, it is first necessary to examine the organizational context in which foundations have pushed these issues as national funding priorities. As Jack Walker (1991) wrote about the expansion of the interest group system in the 1970s and 1980s: "The rise and fall of political insurgencies and their ultimate success in obtaining their goals . . . depend not so much on the character, attitudes, or motives of those who lead or participate in them; rather, they are a function of the amount of assistance they obtain from sympathetic third parties and the reaction of authorities to their challenge" (55). Philanthropic foundations have increasingly been active participants in the policy process, supporting policy views through grants to nonprofits. This is one of the reasons it is necessary to examine immigrant-serving nonprofits using the framework offered by interest-group scholars and pluralism. Foundations support particular policy interests, and they also prefer certain political strategies over others. In the case of immigrant issues, qualitative and quantitative evidence shows that foundations have increasingly supported a collaborative, pan-immigrant strategy versus other alternatives. For nonprofits that adhere to this strategy, foundations have placed enormous financial aid at their disposal; for organizations that opt for other strategies, funding has been less plentiful.

Nevertheless, the bargain forged between foundations and nonprofits is not an easy one: interests do not always align perfectly and are sometimes contradictory. For over a century, immigrants have had to confront the norm of assimilation and the image of the American melting pot, what we today call immigrant integration. Immigrants who have chafed at this norm, failed to adopt English as their preferred language, and maintained traditional dress and culture have faced antipathy as permanent outsiders. Immigrant-serving organizations have faced similar dilemmas: how to remain autonomous, preserve their identity, and maintain the authenticity of their mission while in financial partnership with powerful philanthropic foundations.

This chapter relies on primary documents from philanthropic foundations and other institutional patrons, secondary data on grant making, and qualitative information drawn from interviews with philanthropic foundation leaders and nonprofit organizations that have received grants. Together, these varied sources are used to set immigrant-serving nonprofits in the context of the organization and development of interest groups in U.S. history, including the funding for and against the interests of immigrants. The chapter ends with a discussion of the tension between foundation influence and nonprofit identity, a key theme of this book.

Nonprofits, Representation, and Interest Groups

Even when nonprofits act in a nonpartisan fashion, any involvement in electoral politics forces organizations to confront other political actors and larger political forces. A primary argument of this book, one that is in line with the arguments made by scholars such as Elizabeth Boris, Jeffrey Berry, and others, is that some nonprofit organizations act—and are treated—as a type of interest group in the political sphere. It is important, then, to clearly define what an interest group is, and the ways that some nonprofit organizations share certain characteristics with interest groups.

An interest group is most simply defined as an organization that promotes a commonly held political or policy goal. This is the definition offered by one of the first interest group scholars, David Truman (1951), and followed by many scholars ever since. The definition is useful because it emphasizes the organization, focuses on the commonality of interest, and clarifies that some of the work of the organization aims to influence political outcomes. We typically think of organizations working on behalf of commercial trades, businesses, or professions as interest groups. Starting in the 1950s, Truman and other pluralists helped to draw the theoretical—if not actual—contours of the system of pluralism in the United States where interest groups are largely free—if not equal—to compete over the direction of policy making through political means.

Using Truman's definition, however, many other nonprofit organizations also must be considered as a type of interest group, including many organizations that have been given 501(c)(3) status by the Internal Revenue Services (IRS). Some nonprofit organizations that we have not historically categorized as interest groups perform many of the same functions as traditional interest groups and use many of the same political tactics. As Elizabeth Boris (2006) contended: "Nonprofit groups aggregate diverse values and interests and represent them in the political system through political advocacy and lobbying of the government" (18). As I suggested at the start of the book, immigrant-serving nonprofits that begin to pursue political and electoral tactics may not have been established as an interest group, but over time they take on some of the characteristics of an interest group.

I am not suggesting that every nonprofit organization that pursues political or electoral tactics is a *lobbying* group. Lobbying is a political tactic aimed to directly influence a policy decision, whether it is the passage or execution of a law, regulation, or rule. Lobbying is regulated by the federal government through limits and mandatory disclosure rules. While the U.S. government has sought to use the tax code to encourage the formation of nonprofits, it distinguishes those that pursue a primarily charitable or social-service mission—501(c)(3)s—from other nonprofits formed to pursue social welfare or political interests: 501(c)(4)s and other nonprofit designations. Neither category can generate profits for owners, but how each can advance its mission and fund operations is different. Since the 1930s, lobbying activities by 501(c)(3) nonprofits have been highly regulated by the government (limited to a very small portion of the total activities or expenditures), while 501(c)(4)s have not been required to abide by such strict lobbying restrictions (Arnsberger et al. 2008; Zunz 2014). As a result, financial donations to 501(c)(4)s do not receive such favorable tax advantages from the IRS as are given to 501(c)(3) nonprofits.

Lobbying, in actuality, is merely one of the tactics used by even the most politically oriented social welfare organizations or interest groups based in Washington. Organizations also devote much time to predominantly unregulated activities such as giving testimony before agency committees, writing nonpartisan policy papers, and public communications (Walker 1991). For this reason, some interest groups that devote little time to legal lobbying are incorporated as 501(c)(3) nonprofit organizations and can claim legal and tax benefits from this status. To be sure, some will form a related, but legally distinct, 501(c)(4) nonprofit or political action committee (PAC) in which political activities can occur (Berry 1999; Berry and Arons 2003).

Most electoral work, including registering voters, holding candidate forums, and mobilizing voters on Election Day, is also permitted by law if it is done in a nonpartisan fashion. As long as the 501(c)(3) organization does not endorse a specific candidate or make campaign contributions, it is permitted to be active in many aspects of an election. Despite this reality, many nonprofits are still wary of pursuing any political or electoral work out of fears of reprisal, accusations of malfeasance, or simple confusion about the IRS and Federal Election Commission regulations (Berry and Arons 2003).

Furthermore, despite the similarities in what they are permitted to do, many service-oriented nonprofit organizations are dissimilar to interest groups in two important ways: the source of their funding, and their relationships to other organizations. The traditional interest group pursues the common interests of individual or organizational members, who pay dues for a say in the operations of the organization; tax-deductible donations are not permitted. The organization orients its operations to best represent the interests of those dues-paying members, evaluating which issues to pursue and the ways to pursue them through communications between the professional staff, the board of directors, and members. To overcome the collective-action problem of diffuse benefits, especially policy change that benefits larger numbers of members but only in small and often unobservable ways, some interest groups even offer symbolic benefits, such as member discounts on health care, or organizational magazines, in order to secure the loyalty and consistent dues payments of members (Olson 1971). This mutually beneficial arrangement inextricably links these member-based interest groups to dues-paying individuals. It also has resulted in disproportionate political representation for some classes of individuals, typically those of ample wealth, because of the higher member dues payments they can make to certain interest groups—the upper-class bias in the U.S. system of pluralism (Schattschneider 1960).

Membership has been one characteristic of organizing and pluralism in U.S. politics; so too has a federated organizational structure. Social movements for much of U.S. history have been organized around interlocking and coordinated organizations. The late nineteenth-century Populist movement, the temperance movement, and the civil rights movement all mobilized citizens and advocated for policy change with organizational structures based on a federated system of local, state, and regional chapters. For example, local "tax clubs" made up of community bankers and small business owners initiated advocacy in the 1920s and 1930s to limit estate taxes and repeal the federal income tax (Martin 2013). They worked within a loosely coordinated federated system to advance these policy goals in states across the country.

Most nonprofits, on the other hand, typically do not have members in the same way as interest groups, and often act independently of a federated system of related organizations. Because most are founded independently of others, many nonprofits are not compelled to coordinate their activities with related organizations based in nearby localities or states. Also, those individuals who receive benefits from a service-oriented nonprofit—what we might call clients or constituents—may pay for certain services, but those payments are not exactly analogous to a dues payment. The payment does not form an affiliation with the nonprofit, as it would if the payment were made to join the organization as a member able to vote on organizational business. Some clients may pay nothing at all to the organization for services, and the organization may continue to operate and provide those services because of other sources of revenue. In order for this to work, nonprofits often receive substantial revenue from philanthropic foundations or governments. Ironically, while this philanthropic funding stream may sever the link between the individuals the nonprofit serves and the organization's own financial sustainability, it may create a relationship to other nonprofits. The grantor foundation will likely be funding similar organizations through grants across the state or country, and coordinating technical assistance across these related grantee organizations. As such, the financial link formed between a foundation and a nonprofit may have the effect of incorporating the nonprofit into a quasi-federated system of other grantees that resembles how traditional interest groups function. As I will show later in this chapter, major foundations interested in immigrants act as institutional patrons to create this type of collaboration and coalition-based approach that now closely resembles the traditional federated interest-group system, but with ties to the philanthropic donor rather than to members.

Moreover, notwithstanding the fact that many immigrant-serving nonprofits do not require clients or constituents to pay membership dues, I argue that what is most important is that these nonprofits do represent the interests of the immigrants they serve, and therefore sometimes behave in fundamentally similar ways to interest groups (de Graauw 2008). Whether or not they are a 501(c)(3) organization is of secondary importance, after how they develop an identity in relationship to the community. This approach is drawn from the work of Jeffrey Berry in *The New Liberalism* (1999) and elsewhere. Berry argued that political change in the country over the last half century has witnessed the elevation of identity as an organizing force and motivation for political allegiances and a characteristic of the system of pluralism. Rather than the strong ties to political parties or vocation of earlier generations, for many individuals the end of the twentieth century saw "a more intensely held identity is often that of a feminist, [or] an evangelical Christian" (Berry 1999, 2)—or, in this case, *an immigrant*. Immigrants affiliate with what Berry called citizen groups, many of which resemble immigrant-serving nonprofit organizations. Even without the dues-paying relationship, in meeting their mission these nonprofits reflect the identity and interests of immigrants for several reasons. Explicitly, many immigrant-serving nonprofits were founded by immigrants; many have leadership boards made up of immigrants; and many are also operated by employees and volunteers drawn from the immigrant community that they serve. These organizations are also often physically located in immigrant neighborhoods and are thus symbolic representations of the vitality of the neighborhood and the presence of immigrants. These explicit connections to the community manifest themselves in the implicit representative orientation of the nonprofits' operations, even if that does not always turn into political action. While the mission of an immigrant organization may focus on health, education, or the arts, when the organization petitions for more funding, interacts with policy makers, with the media, or with other businesses or nonprofits, it is providing a voice for those it serves. It articulates the immigrant community's needs and values in this public sphere, and in doing so acts as a representative institution. While some immigrant-serving nonprofit leaders might eschew this role as presumptuous, it is hard to deny that representation is a part of what nonprofits do, even if not every nonprofit is well equipped to do it effectively. Furthermore, because of the uniquely political and civic characteristics of immigrants and immigration, the representative dimension of this type of nonprofit is likely to be even more prominent than it is for nonprofits that provide services to less civically defined constituents, such as children or the elderly.

In view of this representative function that immigrant-serving nonprofits play, they can be seen to fit into a more recent trend in American politics and pluralism. Research suggests that the central role played by member-based and member-funded groups has been waning, edged aside by citizen groups funded out of large donations and grants (Berry 1999; Skocpol 1999; Skocpol, Ganz, and Munson 2000). While national member-based associations and interest groups still wield much influence in political decision making, they are now often joined by a host of other types of organizations with no distinct group of members. Single-issue citizen organizations, think tanks, and research institutes—all nonprofit organizations—have emerged as prominent voices in policy debates, none of them a traditional member-based type of interest group. And rulings by the Supreme Court, such as the infamous *Citizens United* decision in 2010, have opened new doors for a range of organizations to become much more active in elections. Thus, the sharp dividing line between these different types of nonprofit organizations has blurred over the last several decades, suggesting that membership and IRS status may not explain as much about an organization's decision making, operations, or its identify as in the past. This is why I focus more broadly on immigrant-serving nonprofit organizations, primarily 501(c)(3)s but also those that maintain other IRS designations.

Another reason to pay much closer attention to the political role of nonprofits in general is their relative prominence. There are many more 501(c)(3) organizations operating in the country than other types of nonprofits, especially 501(c)(4)s. In 2012, there were over a million 501(c)(3)s, two-thirds of the total and three times the number of 501(c)(4)s.[2] Increasingly, these 501(c)(3) nonprofits are major employers and sources of economic activity in many parts of the country. As the role of nonprofits in many segments of the society and economy has increased, and the dominance of traditional membership-based interest groups has waned, nonprofits have taken on a greater role in representing the political interests of those to whom they provide services. Since these services are often provided to those in need, and those who often lack any other type of formal representation, representing nonprofit constituents is both important but also controversial. The attacks made in 2010 on the low-income-voter registration organization called ACORN were exemplary of the fragile and often contentious role nonprofits play in politics. For some critics, advocacy should be reserved for political organizations who are given the 501(c)(4) status, not the special 501(c)(3) tax status, particularly if those organizations receive government funding. The postelection controversy faced by the IRS in the spring of 2013 regarding how to grant and regulate nonprofit status was further evidence of this contested institutional arena for nonprofits.

To be sure, simply because 501(c)(3) nonprofit organizations may legally engage in many forms of political advocacy does not mean they have the resources in place, the demand from their board or constituents, or the intrinsic interest to incorporate advocacy into their operations (LeRoux and Krawczyk 2013). Nonprofits supported primarily by government grants, which restrict the use of funds for advocacy and elections, may have limited alternative sources of funding to support political representation. And even if an immigrant-serving nonprofit believes it should represent a particular immigrant community, that does not necessarily mean it will see politics or elections as the best avenues for that representation. For those that do, however, private foundations provide a willing partner. For nonprofit organizations that lack other sources of funding to pursue political advocacy, philanthropic foundations can provide opportunities through grants to support these organizations' political and electoral activities. Not all nonprofits that participate in elections do so with the support of foundation funds, but some of the most significant electoral work in 2012 was connected to a complex philanthropic funding structure.

Philanthropic Foundations and the Policy Process

In the last fifty years, as some nonprofit organizations have successfully stepped into policy debates and electoral politics, private philanthropic foundations have also joined the fray; and their more recent role in the movement to register and mobilize immigrant voters and pursue immigrant rights has been prominent. Many of today's most prominent foundations grew out of the accumulation of wealth in the late nineteenth and early twentieth centuries. Business tycoons of the Gilded Age and the following decades such as Andrew Carnegie and Henry Ford sought to stamp their impression on U.S. society by creating private non-profit institutions with the mission to give money to address social causes. The impetus for many foundations of that period was closely tied, if not always in harmony, with the spirit of social reform of Progressive reformers like Jane Addams, Lincoln Steffens, and Edward A. Ross. But it was not until the mid-twentieth century that these foundations emerged as powerful players in the policy process.

Changes in federal laws in the late 1960s sped the ascension of foundations in American policy making (Ferris and Harmssen 2009). In terms of sheer numbers, foundations (including private, community, and public foundations) ballooned, increasing threefold from 21,887 in 1975 to 76,610 in 2010. Foundations also prospered as their invested assets grew rapidly from expansion of the stock market. And perhaps most significantly, the amount foundations gave out each year increased because of new mandates from Congress. Starting in 1969, Congress required private foundations to give out 6 percent (this was amended in 1981 to 5 percent) of their earnings from invested assets each year (Roelofs 2003). Thus, in 2010, the $75 trillion in foundation assets resulted in the awarding of $45 billion in various types of grants, more than the total budget for the National Science Foundation (approximately $7 billion) and National Institutes of Health (approximately $30 billion) combined.

Though legally restricted by the IRS from lobbying or direct advocacy, foundations have long been associated with the policy process (Vaughan and Arsneault 2014). The Russell Sage Foundation traces its policy work back to the turn of the previous century and its interest in financial services policies (Anderson 2008). Concerned with unscrupulous banks and banking practices, Russell Sage helped develop new ideas for reforming public policies on lending. These ideas, and others, put Russell Sage at the forefront of the Progressive Era reforms of numerous U.S. political institutions.

Today, foundations play an active role in debates about policy ideas, or what John Kingdon (1995) famously called the "policy stream." Foundations often act as "policy entrepreneurs," linking funding, ideas, and policy experts together (Mintrom 2000). Within foreign policy circles, foundations create "intellectual institutions and knowledge networks" (Parmar 2012, 8). Some prominent think tanks—often the home to policy entrepreneurs—received over a quarter of their revenues from foundation grants (Weidenbaum 2009).

Foundations are most conspicuously involved in key policy issues by financially supporting the formation and operations of nonprofit organizations (Walker 1991; Mandeville 2007; Sandfort 2008; Zunz 2014). In *The New Liberalism*, Jeffrey Berry's (1999) seminal account of the rise of citizen groups in the 1960s, he wrote:

"For the development of citizen groups . . . the most important reform effort was initiated by the Ford Foundation. . . . The Foundation supported a cadre of sixteen public interest law firms whose avowed intention was to broaden representation before government and to open up the governmental process" (26). Indicative of this approach, Ford helped found the immigrant-serving organization the Mexican American Legal Defense and Educational Fund (MALDEF) in 1968 with a grant of $2.2 million (Kaplowitz 2005). Other foundations followed this model and supported policy and advocacy work in a variety of policy areas, acting as what Walker (1991) called "institutional patrons." The Ford Foundation and the Carnegie Corporation of New York, among others, were instrumental in funding aspects of the educational reform movement during the 1990s, and the Gates Foundation stands above all others in providing money for nonprofits working on educational issues in the 2000s and beyond (Rhodes 2012; Reckhow 2013). In her recent account of education reform, Sarah Reckhow contended: "Major foundations, such as the Gates Foundation, Broad Foundation, Carnegie Corporation, and Walton Family Foundation, have financed the development of a new organizational infrastructure in education policy. . . . Without private funding, many of these organizations would not exist" (3). In similar ways, three foundations (the Robert Wood Johnson Foundation, the W. K. Kellogg Foundation, and the Pew Charitable Trusts) have influenced health policy making (Weissert and Knott 1995), and foundations with left-leaning and right-leaning ideologies were involved at the national and global level in funding groups on either side of the gay rights and gun rights debates (Bob 2012). Finally, the Olin Foundation supported the conservative legal movement of the 1980s and 1990s through helping establish student organizations at U.S. law schools (Teles 2009; Avery and McLaughlin 2013).

Despite the restrictions on lobbying, philanthropic foundations are far from neutral players in the policy process. In education policy, for example, the Gates Foundation has wielded enormous influence over the shape of policy reforms. The foundation's view of what works has focused on centralization of political control—often in a mayor's office—standardization and testing, and market-based options such as vouchers and charter schools (Reckhow 2012). The enormous size of the Gates Foundation has largely shut out other educational options such as stronger elected school boards and stronger teacher unions, and limited the financial opportunities for organizations that advocate for these positions. In other policy arenas, foundations bring similarly strong preferences for certain policy approaches and for funding the organizations that can advocate for and implement policy change. Foundations have changed the system of pluralism in the United States, empowering new political actors, but they have not necessarily changed the unequal character or biased nature of political representation and pluralism.

It was these strong political preferences, in fact, that resulted in the passage of one set of federal regulations on private philanthropic foundations. During the 1960s, foundations ran askance of federal policy makers who viewed the voter registration work that the foundations supported as too partisan and narrowly focused, potentially affecting certain election outcomes, not just increasing the number of registered voters. As a result, new IRS regulations—Section 4945(f)—placed limitations on private (not community or public) foundation grant-making to nonprofits that run voter registration drives.[3] In order to be compliant with the regulation, private foundations can fund 501(c)(3) nonprofit organizations engaged in voter registration only if such registration is across more than five states and not focused on a single electoral cycle. Those nonprofit grantees must also devote a majority (more than 85 percent) of their resources to the core service mission of the organization. Federal regulations restrict nonprofits from transitioning much beyond the hybrid type of organization described in the introduction. But these regulations do not restrain voter engagement, voter education, or voter mobilization, as long as all those funded activities are done in a nonpartisan fashion.

In short, the last fifty years have seen foundations move to the center of important policy debates and various opportunities to form common cause with nonprofit grantees, while operating in an arena shaped by new federal regulations. While foundations may be the hidden or unacknowledged player in public policy making, it is hard to imagine the U.S. system of advocacy and pluralistic representation operating without foundations as the source of so much financial aid. The enormous financial resources have also brought with them control and influence, dictating not only who is funded, but also crowding out competing efforts. In many instances, foundations have helped advance immigrant interests through funding immigrant-serving nonprofit organizations and creating a quasi-federated system of coalitions of coordinated nonprofits. Meanwhile, another group of institutional patrons has opposed certain immigrant issues, particularly related to voting, by supporting a different set of nonprofit organizations. In each case, complex funding structures link interests, money, and nonprofit organizations together around the issue of immigration and immigrants.

The Structure of Funding

In order to focus their influence, foundations concentrate giving in certain policy sectors. In 2010, the Foundation Center estimated that education (23.7 percent), health (21.7 percent), and human services (15.1 percent) were the three policy areas that received the largest amount of funding. Public affairs, the broad policy area where most funding is provided on immigrant issues, made up 12.3 percent of foundation funding in 2010. Within that policy area, foundations provided more than $2 billion for projects related to ethnic and racial minorities, and $265 million for projects related to immigrants and refugee issues. These levels are historic highs for grants related to immigrants. Indicative of this, the trend of funding for immigrant issues has been sharply upward since 2000 (see figure 2.1): foundation grants for immigrants and refugee issues doubled in less than a decade, from less than $150 million to a peak of over $300 million in 2008.

There is also a geographic dimension to foundation giving related to immigrants. Foundations targeted their donations to where most immigrants and refugees reside. In 2011, over 40 percent of donations went to organizations and projects based in the Northeast, followed by the West, the Midwest, and the South. These patterns have remained relatively unchanged since 2007, though in 2008 there was a shift in emphasis to projects in states in the West.

To understand the full structure of funding for immigrant-serving nonprofits, traditional private philanthropic foundations have to be viewed in relationship to other, new philanthropic organizations. In 2012, there were numerous individual foundations, as well as collaborations *among* foundations, that provided grant opportunities to immigrant-serving nonprofits to do civic, electoral, and voting-related work. Funding for these activities often comes through a "Russian nesting doll" arrangement of interlinked organizations and streams of funding (See figure 2.2). Understanding this complex and somewhat convoluted structure

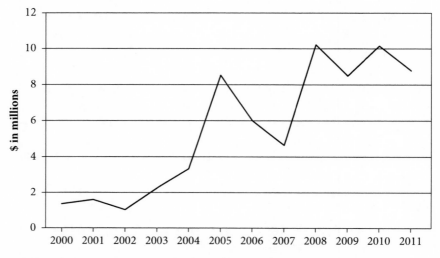

FIGURE 2.1. Trend of foundation grant funds for immigrants and refugees, 2001–2011

Source: Foundation Center.

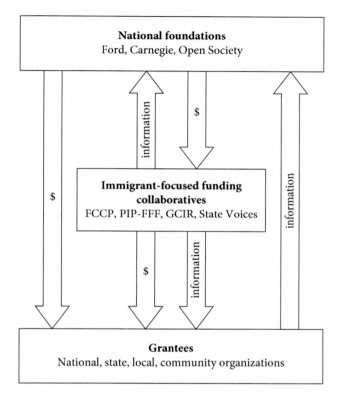

FIGURE 2.2.   Russian nesting-doll structure of philanthropic funding for immigrant issues

can help make better sense of the immigrant integration and voting movement, the way streams of funding promote certain nonprofit strategies over others, and the opportunities and challenges posed to nonprofits in need of support.

At the outer shell, several well-known foundations ("National foundations") provided large, multimillion-dollar grants to make possible much of the work of new intermediaries ("Immigrant-focused funding collaboratives"), which then provided smaller grants to nonprofits, often with budgets that total less than $500,000 ("The grantees"). Money was not the only form of exchange between foundations and nonprofit organizations. Information, technical expertise, and lessons learned were shared back and forth between each level of this complex structure of aid. Thus, as much as the money, other connections deepen the relationship between the grantees and the other organizations in the quasi-federated funding stream. Rather than members, as is the case for most traditional interest groups, grants bind nonprofits together within this system. As such, in accepting a foundation grant, the grantee also will need to align with the general approach or vision held by the foundation, if not entirely, then at least in regard to the execution of the grant. A nonprofit with a mission that is incompatible with that of the foundation is unlikely to ever become a grantee. The following section examines these various organizations and how they emerged over the last decade.

National Foundations

Many foundations have long prioritized issues of democracy and political participation, but interest in these issues grew and sharpened in the early 2000s. One factor that drove particular interest in immigrants and participation was the realization of the demographic changes described in chapter 1. The population of the country was in flux, and there were limited governmentally sponsored efforts to integrate newcomers, particularly those from nontraditional sending countries. In the 2000s, foundations saw the trajectory of demographic change as a growing issue, and over time linked it to the research on low levels of immigrant political participation. For certain foundations, these were not new pursuits; in fact they traced back to the foundations' founding and founders, generations earlier.

Other events also affected the decisions foundations made. The attacks in New York City and Washington, DC, of September 11, 2001—9/11—had ramifications that went beyond a new awareness of global terrorism threats. The realization that these threats had an ethnic and religious dimension resulted in immediate concerns for immigrants and ethnic minority groups. For example, hate crimes were committed against Arab, Muslim, and other Americans who were wrongly linked to the attacks, often merely based on their dress or physical appearance.[4] Certain foundations were keen to address this issue. Hasan Jaber, the executive director of ACCESS—the Dearborn-based Arab American nonprofit—noted that "the one [foundation] that took interest first was the Ford Foundation; after September 11, [they were] the ones who approached us and said we need to do something on civic engagement."[5]

The Ford Foundation, one of the nation's oldest and largest private philanthropic foundations, had assets of over $10 billion in 2012. The foundation owes its large endowment to Henry Ford and the accumulated wealth from automobile manufacturing innovations of the early twentieth century. Ford's assembly line depended on workers with a common set of low-level skills, discipline, and English literacy, attributes the company believed recent immigrants were often lacking. The "Americanization" program, run from 1914 to 1921 by the company's Sociological Department, included language classes, grooming and etiquette advice, and financial incentives, all aimed at imbuing in the recent immigrant a Ford-inspired sense of citizenship (Meyer 1980). For Ford, integration meant immigrant workers casting off a variety of languages, beliefs, and cultures in favor of a common, American version of assembly-line culture.

Henry Ford's views toward immigrants were generally consistent with those of the Progressive reformers of his era. The Progressives' campaign against party machines and political corruption, so often linked to the common cause formed between urban party bosses and new immigrants, shaped certain nativist aspirations for political and cultural homogeneity (McMahon 1999; Lim 2013). The Americanizing of assembly-line employees was seen as working in tandem with Americanizing new citizens and future voters to eschew political parties in favor of the Progressive vision of a benevolent melting pot, free of partisanship and some of the allegedly nasty habits newcomers preferred, such as alcohol consumption (S. Wilson 2011).

The Ford Foundation grew out of the Progressive Era and the rising role played by philanthropists in solving societal problems. But times have changed since Henry Ford's passing, and the foundation, which Ford's son, Edsel, established in the 1930s, has adapted to the contemporary immigrant situation. The foundation framed the issue during the 2000s in this way: "A greater influx of immigrants has come to the United States in the past 25 years than at any time in history, engendering a backlash that has stripped large segments of the immigrant community of their rights. This population confronts large-scale immigration roundups, the denial of due process in deportation proceedings, abusive detention conditions, and increased hate crimes and bias attacks."[6] In line with that framing of the issue, Ford's interest in immigrants was reflected in 2011–2012 with major grants to the Asian American Legal Defense and Education Fund ($100,000), Voto Latino ($750,000), and the National Council of La Raza (NCLR) ($1.875 million).[7] These individual grants made up a small portion of the foundation's total giving but are an indication of its strong and persistent interest in the immigrant issue.

The Ford Foundation has long worked in close partnership with the Carnegie Corporation of New York. Carnegie, also one of the largest foundations in the country, was famously founded by Scottish immigrant and steel magnate Andrew Carnegie. Carnegie celebrated the role of the immigrant in American society and championed assimilation. In fact, upon its founding, the Carnegie Corporation initiated a major 1918 study of Americanization, the "Study of Methods of Americanization or Fusion of Native and Foreign Born." Much like Ford, though without as many allusions to the corporate bottom line, Carnegie and the study group emphasized educating or re-educating immigrants about accepted American attitudes and the English language. In one section of the report, Frank Thompson (1920) framed the immigrant problem as one related to the shift to Southern and Eastern European immigration. He wrote that the problem had two important elements: "the preponderance of immigrants from non-English-speaking nations; and . . . our newer immigrants have come from countries having a high degree of illiteracy" (30). Thompson went on to argue that the second of these issues might be addressed with the new 1917 immigration law that tested potential immigrants for literacy before granting admission to the country. The first would be addressed with more resources for adult education and, Thompson hoped, more diligent class attendance by immigrants. The report's findings shaped future national immigration policy and the creation and funding of a host of new organizations during that era.

Ever since, the Carnegie Corporation has maintained the vision of its founder and emphasis on what it later called immigrant *integration*. The foundation had also been interested in voting issues since the 1990s, at that time focused on campaign finance debates taking place in Washington and many state capitals. Only a year before the 9/11 attacks, the 2000 Supreme Court decision in *Bush v. Gore* exposed deep weaknesses in U.S. election law and voting procedures. Partly in response to this problem, Carnegie made numerous grants to organizations working on election technology and implementing reforms to state education procedures, particularly those related to disenfranchisement of groups of voters.[8]

During the 2000s, Carnegie reemphasized immigrant integration and participation, a priority that had been mostly absent from its recent portfolio. As late as 2000, the foundation only tangentially mentioned immigrant issues as a part of its core programs; but it quickly added immigrant integration to its funding priorities by the middle of the decade.[9] According to the foundation's 2004–2005 annual report, "A relatively new emphasis of the Strengthening U.S. Democracy program is immigrant civic integration. A network of national and local organizations serving immigrants has received support to provide legal assistance and advice about naturalization" (5).[10] But Carnegie's agenda was not narrowly focused on a handful of grants—the foundation had ambitious aims related to immigration and immigrants. Geri Mannion, who led many of the Carnegie Corporation's efforts in the immigrant rights movement, elaborated the approach in a 2008 publication: "An [immigrant's] ability to fully integrate into our society is being challenged by an immigration system that is clearly broken. In collaboration with donor partners such as the Ford and Horace Hagedorn foundations, Atlantic Philanthropies and the Open Society Institute, the Corporation's goal is to work with its grantees and support their collaborative efforts to integrate immigrants so that all of America can continue to benefit from the skills, ideas and dreams of its newest citizens."[11]

These far-reaching objectives were reflected in grant data from Carnegie. Based on information from the Foundation Center, starting in 2007 there was a sharp increase in funding for this area, totaling over $14 million in 2012 (see figure 2.3). Major grants were given by Carnegie to the Public Interest Projects

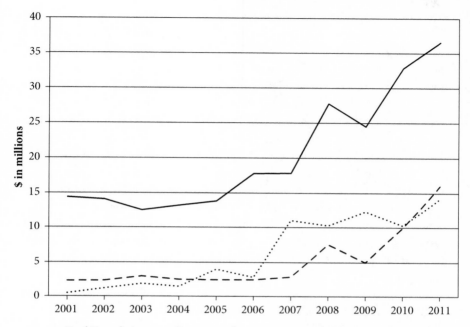

FIGURE 2.3. Select foundation awards for immigrants and refugees, 2001–2011
Source: Foundation Center.

(PIP) in 2008 (a grant for $6 million and another for $6.5 million), in 2011 (a grant for $3 million and another for $5 million), and then in 2012 (a grant for $5 million) to support immigrant issues. In 2012, Carnegie also gave large grants to the Immigrant Legal Resource Center ($5 million), America's Voice Education Fund ($1.5 million), and the Center for Community Change ($1 million), all dedicated to immigrant rights and immigrant civic integration work.

Immigrant-Focused Funding Collaboratives

Ford and Carnegie, along with the Open Society Foundations, the Knight Foundation, Unbound Philanthropy, and other foundations, prioritized immigrants, voting, and civic engagement during the 2000s, but, as Mannion suggested, they did so not only individually but also in partnership, or what Sarah Reckhow (2012) called "convergent grant making." Rather than institutions pursuing their often-overlapping missions independently, this approach to grant making draws foundations together in order to avoid redundancy and to share information about programmatic successes. One effort to better bind the various independent foundation efforts together in common cause was the formalization of a group called the Funders Committee for Civic Participation (FCCP). The organization had been established in the 1970s, but not until the mid-2000s was a professional staff chosen. According to the executive director, Deb Ross, "a key aspect has been sharing funding strategies to increase the impact and avoid duplication."[12] Ross explained that for the approximately two hundred foundations at the local, state, and national levels, "immigrant civic engagement is a big issue, because we have a priority on equity issues." The FCCP pursued its mission primarily through convening member foundations for weekly phone calls and national meetings, sharing information on election reform, ballot initiatives, and the census/redistricting process. Rather than being concerned with distributing funds, the strategy was focused on distributing information and sharing ideas.

Another collaborative that bound together the work of foundations was Grantmakers Concerned with Immigrants (GCIR). Founded in 1990 by Mary McClymont, then with the Ford Foundation, GCIR aimed to help address the aftermath of the passage of the Immigration Reform and Control Act in 1986. GCIR initially focused on the backlash against immigrants and the impact of the welfare reform policies of President Bill Clinton, but it was not an easy sell to many foundations, even those with deep interests in social issues. According to the organization's executive director, Daranee Petsod,

> When GCIR was formed in 1990, our membership grew slowly and quietly. From the beginning, we have sought to connect immigration to priority issues for foundations, focusing on helping "newcomers," responding to "changing demographics," and building "strong, healthy communities." Today, a growing number of our members have an immigrant- and/or refugee-specific funding area, although the majority integrate immigrant and refugee issues into their existing funding portfolios—from poverty alleviation to education to workforce development.[13]

By 2012, more than three hundred foundations were members of GCIR, which specialized in "research, communications, programming, and technical assistance" and did "a large body of work on . . . immigrant integration." In line with the focus on integration, its work was increasingly tied to elections, and it published major reports and held meetings during election years.

Running parallel to FCCP and GCIR was one of the other collaborative in-novations that emerged out of this period of increased foundation focus on im-migrants. Foundations established the Four Freedoms Fund (FFF), a part of the Public Interest Projects (PIP also had separate "funds" that work on juvenile justice, low-income communities, human rights, and gender equity), to collaborate on ac-tual funding, not merely sharing and disseminating information. According to a report from the Carnegie Corporation, the national foundations mentioned earlier

> found they were hard pressed to serve the immigrant community whose most dire needs called for local action. Seeking effective new strategies to get needed money down to grassroots groups they couldn't reach, rep-resentatives of several large foundations got together to think through better ways to facilitate funding and move immigrant civic engagement and integration forward. . . . Observing how small immigrant organiza-tions regularly banded together to be more efficient and effective, [Mi-chele Lord, then of the Ford Foundation,] suggested starting a parallel funding collaborative on a national level.[14]

The initial grants were for $2.8 million to create the FFF. According to the FFF, "The Four Freedoms Fund works by pooling large grants from individual foun-dations and making smaller grants to state and local immigrant advocacy orga-nizations for strategic planning, board development, fundraising, policy analysis, organizing and media training" (4). This approach, the FFF argued, "simplifies the process of making a large number of grants to grassroots groups, while en-couraging funder collaboration for strategic grantmaking."

Under the auspices of PIP, the FFF funded individual organizations and several electoral coalitions that then sub-granted to individual organizations. FFF grants to nonprofits that were focused on immigrant and refugee issues increased four-fold in ten years, from less than $2 million in 2000 to close to $10 million by the end of the decade. FFF used this foundation support to fund smaller nonprofit organizations. Based on publicly available IRS data for 2010, FFF provided large grants to South Asian Americans Leading Together ($175,000), the New York Im-migration Coalition ($225,000), and Latino Justice / PRLDEF ($150,000).

Another innovation during this time was the creation of State Voices. In 2008, State Voices began to work on civic and voter engagement, specifically to pro-vide technological support to organizations, including those serving immigrants. The organization's website stated that the founders "knew grassroots nonprofits could improve their effectiveness by working together, and they knew this sort of sophisticated collaboration would require a stable structure. The state table model was born."[15] The "state table model" was "a place where organizations could come together to share resources, communicate openly, build trust, engage in real field collaboration, and share their battles."[16] The organization started with tables in eleven states but by 2012 had grown to twenty-two states linking six hundred organizations. Each state table was overseen by a particular organization in the state: the Grassroots Institute of New Jersey for New Jersey, Blueprint NC for North Carolina, and Michigan Voice for Michigan.

State Voices received a portion of its revenue from foundations. FFF provided it grants worth $400,000 (2009) and $600,000 (2011). State Voices, which also received a $1.5 million grant directly from Atlantic Philanthropies and a $300,000 grant from Ford, then gave out its own grants, typically less than $100,000, to state and local groups such as the Ohio Voters Fund, the Center for Nonprofit Voting, and APIA Vote.

State Voices also developed a unique strategy on voter engagement. It focused much of its giving on technology, often to open access to the very database and outreach tools mentioned thus far in this book. In particular, State Voices worked closely with the Voter Activation Network (VAN), a digital product distributed by Catalist (Ambinder 2009). Laura Quinn and Harold Ickes created Catalist, a private for-profit company, in 2006 with seed money from George Soros (not funding by the Soros-affiliated Open Society Foundations).[17] The VAN was a massive database of voter information that Catalist rented to labor unions, political parties, and nonprofits such as State Voices. In states that did not have an established state table, State Voices established a "Tools for All Fund" in order to give technological support and data access to interested nonprofits.

Grantees

Sitting at the center of the nesting-doll or quasi-federated structure of funding are individual nonprofit organizations or grantees, what I call immigrant-serving nonprofit organizations. It is difficult to fully disaggregate foundation grants for immigrant-serving nonprofit election work, because many grants are for multiple purposes, and information on individual grants is not always publicly accessible. For the largest recipients of grants in 2011 across immigrant and refugee issues, the organizations ranged in purpose: a number focused on legal protections and civil rights (the Immigrant Legal Resource Center and Asian Pacific American Legal Center of Southern California, and the National Immigration Law Center), others focused more on refugee resettlement or immigrant services (the International Rescue Committee, and Catholic Relief Services). Much of the funding for voter engagement, as explained above, came from Public Interest Projects, which redistributed the $8.47 million in grants received by smaller organizations.

In addition to the work of intermediaries such as PIP, FFF, and State Voices, large foundations also provided grants directly to grantee nonprofits. Three examples—ACCESS, the Consortium of Hispanic Agencies, and One Arizona—will help illustrate how this funding supports nonprofits serving different communities of immigrants in different parts of the country. First, ACCESS, the Arab Community Center for Economic and Social Services, described at the start of the book, received early funding from the Ford Foundation, and in 2011–2012, in addition to grants from Carnegie, Ford, and the Open Society Foundations, received grants from the FFF and State Voices.[18] An affiliate of ACCESS, the National Network of Arab American Communities (NNAAC), also was awarded considerable grant support. According to NNAAC's director, Nadia Tonova, "those [funding] organizations are our lifeline, not only for elections, but other work; without them we would not be able to function."[19] NNAAC coordinated advocacy and electoral engagement for ACCESS and also the work of twenty-three partner organizations across the country. NNAAC even used foundation support to provide sub-grants ($2,000–$3,000) to smaller organizations to pursue electoral engagement; the funding was used, for example, to hold election-related events or provide small stipends for interns. This range of funders makes ACCESS and NNAAC unique and their electoral engagement portfolio as deep and broad as nearly any in the country.

Second, the experience of the Consortium of Hispanic Agencies, based in Detroit, was also indicative of the complex ways foundations interacted with grantees around voter engagement. The consortium's mission was to link together six local agencies: Community and Health Social Services, Detroit Hispanic Development Corporation, Latin Americans for Social and Economic Development, Latino Family Services, Mana De Metro Detroit, and SER Metro Detroit. The consortium had loosely tied the work of these agencies together since the 1970s, but even after a new policy agenda was agreed upon in the 1990s, the consortium deemed its advocacy work ineffective.[20] Executive director Norman Bent summarized the dilemma that "individually they could not do advocacy; after the 1990s agenda was drafted it created momentum, but died down over ten years."[21] In response, the organizations collectively asked: "How do we strategize? How do we focus?" The consortium began by establishing committees around different important issues, but it soon realized "we can't focus on all nine issues; how do we prioritize?" According to Bent, initial advocacy was aided by foundations: "Skillman Foundation was the first, then Kellogg, and minor dollars from NCLR [National Council of La Raza]." In January 2012, the consortium received a four-year, $1 million grant from the Kellogg Foundation to "build the necessary infrastructure to strengthen collaborations and implement a Latino agenda for Southwest Detroit."[22]

The consortium of organizations understood that politics was more than sim-ple advocacy: voting and elections mattered too. Bent recalled: "So ... we realized, [the question was,] how do we get involved in civic engagement? [Our county in Michigan] was one of the only counties that grew in the 2010 census. . . . [It had] a very high number of eligible individuals, but only a small percent participated." The organizations in the consortium believed that they "had to change that, had to work on leadership development, get representation in governance, and build a pipeline. . . . We felt that we had to get involved in the election piece."

The consortium also knew that since "existing funds were for organizing," there was no external support for its plans to expand voter engagement. Accord-ing to Bent, "Kellogg has been open to [the] voter mobilization piece; however, the funds were already allocated for other things." Fortunately, there were other options: "State Voices came in handy. . . . [Its] role was to provide that funding," with matching funds from the NCLR. "State Voices funds provided money to hire a part-time coordinator, to hire students to go door to door." The consortium used those new foundation dollars to hire nearly eighty student volunteers dur-ing the summer to canvas neighborhoods.

This overlapping and complementary foundation funding allowed for a wide array of new activities to expand what the consortium could accomplish. New funding permitted the consortium to transition from a service-oriented organi-zation to the hybrid type of organization, taking on characteristics of and elec-toral tactics used by a traditional interest group. It is reasonable to speculate as to whether this would be possible without the coordinating work and new resources provided by collaboratives such as GCIR, FCCP, and State Voices.

In other parts of the country, similar events occurred and illustrated the third example, One Arizona. Leticia De La Vara explained that following passage by the Arizona State Legislature of SB 1070, the infamous anti-immigrant state policy, nonprofits in the state were uncoordinated and ineffective in a response. De La Vara said, "Funders came forward to ask for the coalition" to coordinate a re-sponse. One of those funders was FFF, which had received support from the Un-bound Philanthropy foundation to support organizations in Arizona.[23] Through a coalition approach supported by FFF called One Arizona, the expense of cer-tain aspects of voter engagement—such as data management software—could be shared, and efficiencies gained across organizations. De La Vara said that by cre-ating One Arizona they gained "unified branding under certain Latino-specific" messages and "combined funding efforts for television, news, and radio." So, not only do foundations help service-oriented nonprofits transition to hybrid or-ganizations; they also help to found new organizations with political identities.

ACCESS, the Consortium of Hispanic Agencies, and One Arizona were in-dicative of the experience of a group of nonprofit grantees, each able to fund new or enhanced electoral activities related to the people they served. These grantees shared a priority with major private foundations and received considerable financial support accordingly. Foundations provided funding, of course, but the other aspects of their influence cannot be underestimated. Foundations have created a quasi-federated structure that permits them to reach across community and state boundaries, link various nonprofits together, and leverage the expertise gained from previous grant making. Increasing rates of political participation by immigrants also must be attributed in part to this complex structure of funding to support immigrant-serving nonprofits.

But the beneficiaries of the convergence of grant making for immigrant rights and integration also reflected other foundation preferences. All three of the organizations described above are pan-ethnic organizations, merging the interests of Arab Americans or Hispanic Americans across ethnic boundaries. Of the top fifty grantees in 2011, all reflected a pan-ethnic or pan-immigrant orientation. For example, the National Immigration Forum and Immigrant Legal Resource Center, which received a large amount of funding from grants, represents broad immigrant interests, and the Asian American Justice Center, also the winner of large grants, represents the interests of Asian Americans, in general. There are obvious reasons for these preferences: pan-ethnic organizations may reach a wider audience and array of immigrant constituents, and supporting them may promote collective action and interethnic harmony. Large foundations may also find it logistically difficult and inefficient to provide small grants to hundreds of ethnic-specific nonprofits, preferring instead to make just a few large grants to the intermediates mentioned earlier that can then re-grant to smaller organizations.

These preferences also hark back to the founding of the Ford Foundation and the Carnegie Corporation, and a particular view toward immigrants that emphasizes acceptance of American values, adoption of English, and citizenship. Historic assimilationist values echo in the more recent attention to pan-ethnic and pan-immigrant common cause. Yet, as chapter 1 showed, pan-ethnic identity is a social construction that many immigrants are ambivalent toward or reject outright. Many immigrants identify with their country-of-origin background—for instance, 62 percent of Asian Americans do so—and many immigrants likely affiliate with at least some organization that shares their identity. To suggest that nonprofits all pursue a common immigrant agenda or view immigration issues alike would be misleading.

And these preferences by foundations were not always so strong, nor have they been uniform across interest areas. For example, philanthropic funding on women's issues favored fragmentation, rather than consolidation, such that in the 1970s and 1980s foundations tended to disperse their support for women's issues, aiding nonprofits separately serving poor women, lesbian women, and abused

women (Goss 2013). Foundation support for immigrant issues had been similarly distributed as late as the 1990s. In 1998, though pan-ethnic nonprofits won
many large grants, the Jewish Fund for Justice, Chinatown Action for Progress, the
National Coalition for Haitian Rights, and the Mexican American Legal Defense
and Education Fund were also in the top fifty of grant recipients in the category
of immigrants and refugees. Yet relatively few of these ethnic-specific nonprofits have benefited from the recent expansion and convergence of grant making.
Nonprofits that specifically represent Indian Americans, Chinese Americans, or
Egyptian Americans—despite the considerable size of each population—have
been largely shut out of the opportunity to expand their civic engagement and
voter mobilization activities through grants. In some cases, these ethnic-specific
organizations may link to pan-ethnic coalitions that receive foundation support
through a state or local coalition, and thus receive some aid. But we must ask
whether in doing so they were compelled to acquiesce to the priority that foundations place on the pan-ethnic perspective. In order to receive support, must they
choose between the ethnic identity of their immigrant constituents and a potentially conflicting view of ethnicity held by national foundations? The answers to
these questions relate to the decisions made by immigrant-serving nonprofits
regarding politics and elections.

Foundations, Voter Fraud, and Immigration

The prominent philanthropic efforts described above to support immigrant-
serving nonprofit organizations occurred alongside, and were likely propelled
by, giving on other issues, some potentially hostile to the interests of immigrants.
The work by nonprofits to change voting laws was initiated and supported by a
different array of philanthropic foundations and equally novel financial intermediaries. Some of the leading foundations supporting this conservative policy
development were the Lynde and Harry Bradley Foundation, the Sarah Scaife
Foundation, and the John M. Olin Foundation (Dye 2001). The Koch family
foundations (a group of foundations supported by various family members of
Fred Koch), Freedom Partners, and FreedomWorks also played a major part in
policy advocacy aiming to alter U.S. immigration policies.

To be sure, the major political phenomenon of the 2008–2012 period was the
rise of the Tea Party or, more aptly, tea parties (Brown 2015). In the immediate
aftermath of the 2008 election of President Barack Obama, individuals established over nine hundred Tea Party–themed and affiliated organizations across
the country (Skocpol and Williamson 2012). Propelled by talk radio and supported by the political nonprofit FreedomWorks and several private foundations,

many, though not all, Tea Party organizations were ideologically conservative or libertarian, hostile to the federal government, and largely opposed to immigrants and immigration (Skocpol and Williamson 2012; Disch 2012; Fallin, Grana, and Glantz 2013). Tea Party organizations aimed to elect anti-immigration candidates at the state and national level and pursued policy change to tighten border control, buttress illegal immigration enforcement, and advance other measures viewed as antagonistic to immigrants, such as voter ID laws.[24]

This political movement of the late 2000s also harked back to an earlier period of political reform in the United States. As noted above, the Progressive reformers of the early twentieth century were hostile to urban political machines and targeted immigrants and immigrant voting (Su 2012). One leading Progressive scholar of the time, Edward A. Ross, wrote: "The worst element in the community makes use of the ignorance and venality of the foreign born voters to exclude the better citizens from any share in the control of local affairs" (Ross 1913). Ross and other reformers focused on federalizing the naturalization process to circumvent "corrupt" local judges and imposing English literacy tests as a requirement for voter eligibility. At the same time, in some southern states, virulently anti-Catholic views intertwined with racial and ethnic prejudice to fuel anti-immigrant activism and the lynching of Italian Americans, Mexican Americans, and Chinese Americans, as well as African Americans (Webb 2002; Carrigan and Webb 2003). The Ku Klux Klan blamed immigrants for opposing Prohibition and cashing in on illegal bootlegging (MacLean 1994). And many nativist southern Democrats opposed the campaign for president of Al Smith from New York largely because of his Catholic faith and related questions about his patriotism (Feldman 2013).

Some in the Tea Party followed a strikingly similar approach in the twenty-first century, questioning the legitimacy of President Obama because of his background, his purported religion, and his purported place of birth. And, as Postel (2012) argued, "Tea Party influence in more than a dozen states has resulted in legislation to rescind motor voter [voter registration] laws, expand felony disqualification lists, add new residency and identification requirements, and impose other hurdles that make it more difficult to vote" (36). These changes in how and when citizens could vote and who was permitted to vote were chief policy objectives of the Tea Party and some of its institutional patrons.

Tea Party advocates pushed beyond simple bureaucratic changes in voting laws. Some Tea Party groups relied on the racialized language—or what Hofstader (1965) called the "paranoid style"—that has dominated debates about immigration used in previous elections (McIlwain and Caliendo 2012). The most radical among the Tea Party groups decried what they called "anchor babies" and advocated for changes in the Fourteenth Amendment of the Constitution to eliminate the practice of birthright citizenship, in order to do away with the long-standing legal practice of granting citizenship to all those born in the country (Postel 2012). And these anti-immigrant views were reflected to some extent in beliefs of the rank-and-file membership or supporters of Tea Party organizations. Public opinion research showed that among the most stridently affiliated with the Tea Party, a majority believed new immigrants increased crime (55 percent) and new immigrants were too powerful (54 percent) (Parker and Barreto 2013). A majority also believed birthright citizenship should be repealed (56 percent) and that the DREAM Act—the legislation written to provide a pathway to citizenship for younger undocumented residents and reform immigrant regulations—should not be passed (54 percent). In the run-up to the 2012 election, organized anti-immigrant advocacy often ran parallel to and was abetted by advocacy on behalf of Tea Party organizations and affiliated campaigns. For example, the Texas-based 1776 Tea Party was "the national faction most directly connected to the anti-immigrant movement" (Burghart 2012, 72).

Some national foundations, though, approached immigration in a different fashion, often aligned with the traditionally conservative, pro-business view of immigration as advantageous for robust trade and economic growth. Many of these foundations, with no direct links to the Tea Party, conceptualized civic participation in different ways as well. Indicative of this mixed view of immigration was the Bradley Foundation. The foundation described its programmatic interests in 2012 as aiming "to encourage projects that focus on cultivating a renewed, healthier, and more vigorous sense of citizenship among the American people, and among peoples of other nations, as well" and explained further that "it is important to note that our view of citizenship is not primarily concerned with promoting civics education, voter awareness or turnout, or similar activities narrowly focused on voting and elections."[25] Bradley's view of citizenship did not directly mention immigrants, but the allusions to voting and elections could not be ignored. Moreover, Bradley had supported immigrant and immigration-focused nonprofits. In total, the foundation gave out $31 million in 2011 to a variety of organizations and issues, including some focused on immigrant issues. Bradley provided grants in 2011 to the Latino Community Center ($75,000), the English Language Partners of Wisconsin ($35,000), and the Hispanic Free Market Network ($50,000).

Bradley also gave funding to organizations that were perceived to be unsympathetic or outright hostile to immigrants. Bradley gave a $35,000 grant to True the Vote, the organization actively seeking to discredit signatures from voters used during the 2011 electoral recall effort targeting Governor Scott Walker in Wisconsin. True the Vote was involved in other policy advocacy aimed to reduce alleged voter fraud in Texas, Florida, and elsewhere (Skocpol and Williamson

2012). The grant from Bradley was ultimately rescinded after True the Vote did not receive the necessary nonprofit status by the IRS (Saul 2012). The Bradley Foundation also supported the American Legislative Exchange Council (ALEC) with grants totaling over $200,000. ALEC was a think tank that developed policy recommendations and "model legislation" that numerous state legislators used to propose changes in voting laws and make controversial changes in gun laws (Bravender 2012).

Perhaps most suspiciously, and troubling to many, Bradley provided a grant for $10,000 to the Einhorn Family Foundation. Einhorn used the grant to purchase billboards in Milwaukee that read, "Voter fraud is a felony"—interpreted by some as a form of voter intimidation.[26] Because the billboards were located in low-income neighborhoods and were posted anonymously by a "private family foundation," there was great concern about who was behind these efforts and what their objectives were. (A similar billboard was placed by the Tea Party–affiliated group Empower Massachusetts [Skocpol and Williamson 2012]). A local newspaper later discovered that Einhorn was behind the purchase, and that the Bradley Foundation grant was the source of the funding.[27]

The Sarah Scaife Foundation, one of a number of foundations overseen by Richard Mellon Scaife, also was involved in immigration issues. Scaife gave out $15 million in grants in 2011 and used a portion of those grants to support immigration policy research organizations. Specifically, Scaife gave a $125,000 grant to the Center for Immigration Studies, a research think tank. The center contended that "data collected by the Center during the past quarter-century has led many of our researchers to conclude that current, high levels of immigration are making it harder to achieve such important national objectives as better public schools, a cleaner environment, homeland security, and a living wage for every native-born and immigrant worker." The center made it clear, though, that while "these data may support criticism of U.S. immigration policies . . . they do not justify ill feelings toward our immigrant community. In fact, many of us at the Center are animated by a 'low-immigration, pro-immigrant' vision of an America that admits fewer immigrants but affords a warmer welcome for those who are admitted."[28] The center also received substantial funding from the Scaife family–affiliated Colcom Foundation (over $20 million in 2010 and 2011 alone) and smaller gifts from Bradley ($25,000).

Scaife was a consistent funder of the National Center for Public Policy Research, or NCPPR (approximately $100,000 between 2007 and 2011, according to the Bridge Project). In the 1990s, the Bradley Foundation was also a big supporter of the NCPPR, as were the Carthage and Randolph Foundations. In the spring of 2012, the NCPPR announced that it would create a "New Voter Identification Task Force" after ALEC decided to stop pursuing voter ID policies. NCPPR took up leadership on efforts to persuade state legislators to change election laws, often related to concerns about noncitizens voting illegally and requiring new forms of ID to protect the integrity of voting. In each case, immigrants, as well as low-income, elderly, and younger voters, would bear the brunt of changes in voting procedures, especially new ID requirements. These efforts had mixed effects on ultimate legislative outcomes, but the organization's role was significant and the funding it received important to consider.

Though the funding infrastructure on the conservative side was less elaborate than for those funders supporting immigrant rights and civic participation, there are clear analogies between the two movements. The foundations on top of the conservative edifice have similarly long histories and broad-based objectives to influence policy, though from decidedly different ideological vantage points. And each of these foundations used intermediaries to help funnel money to the grass roots of the policy process. In the case of these conservative foundations and philanthropists, FreedomWorks served a role similar to the roles of FFF, GCIR, and FCCP combined. Though FreedomWorks operated mainly with non-tax-deductible private donations as a 501(c)(4) nonprofit, rather than establishing itself as a 501(c)(3) nonprofit, it ultimately provided many of the same financial and nonfinancial links between philanthropists and organizations directly engaged in advocacy and electioneering.[29] As its mission statement declared: "FreedomWorks recruits, educates, trains and mobilizes millions of volunteer activists to fight for less government, lower taxes, and more freedom."[30] FreedomWorks pursued its mission in support of these nonpartisan issues, but it also engaged more directly than FFF and the other intermediaries mentioned earlier in giving partisan campaign donations. According to the Center for Responsive Politics, FreedomWorks had nearly $20 million in unregulated outside political spending and $2 million in regulated campaign contributions through its associated PAC, FreedomWorks for America. To be sure, FreedomWorks was overseen by former Republican House majority leader Dick Armey, and most of its donations and campaign spending directly or indirectly supported Republican and Tea Party–affiliated candidates for office. The more explicitly partisan and aggressively political approach of FreedomWorks distinguished it from those groups working to advance immigrant rights.

While FreedomWorks for America pursued its campaign directly, a new organization called Freedom Partners funded organizations as a quasi-philanthropic foundation. Organized as a 501(c)(6), or trade association, in 2011, Freedom Partners quickly raised over $250 million from two hundred members who each made a $100,000 dues payment to join. Freedom Partners gave out grants to many nonprofits pursuing conservative causes, including gun rights, opposition to the Affordable Care Act (Obamacare), and immigration (Allen and Vandehei 2013).

The LIBRE Initiative, a 501(c)(4) nonprofit with a mission to "equip the Hispanic community with the tools they need to be prosperous," earned a $3.1 million grant from Freedom Partners.[31] LIBRE presented the conservative perspective on immigration that focused on stronger border security and market-based allotment of visas based on employer needs. LIBRE also advocated for citizenship for those born in the United States to legal-immigrant parents and argued that "college-bound undocumented immigrant students who have proven themselves should be afforded the opportunity to earn a professional degree in our nation's higher education system, especially those interested in pursuing STEM degrees." LIBRE's views toward immigration and immigrants were decidedly different from those of many in the Tea Party movement.

While total grants were smaller compared to those given by Ford, Carnegie, and the Open Society Foundations, and the overall infrastructure was not as institutionalized, the impact of conservative foundations may have been just as powerful. According to the Brennan Center, between 2011 and 2012, forty-one states debated proposed voter ID laws, and nineteen states enacted some form of change associated with voter ID.[32] These laws provided new barriers to voting and political hurdles for immigrant-serving nonprofits to confront in mobilizing their constituents in 2012 and beyond. But it was not merely policy change that affected immigrant integration and voting. The funding of propaganda, billboards, and often fiercely anti-immigrant rhetoric greatly shaped the political environment in which immigrant-serving nonprofits worked in 2012. It may not have even been necessary to change every state law to require new forms of ID to vote, or to change when voting commenced and concluded. The atmosphere of 2012 was strongly influenced by the aggressively anti-immigrant voice of nonprofit groups and activists funded by conservative foundations.

The Fragile Bargain with Foundations

Foundations and other patrons have thus been active on many sides of the immigration and immigrant issue, supporting nonprofit organizations through grants and the legitimacy this support transfers to the grantee. Given this interwoven relationship between various types of foundations and immigrant-serving nonprofits, how influential are foundations in supporting and opposing civic and voter engagement activities? It is impossible to know the extent to which immigrant-serving nonprofits, in the absence of foundation grants, would act or fail to act, though in the statistical analysis in chapter 5 I attempt to partly control for this variable. For one, foundations provided substantial funding, but most immigrant-serving nonprofit organizations do not receive grants. Fewer than three thousand grants were issued in 2010, and a portion of those grants were given to the same set of organizations, meaning most immigrant-serving non-profits went without support. Many organizations lacked sufficient staff or expertise to access funding opportunities, or even to submit an effective grant proposal.

Second, the sustainability of activities supported by foundation grants is questionable. Much of the funding provided by foundations is short-term in nature, two- or three-year grants. This concern was articulated by Nadia Tonova of NNAAC, who explained to me: "Foundations don't typically fund for the same [organization] for a long period of time. It is a concern, which is why we are looking at diversifying our funding streams and other sources, whether it is new foundations or moving away to other revenue streams."[33] Unless the grantee is able to institutionalize these funded activities through more predictable financial support, there are great risks that voter engagement projects will ebb and flow with somewhat unpredictable funding opportunities. Wise foundations encourage this type of institutionalization, but political activities are difficult to fund from other sources. To be certain, institutionalization has been a mantra of these immigrant-focused efforts during the last ten years. When I asked about this, Ted Wang, a program director with Unbound Philanthropy, said, "We think about sustainability all the time."[34] And according to one report, "The Four Freedoms Fund was quite intentional in its effort to build and sustain the immigrant civic sector. Not only did the Fund provide financial support to increase core staffing, it also devoted considerable attention to organizational capacity-building by creating opportunities for coalition leaders to meet and interact with one another on a regular basis" (Montalto 2012, 9). Another strategy focuses on working with groups that provide other non-electoral services with separate funding streams that can enable voter work on occasion. Ted Wang said that Unbound Philanthropy wants to "figure out what is [the grantee's] niche; they have to be sustainable through other programs. I can't think of any organizations that are just electoral engagement." But despite these efforts, full institutionalization is exceedingly difficult and expensive. Government grants rarely will support political work, even the most nonpartisan civic engagement, meaning other sources of funds have to be sought. For small nonprofits, particularly those that have a service-based mission and a small pool of donors, when foundation grants end, so too may electoral engagement.

This raises the third major dilemma of foundation funding. Critics contend that the role foundations play represents an elite-based or top-down form of policy making that limits the voice of citizens. Some question the role that foundations play as a link between the wealthy and the policy process, especially during policy formulation (Dye, Zeigler, and Schubert 2012). By establishing particular priorities—priorities that some critical theorists contend are aligned with an overtly market-oriented ideology (Roelofs 2003, 2007)—and funding provided to those interested in pursuing those priorities, foundations dictate major steps of the policy process and perpetuate certain values to the exclusion of others. Foundations have added new players to the system of pluralism, but they have not promoted a truly open and equal system of pluralism. Those organizations with a different set of priorities often go unfunded or largely ignored.

The reliance on foundations also may change the way organizations relate to and represent their constituents. The weakening control of traditional membership-based associations over the policy process has been tied to the rise of citizen groups, and their tendency to turn to foundation and private financial support (Skocpol 1999). The American political system had long been defined by voluntary organizations that were financially supported and dependent on individual members. The rise of citizen groups that need not depend on individual dues payments, because of the existence of other sources of finance, especially foundations, may have changed the extent to which organizations provide a pluralistic or representative voice to a wide range of individuals and social groups. Skocpol argued it should come as no surprise that, because of these changes, "public agendas are skewed toward issues and values that matter most to the highly educated and the wealthy."

One of the critical questions facing an immigrant-serving nonprofit is whether accepting foundation support for voter or electoral engagement activities is worth it. Does foundation support weaken the extent to which the nonprofit can reflect the identity of the community it serves, in favor of the priorities of the foundation? This question is more than theoretical; nonprofit leaders routinely ponder this problem. For example, Amardeep Singh, program director of the New York–based Sikh Coalition, said that "we have had an intentional strategy . . . of ensuring that the significant majority, 65–80 percent of funds, are from our community. We don't want the foundation world to have a significant say in how much we grow, or what we grow into. If we don't grow as a result, that is OK."[35] Singh went on to clarify that the problem is not necessarily whether foundations want to provide support—they do so conscientiously and often consistently with the mission of the Sikh Coalition—but one of priority setting: "The concern is . . . someone not from my community deciding what is a priority for my community; the community in terms of its dollars should be deciding whether we should grow or contract." Decisions about organizational form are often based on how organizational leaders perceive the identity of those they serve. Nonprofit leaders strive to best represent the interests and priorities of the community; how the organization receives its funding is related to those interests and priorities.

Others interviewed for this book corroborated Singh's views. John Albert of the New York–based Taking Your Seat, an organization that represents South

Asian Americans, said that his all-volunteer organization lacked the staff exper-tise to pursue major grants, but while it "would love to have access to founda-tions, what we gain in autonomy is so precious to us."[36] Albert said that the failure to apply for and be granted funding from foundations permits his organization the freedom to pursue its mission in the best interest of the small community it represents. Autonomy from philanthropic donors, operating outside this feder-ated system, allows Albert to authentically reflect the beliefs and identity of those he serves.

Thus, these separate and independent factors might dissuade a nonprofit from pursuing a grant proposal to fund electoral engagement. Autonomy and authenticity are deeply protected assets for any nonprofit and are particularly strong principles held by the leaders of immigrant-serving nonprofits. These principles sometimes transcend the allure of foundation support to determine many organizational decisions. Subsequent chapters of this book build on this idea to conceptualize a theory of immigrant-serving electioneering.

Conclusion

The way immigrant-serving nonprofits decide to participate in elections must be examined in the context of several organizational traditions in American poli-tics. One tradition relates to the enormous private funding on the left and the right for organizations pursuing often competing aims related to immigrants and immigration. The country has always been a nation of organizers, compet-ing (at least in theory, according to pluralists) in an open political market to ad-vance diverse interests. This is in part why the federal government encourages the formation of nonprofit organizations through the tax code, and regulates what various types of nonprofits can and cannot do related to politics and policy. In reality, IRS status limits only a few political tactics—specifically lobbying, cam-paign contributions, and making endorsements—but finding the resources to support other legally sanctioned tactics remains a barrier for some nonprofits. Philanthropic foundations have emerged to fill this funding gap. Ford, Carnegie, and FFF, on one side, Bradley, Scaife, and FreedomWorks on the other—to name just a few—provided the funding necessary for many nonprofits to engage in the political process, either through policy advocacy or electoral mobilization. This funding fits into a long, historical record of philanthropic interest in immigrant issues and is an open invitation to some nonprofits to participate in politics.

Yet a second and competing tradition in American politics has been the para-noid style and conspiratorial views of the motivation of outsiders. Progressive Era reforms aimed at ridding politics of corruption were often associated with concerns that immigrants were, at best, not being fully assimilated into the norms of American life or, at worst, foreign conspirators and a threat to the essential spirit of a unified nation. Nearly a century later, these same concerns animate the interest in immigrants and political participation from both the left and the right. Immigrant-serving nonprofit organizations, aware of these traditions in American politics, make electoral decisions in this historical organizational context.

The external context of politics and funding matters to nonprofits, but politics and funding also relate to internal issues as well. For a nonprofit organization, the prospect of a million-dollar grant should raise important questions about identity and operations. How does the funding relate to its IRS status? Can a grant increase the organization's ability to meet its mission and serve the community? Or will accepting a grant change its priorities and identity in a way that is harmful? There is no easy way to resolve these tensions between the enormous power of philanthropic foundations and the intrinsic value of the independence of an individual immigrant-serving nonprofit organization. In many cases, the interests of a foundation and a nonprofit may align well, resulting in a successful and mutually beneficial grantor-grantee exchange. Many nonprofit leaders speak glowingly about the positive contribution foundations have made to immigrant rights and voter participation. But leaders who eschew funding opportunities out of deep concerns about what they sacrifice when they accept a grant, or leaders who lack the resources to successfully respond to a request of proposal (RFP), likely exist but are harder to identify. The difficulty of reaching them to complete a survey or respond to research questions, though, does not negate the theoretical dilemma and practical problems elaborated by Amardeep Singh and John Albert in this chapter.

In more practical terms, the groundwork for the 2012 election was set by these complex efforts to support organizations that mobilized voters and advocated on multiple sides of the immigrant issue. Organizations also approach elections in the context of the demographic change and differences described in the previous chapter. But one final context must also be examined. Demographics and funding opportunities matter, but so too do the unique political circumstances and campaigns that vary from district to district and state to state. Campaigns differ in how competitive they are, whether there are immigrant candidates, or whether immigrant issues are salient topics for debate. Immigrant-serving nonprofit organizations must consider that campaign context when they make decisions about participation. The next chapter dives into 2012 through examinations of illustrative campaigns in the six states of this study.

3

"YOU DON'T VOTE,
YOU DON'T COUNT"

Demographic change and organizational patrons establish the context in which immigrant-serving nonprofit organizations make operational decisions. Each of these factors pulls some organizations into the center of electoral politics and pushes others to the margins. A growing immigrant community may embolden one organization to begin mobilizing local voters, while the failure to win a grant may dissuade another from devoting staff time to holding a voter registration event. The broadcast of anti-immigrant political advertising may silence an organization in one city, and in another county an immigrant coalition may encourage an organization to collaborate on translating voter information.

A third context must also be considered: the political campaign. All these electoral decisions occur during very different political campaigns at the national, state, and local levels. Some candidates for local office are themselves immigrants; in other local campaigns the candidates vilify immigrants to rally supporters. Wealthy immigrants may make key campaign contributions to support a candidate in one state, while policy makers in another state erect new obstacles to immigrant-serving nonprofits registering voters. Drawing on information from the six states that are the focus of this book, this chapter demonstrates the ways immigrant-serving nonprofit organizations interact with state and local campaigns during the primary and general election phases. The cases presented here further develop important themes of this book, including (1) the importance of demographic change and redistricting for elections; (2) the varying ways immigrant candidates confront electoral politics; (3) the policy and campaign threats for immigrants and the organizations that serve them; (4) the importance of partisan, inter-immigrant, and interethnic conflict; (5) the roles of media and technology; and (6) the importance of money and resources. Each of these themes shapes the opportunities and challenges for immigrant-serving nonprofit organizations as they negotiate the complex politics of campaigns and elections. Throughout, I rely on original interviews with organizational leaders, analysis of primary documents, and extensive secondary sources and news accounts.

The 2012 Election Campaign

Through the winter and spring of 2012, Democrats and Republicans were busy choosing presidential candidates to run in the fall. Ironically, both candidates had fathers born outside the country, Mitt Romney's in Mexico and President Obama's in Kenya. While the president went without a Democratic challenger at the top of the ticket, Romney fought off primary opponents who contested his stance on immigration, including his "self-deportation" proposal for undocumented immigrants to voluntarily return to their home countries. Meanwhile, Obama delivered on a campaign promise from 2008 and rallied the support of many immigrants[1] by announcing a new immigration policy, called Deferred Action for Childhood Arrivals (DACA), which ordered the Department of Homeland Security to implement certain aspects of the DREAM Act.[2]

For immigrants, the campaigns that had the most direct impact on their political lives occurred much more locally. The mandatory ten-year redistricting process resulted in newly competitive electoral races at the congressional level. For most immigrant communities, whose numbers are too small to influence the presidential campaign, congressional races are where they and their organizations can wield more power. Particular races from each of the study states demonstrate the complex politics that emerge when mainstream candidates run in districts with large immigrant populations and when candidates who are first- or second-generation Americans seek out support from inside and outside their own community. At the same time, other forces were at work to resist these trends, enact new barriers, and squelch the success of immigrants.

New Jersey

As in other districts across the country, redistricting shaped the Democratic primaries in New Jersey. At noted in chapter 1, New Jersey lost a seat in the House of Representatives as other states far outpaced its growth. This resulted in a newly drawn congressional map that placed two sitting members of Congress into the

Ninth District in the northern part of the state. Both Democratic congressmen, Bill Pascrell and Steve Rothman, sought the party's nomination for this new district.

At the center of the newly drawn borders was the city of Paterson—Pascrell was the city's former mayor. Paterson has been, next to Dearborn, Michigan, one of the country's most important centers of Arab American immigrants and culture, particularly for Egyptian Americans. While Arab Americans make up a tiny minority of registered voters in most districts, in this part of New Jersey they were a powerful potential voting bloc.

All newly redistricted races featuring two incumbent candidates from the same party draw attention, but this race was particularly eventful and focused extensively on the identity politics of nationality, ethnicity, and religion. Both candidates, Pascrell and Rothman, had first been elected to the House in 1996. They had nearly identical congressional voting records, and they were reported to be close friends, based on frequent train trips on Amtrak to and from Washington (Farrell 2012). During the early stages of the primary campaign, Rothman was able to raise slightly more campaign funds than Pascrell, but both had ample financial support. The race ultimately turned on three factors: endorsements, mobilization, and the contentious politics of immigrants. First, at the national level, important Democrats allied themselves with each candidate. Former President Bill Clinton stood with Pascrell, based in part on Pascrell's support for Hillary Clinton's presidential run in 2008. Though President Obama did not make an official endorsement, his chief adviser, David Axelrod, endorsed Rothman, who in 2008 had been the first in the New Jersey congressional delegation to support the Obama candidacy. In 2012, each Democratic candidate in the Ninth District was calling in major political chits to spur party members to support his campaign.

The lack of consensus between the Democratic Party's two leaders, the current and former president, meant that there was no clear signal sent to local Democratic voters. Other issues further stoked the campaign, including the courting and mobilization of Jewish and Arab American donors and voters. In this primary election, Arab American voters were mobilized by powerful, national Arab American organizations such as the Washington, DC–based Arab American Institute (AAI) and a grassroots coalition of local leaders. At the national level, AAI had developed a program called Yalla Vote in 1998. The Yalla Vote strategy had been employed in local communities ever since to empower Arab American voters, particularly after 9/11. Prior to 2001, Arab American voters had split evenly in many races between Democrats and Republicans. George W. Bush, for example, won the state of Michigan in 2000, in part because of the support of Arab American leaders and voters. But after 9/11, and years of rhetoric from GOP party leaders that ranged from guarded ambivalence to outright hostility, it became increasingly difficult for Republicans to gain Arab American votes. Yalla Vote also emerged at a time when increasing numbers of Arab Americans of the Muslim faith were entering the country, and partisan policy differences over civil liberties began to push the community toward the Democrats. Many of these new immigrants were young and had stronger ties to their home countries than did the older, established generation. These links and the headlines from centers of the Arab Spring in Egypt, Libya, and Syria fueled attention to politics. Emily Manna, a community relations associate with AAI at the time, explained that the "Arab Spring has reinvigorated youth activism."[3]

Complicating matters for AAI and other nonprofits was the realization that Muslim American immigrants, particularly the younger generation, resemble other immigrant communities: they tend to register to vote at lower levels than the general population, and at much lower levels than nonimmigrant Protestants and Jews in particular. Hoda Elshishtawy of the Muslim Public Affairs Council explained: "Younger American Muslim community, those in the first generation, are weary of the political process. . . . [They] don't have positive experiences with the political process" in their home country.[4] According to Gallup polling, in 2009, a slim majority (51 percent) of Muslims ages eighteen to twenty-nine were registered to vote, far below the levels for the general population (65 percent) and for Protestants (78 percent) and Jews (73 percent).[5] The challenge for an organization like AAI was more than simply calling for additional engagement in the political process; nonprofits had to devise very particular mobilization plans, fitted to the broad community while also cognizant of the nuances that exist within the community between Arab Muslim Americans, non-Arab Muslim Americans, and Arab Christian Americans. As Voto Latino did for younger Hispanic American voters, AAI had to reflect the complex identity of the voters it served.

Most important to this New Jersey primary race was the early and active engagement of leaders drawn from a number of local advocacy groups. These leaders began to mobilize as soon as the redistricting process resulted in a likely Rothman-Pascrell contest. Recognizing the track record Pascrell had in the community, and what the Arab American community might give up if Pascrell lost the race to Rothman, leaders such as Salah Mustafa aimed to register a record number of new voters. Mustafa had been active with two previous organizations, the Arab American Anti-Discrimination Committee of New Jersey and the New Jersey chapter of the Council on American-Islamic Relations (CAIR), and he came together in 2012 with other local leaders in an ad hoc coalition.[6]

The new Ninth District of New Jersey, Mustafa acknowledged, did not just have a large Arab American population; it also had non-Arab Muslims from Pakistan, Albania, and Turkey. Rallying this ethnically and linguistically diverse group that shared a Muslim identity, but often little else, required the mobilization efforts to be aligned across ethnic boundaries. According to Mustafa, "What we wanted to send out was very specific and targeted. It had to reach a very specific audience. We knew what we wanted to say, we knew how we wanted to say it, use motivational sayings from the Koran—it was very specific." The ad hoc coalition sought to communicate that they believed "this is the most important election in the history of the Arab and Muslim in New Jersey."

The coalition had a three-pronged strategy to mobilize the community for the May primary election: (1) careful data management; (2) authentic voter mobilization; (3) invitations to candidates. Early on, a national group offered Mustafa's coalition access to the VAN database from Catalist with information on all the residents of the district, but Mustafa said "as we looked at it with other people, it just didn't seem to fit, seemed to be off." The matching of names to ethnic background was not complete: known Arab and Muslim Americans in the district were not labeled as such. Without accurate name matching, it is difficult for an organization to effectively target specific voters, resulting in wasted time and resources. So Mustafa and others in the coalition started with the database from scratch, and for three weeks recoded all the names for ethnic background. Because they were seeking out Muslims from different ethnic backgrounds, this required relying on volunteers with Bengali, Turkish, and Bosnian language fluency to comb through and find thirty thousand targeted Muslim voters, many non-Arabs, all registered Democrats or independents. For example, Mustafa related what he learned from a Turkish volunteer aiding him in the database work: that "Mine, *M-i-n-e*, is a very popular name for Turkish women, so every time you caught that you knew." Further, he soon discovered: "Bosnian names, you'd never guess they were Muslim names!" This is an important finding for understanding how immigrant-serving nonprofit organizations participate in electoral politics. Chapter 2 showed how national funders helped provide the money and resources necessary for local organizations to mobilize immigrant voters. These outside resources may be necessary, but not always sufficient. For this New Jersey Muslim American coalition, simply getting access to the electoral resources was not enough. The coalition also had to have the human resources in place, almost entirely volunteers, to make sense of the database.

With this voter list reassembled, the coalition began making phone calls and knocking on doors, the staples of any voter mobilization plan. They used donated office space to house a makeshift phone bank to call every phone number that was in their database. They used volunteers from each Muslim community when possible to knock on doors and use the language the database predicted the resident would speak. Most important for new and older voters, according to Mustafa, was to speak Arabic: "The key was for folks who were new to voting, the key was using Arabic. If you could start the call with *Assalamu alaikum* [the Arabic greeting translated as 'Peace be with you'], it was gold, people just light up on the phone." Making that mobilization call or in-person interaction with an authentic voice from the community resulted in great interest in the race and, research suggests, possibly higher voter turnout (García Bedolla and Michelson 2012).

Finally, the center of the northern New Jersey Muslim community, analogous to the church for the large Catholic community and the synagogue for the large Jewish community, is a handful of mosques. Friday prayers, attended in large numbers by older residents in the Ninth District, provided a predictable audience for mobilization. Research shows that Arab Muslims who regularly attend their local mosque vote at higher levels than others, though this relationship does not hold for South Asian or African American Muslims (Jamal 2005). The New Jersey coalition invited both of the Democratic candidates to attend Friday prayers and speak to the attendees. Mustafa explained to me that he believed the decision to allow Pascrell, in particular, to enter the mosque through the front door, rather than through a side door, which is more typical for a guest, cemented the support for his candidacy. Pascrell visited and spoke on the last six Fridays before the election. Mustafa also explained to me that this decision was not uncontroversial. As chapter 2 showed, electoral politics are fraught with risks, and such a direct link to the local campaign could expose the mosques to criticisms about overstepping boundaries. In the end, Mustafa concluded that while many mosque leaders expressed doubts about such an open form of campaigning, fearing the inevitable claims made by their critics, in the end they embraced the coalition's work to mobilize the community.

In addition to the nonpartisan mobilization of Arab Americans to register and vote, Pascrell also received financial support from the Arab American community. John Zogby, the longtime president of AAI, held fund-raisers among Arab Americans in the district that netted approximately $150,000, largely for the Pascrell campaign (Assaf 2010a). The Turkish Coalition PAC also donated $7,500 to Pascrell.[7] The coalition was able to help mobilize Arab and Muslim American voters, as well as donors and major organizational supporters.

At the same time, Congressman Rothman was busy courting voters, and he also received support from a variety of immigrant organizations and communities. Rothman beamed early on in the campaign: "It's particularly exciting to attract the support of so many of the area's outstanding Hispanic leaders. My record on issues of interest to the Latino community is extremely strong and I'm ready to continue to fight on their behalf in Washington."[8] Rothman also promoted his pro-Israel credentials and support among Jewish American voters.[9] AIPAC, the powerful pro-Israel lobbying group, provided substantial support for Rothman's campaign as well, helping to garner $175,000 in donations from pro-Israel donors.[10] Unlike other parts of the country where immigrants tend to line up together on one side or another of a campaign, favoring a particular immigrant candidate or a particularly sympathetic nonimmigrant candidate, in this highly diverse community in New Jersey, immigrant and ethnic communities were deeply split.

These divisions can be seen in other aspects of the campaign, especially in how new media influenced the race. In addition to an endorsement from the statewide paper the *Star-Ledger*, Pascrell received the support of Aref Assaf, one of the paper's opinion editorial writers and president of the Arab American Forum, a New Jersey–based nonprofit think tank. Assaf used his blog to raise questions about how local rabbis were mobilizing Jewish American voters. In February 2012, Assaf, responding to newspaper accounts, questioned the legality of New Jersey rabbis encouraging Jewish Republicans to vote for Rothman. Assaf wondered online whether imams would be as politically active with their followers. Assaf called Rothman "Israel's Man in District 9," and the race quickly became defined less by policy differences, of which there were few, but by religious and ethnic divisions (Assaf 2010b).

On the other side, Pascrell was challenged by a nonprofit organization called the Investigative Project on Terrorism. This group, run by Steve Emerson, a former AIPAC staffer, used its website to claim that "Islamists on Capitol Hill have few better allies than Rep. Bill Pascrell, D-N.J. A former mayor of Paterson, Pascrell, 75, is in his eighth term representing Passaic County in New Jersey's 8th Congressional District. He is an outspoken critic of congressional efforts to investigate Muslim radicalization in the United States and a top ally of the Council on American-Islamic Relations (CAIR)."[11] Emerson also criticized Pascrell for not denouncing Assaf's opinions in the *Star-Ledger*. By focusing on Pascrell's record, as well as his organizational ties to CAIR, the Investigative Project on Terrorism tied nonprofit mobilization and advocacy to this race. In other parts of the country, CAIR was repeatedly pulled into campaign debates as an easy target and trigger for underlying anti-Muslim animosity.

Another organizational player in this race was a group called "I Vote Israel," which sought to register Americans living in Israel to vote in U.S. elections in support of candidates who it believed were most supportive of Israeli interests. I Vote Israel wrote on its website:

> An estimated 200,000 to 500,000 US citizens currently reside in Israel. Of these, a substantial number are eligible to vote in key swing states, such as Florida, Ohio, and Pennsylvania. By mobilizing this never-before targeted micro-group we can be a decisive factor in the 2012 elections, ensuring a Congress and White House who will stand by Israel. Beyond the direct electoral significance, mobilizing and energizing American voters

in Israel will play a key role in influencing the votes of friends, family, and supporters of Israel back in the US; voters whose vote would otherwise be driven by domestic concerns rather than concern for Israel.[12]

Mobilizing voters living abroad coincided with Mitt Romney's summer trip to Israel, where he raised campaign funds from Americans living there.

In the end, Pascrell won the primary election. Following his victory over Rothman, I Vote Israel released a web-based video that indicted Arab Americans for "flexing their political muscle" and referenced the Yalla Vote campaign of AAI as associated with "radical anti-Israel elements of the NJ Arab community" (Hoffman 2012). The video included images of pro-Pascrell posters that were printed in Arabic and accused Pascrell of supporting terrorists. Campaign posters and election materials are often printed in non-English languages, but the juxtaposition of Arabic writing in favor of Pascrell with terrorism threatened to incite deeper fears and hostilities toward Arab and Muslim Americans. This purposeful attempt to associate support for one candidate with anti-Americanism posed serious questions about how hospitable the district was for immigrants of Arab, Muslim, and other backgrounds.

This race also showed how the redistricting process—often driven by demographic change—can reposition certain immigrant groups and organizations as kingmakers; but with newfound power come new threats. In other parts of the country, the rising numbers of immigrants and ethnic minorities coincided with efforts to make voting more difficult—for many, a coordinated effort at voter suppression guised in a cloak of protecting the country from fraud. In New Jersey, immigrant-serving nonprofits demonstrated how certain electoral tactics could draw out voters and mobilize a community to action. The race in New Jersey also showed the increasingly important role played by new media, advertising, and technology. As in other segments of politics, each of these factors has greatly shifted the terrain for immigrants. New organizations can capitalize on the low cost and easy use of technology to mobilize large numbers of voters in ways that in the past were possible only for large organizations. The same technology can also easily be used to mobilize the opponents of immigrants and share deeply anti-immigrant images with the world.

New York

As in New Jersey, 2010 redistricting determined who was in and out for New York in 2012. In the New York City borough of Queens, because of the decennial reapportionment that saw the state lose two seats, long-serving Democratic congressman Gary Ackerman witnessed his old Fifth Congressional District chopped up by the new congressional map. Unlike his counterparts in New Jersey, Ackerman opted not to run for reelection.

The new Sixth District was now the site of one of the largest concentrations of Asian American voters in the country. Approximately 40 percent of voting-age residents of the district were of Asian ancestry, and many of those were recent immigrants. Some census tracts in this new district saw between 50 and 100 percent growth in the Asian population between 2000 and 2010, and many tracts had upward of 70 percent Asian residents.

Though quickly growing in numbers in New York, Asian Americans have long had a tenuous and marginalized part to play in city politics. In the 1980s, then-mayor Ed Koch dismissed protests led by Chinese Americans against a proposed jail in the Chinatown neighborhood of Manhattan with his infamous retort: "You don't vote, you don't count" (Hsiao 2001). At the time, despite a large Asian American community, few Asian Americans had been elected to citywide office, let alone higher office, and many attributed this to low voter registration and turnout. Koch expressed the cynical but real side of local and immigrant politics. Turnout equals influence.

Since the 1980s, the city's population and politics have changed. With Ackerman out of the race, a handful of city officials signed up to compete in the Democratic Party primary, including one from the Chinese American community, who happened to be the most prominent and best-funded of them all: Grace Meng. A second-generation Taiwanese American lawyer married to a Korean American, Meng had been the youngest Asian American elected to the New York State Assembly, having won the seat that her father had held previously (he was the first-ever Asian American member of the New York State Assembly) (Chen 2012). Based in part on this résumé, Meng won the endorsements of Asian American political organizations such as Korean Americans for Political Advancement (whose steering committee she sat on), the Bangladeshi American Community Council, and the Alliance of South Asian American Labor.

On the issues, Meng and her Democratic opponents were in broad agreement. During one candidate forum, the three leading candidates addressed an issue with particular resonance in the immigrant community (Campbell 2012a). The forum moderator raised the issue of enforcement of a state law that required some portion of commercial signage to be written in English. Many store signs in the district were written entirely in some other language, raising public safety issues and difficulties for fire and police department responders. The issue also connected to deeper questions of ethnic identity, assimilation, and sentiments of hostility toward what usage of non-English languages means in a diverse community. For a century, immigrants have faced the question of whether they should continue to use other languages in cultural activities, commerce, and even politics, or whether civic affiliations should lead them to the full adoption of English.

All three candidates voiced general concern for the issue, but none, including Meng, was fervent in the defense of the rights of store owners. In general, while she had been an outspoken advocate for immigrant issues as a member of the state assembly, Meng's campaign for the Democratic nomination subtly downplayed immigrant and immigration issues. For example, her campaign literature often omitted her surname, favoring instead simply "Grace," a decision that commentators believed was a nod to her non–Asian American constituency (Grossman 2012). And on her campaign website, she summarized her views on many public policy issues but did not highlight her views on immigration reform or the particular rights of immigrants. Her explanation of her views on civil rights focused on women's rights and gay and lesbian rights, yet she left out any clear mention of the civil rights concerns of immigrants.

Meng's run for Congress was made possible by redistricting and the growth of the Asian American community in the borough of Queens, as well as the support of Democratic officials in the city and leaders in other ethnic communities. Eighteen percent of the new district was Hispanic American, and Meng was endorsed by several New York Hispanic leaders and a leading Spanish-language newspaper, *El Diario* (Campbell 2012b). She also won endorsements from the outgoing congressman, Gary Ackerman, and from Governor Andrew Cuomo, who recorded an automated campaign ("robo") phone call: "Hello, this is Governor Andrew Cuomo. I'm calling to urge you to vote for my friend Grace Meng for Congress in tomorrow's Democratic primary." He clarified to district voters, "I'm a Queens guy as you know, born and raised."

While Meng may not have directly communicated her messages on immigrant issues, her campaign team targeted many first-generation Asian American voters. According to the *New York Times*, the Meng campaign focused on turning out twenty thousand likely voters whom it aimed to reach ten times by a combination phone, in-person visits, and traditional mail in the days leading up to the election. Outside of her campaign, one of the most active immigrant groups in the race was the MinKwon Center for Community Action, the Korean American nonprofit organization described at the start of the book. MinKwon did voter canvassing of Asian American district voters, making one thousand phone calls. "We are hoping to build up our community maturity, in terms of politics," including fund-raising, the organization claimed (Chan 2012).

Meng ultimately won the primary with 51 percent of the vote. Whether the victory represented the political maturation of the Asian American community in electoral contests was debatable. Meng won despite very low voter turnout: less than 15 percent of registered Democrats turned out for the June primary election (Kaplan 2012). If she was to win the general election in November, her campaign and her allies in the community would need to improve their get-out-the-vote activities to ensure that a larger percentage of Asian American and non–Asian American Democrats registered and then voted. As was the case in New Jersey, much of this ultimately would come down to how active and effective immigrant-serving nonprofits would be.

This race also raised a second issue for immigrant candidates: How closely should they align themselves with their own immigrant story? For candidates such as Grace Meng, who had a track record in state politics and an interest in a variety of policy issues, how might she balance the different aspects of her public appeal? For the immigrant-serving organizations that supported her, and for organizations that supported first- and second-generation immigrant candidates in other parts of the country, they too had to balance their interests in a particular candidate's compelling background with the specific issues that candidates would pursue if elected. Having an immigrant candidate in the race adds a dimension and shapes the campaign context in which the immigrant-serving nonprofits make decisions about electoral engagement.

Florida

While demographic shifts resulted in losses for New York and New Jersey, Florida's rapid growth in population—the Puerto Rican population in the state alone doubled between 2000 and 2010—netted two additional seats in the House of Representatives. Following redistricting, new Hispanic-majority districts appeared across the state. One particular new district, the Ninth, snaked through central Florida, Osceola County (and parts of Orange and Polk Counties), and the sprawling urban center of Orlando. The new district was 41 percent Hispanic, mainly Puerto Rican American, and strongly Democratic leaning (Powers 2012). While Southern Florida has long been home to a large Cuban American population, more recent arrivals from Mexico, the Caribbean, and Puerto Rico made the state a growing and changing gateway for immigrants and other newcomers. These recent demographic changes resulted in shifts in the political power of various immigrant communities in elections.

In the state's Ninth Congressional District, Alan Grayson, the white, non-Hispanic Democratic nominee, was seeking to regain a seat he had lost in 2010. Grayson had remained on the national stage during his hiatus from Congress through media appearances on cable news. He returned to Florida and received endorsements from Puerto Rican American organizations, including the Committee for the Rescue and Development of Vieques, but faced an uphill battle to win again in this newly drawn and majority-Hispanic district. According to a story in the *Orlando Sentinel*, a representative of another important organization, the National Congress for Puerto Rican Rights, and a Democrat, Zoraida Rios-Andino, said: "I have nothing against Congressman Grayson. I think he did a good job. But he should be running in another district. . . . That is the whole issue of the redistricting crisis: Puerto Ricans need their own congressman" (Powers 2012). Rios-Andino was supporting the Independent candidate and Puerto Rican American Miguel Nieves, and her comments expressed an underlying sentiment in parts of the country with rapidly changing demographics. Voting is one thing, representation is another.

Grayson's likely opponent was to be Republican John "Q" Quiñones. Quiñones, a Puerto Rican American, served in the Florida House of Representatives from 2002 to 2006 and then as a commissioner in Osceola County. Quiñones featured his background on his campaign website, explaining that "my parents and I came to Florida in 1980 from Puerto Rico in search of a better life. . . . [My wife] and I are raising our children Alexa and Natalia in that same Puerto Rican tradition of faith and hard work." Even though one does not "emigrate" from a U.S. territory such as Puerto Rico, Quiñones embodied the identity of an immigrant, and this shaped his campaign. He was viewed as a popular option for a Republican victory in this Democratic-leaning district, and he received the endorsements of the Republican governor of Puerto Rico and Romney ally Luis Fortuno, former congressman Adam Putnam, and the National Rifle Association.

Quiñones faced Todd Long in the August Republican primary. Long, the main white Republican candidate in the race, was a perennial yet unsuccessful conservative candidate, and his chance of defeating Quiñones in this new and largely Hispanic district was viewed as a long shot. With Quiñones in the race, the Washington-insider newspaper *Roll Call* predicted a November win for the Republicans.

With his party's nomination sealed and considerable cash on hand from campaign donors, Grayson began buying advertisements in advance of the Republican primary. News reports showed that Grayson bought $300,000 of media ads that accused Quiñones of raising taxes while in office (A. C. Smith 2012). Campaign mores usually preclude a direct confrontation between the parties until after candidates have been chosen. At this point, Republicans had not yet voted in the Quiñones-Long primary election. As such, national figures, such as former Florida governor Jeb Bush, criticized Grayson for meddling or seeking to pick his opponent.

Most interestingly, during one of the television ads, Grayson's allies showed Quiñones in a *pava*, a traditional Puerto Rican hat worn by the working class. Grayson supporters created a website called "johnqraisestaxes" with the advertisement and a prominent image of Quiñones wearing the *pava*. Quiñones complained of ethnic baiting on the part of Grayson, that the portrayal of him in the hat implied he was foreign and un-American. The Grayson campaign explained that the use of the picture showed the hypocrisy of Quiñones wearing the hat of the working class yet passing tax increases that would do harm to those very people (Montalvo 2012). But Grayson's ad might have had a second motivation. Because Hispanics in this district were mainly registered Democrats (a quarter were registered Republicans and a quarter were Independent), and party primaries in Florida are closed—meaning registered voters can vote only in the primary of their chosen party—the Grayson strategy might foment anti-Hispanic sentiments among district voters, with little concern for backlash from Hispanic voters, many of whom could not vote in the Republican contest (Fox News Latino 2012).

Possibly lost in the summer break and run-up to the Republican National Convention, the Grayson ad attracted little national attention and no sizable organized resistance from Hispanic organizations. For those who watched the ad, it is impossible to know if they were swayed by the tax accusations or the ambiguous meaning of the hat, or whether the ad had no effect at all. But the choice of the image cannot be viewed as coincidental, and reflects an underlying challenge faced by candidates with an immigrant background. Candidates such as Grace Meng and John Quiñones make choices about how they want to portray themselves, but are also subject to portrayals by their opponents.

In the end, despite predictions and endorsements favoring his opponent, Todd Long handily defeated Quiñones, 47.3 percent to 28.3 percent, and won the Republican Party's nomination to face Grayson in the November general election. Ironically, two Puerto Rican Republican candidates, Quiñones and school board member Julius Melendez, together won forty-three percent of the vote, potentially splitting the Republican Hispanic vote and maybe precluding a Hispanic candidate from winning. One was left to wonder: Did Grayson's foray into the Republican primary succeed, or was Todd Long's affiliations with the conservative wing of his party the key to victory?

The case of the Ninth District in Florida illustrates another dimension of the immigrant story in 2012. Florida, long assumed to be the domain of Cuban Americans, has been changed by the increasing number of non-Cuban Hispanics. Puerto Rican Americans in the center of the state, and Mexican Americans and Caribbean Americans in different districts have altered the standard calculus that more conservative Cuban American voters determine Florida elections. Many of these newcomers, who trend Democratic in the state, now wield power in numbers. But redistricting does not always result in predictable outcomes. Alan Grayson's success in this Hispanic majority district, created by a Republican-majority legislature, related to the particular ways that background can be framed. While probably not the only reason for his loss, depicting Quiñones in the ethnic garb, potentially an asset in a general election campaign, may have crippled his campaign in the non-Hispanic-dominated Republican primary. In either case, redistricting aimed in part at creating opportunities for minority voters to elect minority candidates failed to produce a general election contest where that choice could be made.

In these complex races, immigrant-serving nonprofit organizations decide how to participate. The discomfort some Puerto Rican American organizations had with Grayson showed another way that identity matters. While most never make a formal endorsement, organizations consider what it might mean to have someone from the community elected. Local organizations might agree with Grayson on issues but be troubled that the demographic change in the district did not result in an immigrant candidate winning the election. Quiñones may not have allied with many organizations on policy issues, but he reflected an aspect of the immigrant identity that his opponents never would, and certainly did not deserve the questionable campaign advertising used to undermine his campaign. For immigrant-serving nonprofits, promoting the identity of the community during an election often means mobilizing turnout of voters, yet for communities that are growing in numbers, it also increasingly means supporting candidates, like Grace Meng, who also can reflect the immigrant identity in Congress.

Taking place at the same time that Alan Grayson was challenging Democrats and Republicans alike were efforts in Florida to change voter registration procedures and who was eligible to vote. Fearful that illegal immigrants were registered to vote in larger numbers, Governor Rick Scott ordered county supervisors to clear voter rolls of those suspected of not being citizens. The "purge" netted only a few thousand potential noncitizens, and many of those were the result of simple clerical errors, with little evidence of a major statewide problem with inaccurate electoral records or noncitizens preparing to vote. Attempts to change Florida's voting laws and pursue illegal immigrant voters mirrored policy advocacy in other states and was spearheaded by organizations like True the Vote. These efforts received praise from those who believed current voting procedures were ripe for fraud, and criticism from those who believed these changes were an underhanded way to disenfranchise voters, particularly those who already have difficulties voting, such as the elderly and immigrants.

These efforts on voting also had an important impact on immigrant-serving organizations. One of the most substantial, and potentially damaging, changes made to Florida voting law in 2011 related to the work of nonprofits. In the amended law, nonprofits—what are called third-party voter registration organizations—as well as their volunteers, faced severe penalties if they provided false information on newly registered voter forms, including a $5,000 fine and up to five years in prison

(Kasdan 2012). The state did not specify what constituted "false," or whether the violations could be unintentional, but each person registering voters would be required to sign a statement agreeing to the new provisions. The law also changed the required reporting period for organizations to send completed registration forms to the appropriate state office from ten days—the national norm—to forty-eight hours, leaving much less time to verify the accuracy of every newly registered voter form. Fearful of the potential fines and felony charges, and uncertain what would violate the new "false" standard, organizations with long histories of voter registration, including the League of Women Voters, opted to disband their voter registration activities in the state (McQuade 2011). Many immigrant-serving nonprofit organizations followed suit and redirected their work toward other electoral activities or opted out altogether. Though the state court ultimately struck down the forty-eight-hour provision at the end of August, the ominous atmosphere surrounding nonprofit voter registration had already been firmly established.

Michigan

While True the Vote pursued action in Florida, in Michigan the state already had a voter identification bill on the books, which the state supreme court had ruled constitutional in 2007. The law required voters to present a photo ID in order to vote, or sign an affidavit that they did not have an ID. But in June 2012 the state assembly, led by the Republican majority and likely influenced by the success of ALEC in other parts of the country, sought to amend that law in order to require voters to affirm their citizenship prior to voting.[13] In addition, in a manner nearly identical to what had passed in Florida, the bill would require "third-party voter registration organizations" to register with the state. Each organization that wanted to register voters, whether as a large or small part of its operations, would be required to submit the names and addresses of each employee who would participate in registering voters. The state would then maintain this information in a database. Furthermore, each organization would be required to go through a state training program that would teach "the proper procedure for taking a voter registration application." All staff and volunteers who participated in registering voters would be required to sign a statement that they had been trained and would abide by the registration law. If a nonprofit organization did not comply with these regulations, it was subject to an unspecified penalty.

Whether or not these procedures would make elections in Michigan less prone to fraud is disputable—there were few indications that fraud was an endemic problem in the state or, in fact, anywhere in the country in previous elections—but the regulations would have an impact. In order to comply with the proposed regulations, all nonprofit organizations would have to submit paperwork, not just once, but every time they hired a new employee or found a new volunteer. This would demand time and staff devoted to compliance and might discourage individuals from volunteering. Moreover, the bill was unclear about how the training would be conducted, and nonprofits would likely have to wait until training procedures and locations were established. It is reasonable to assume that, fearful of the penalties for noncompliance, many nonprofits would simply opt out of registering voters.

Immigrant-serving nonprofits in particular feared the consequences of this law in Michigan and similar efforts in other states. New procedures, even innocuous-seeming ones, could dampen enthusiasm among voters for whom submitting identification to the government means more than just showing an ID. For new immigrants, or those who have family members stuck in the visa process or in the country without documentation, efforts to require more identification could tip them toward staying home on Election Day. Cognizant of these fears, nonprofit groups challenged the Michigan legislative changes. At the same time, some saw early voting procedures in the state as a lifeline.[14] If an organization could persuade eligible voters to vote early, by mail or in person, the deep fear of immigrant voters being turned away because of real or questionable claims about proper identification might be addressed. Many responded by pursuing aggressive early voting campaigns, hoping that day-of-voting difficulties could be avoided. Indicative of this, Doua Thor, executive director of Southeast Asian Resource Action Center, said, "A lot in our community don't speak English, so early voting or mail-in voting is good, particularly for seniors."[15]

Ultimately, Michigan's Republican governor, Rick Snyder, vetoed the amended voter ID bill, preventing these new restrictions from taking effect. Nonetheless, the threat presented to organizers may still have affected voting and the election. From one perspective, some organizations were energized by these attempts to change the law and used them to rally support and mobilize voters earlier than normal. From another perspective, the climate created by the failed voter ID legislation may have also driven down interest in voting among some registered voters. Most voters do not follow the particular ups and downs of legislative policy making; rather, they follow the general mood of politics expressed in the media or in personal networks. For some, news of the gubernatorial veto may not have registered as a rebuke to these voter ID efforts, leaving only the vitriol of the bill's sponsors as a powerful disincentive to civically engage. No exit polling was conducted that could fully measure the effect of the voter ID efforts on voter turnout, positively or negatively. Also, in the absence of the new law, no major cases of voter fraud in Michigan emerged during the campaign and after the election. The governor's veto did not produce the rampant abuses of voting procedures that voter ID advocates feared. But the potential policy changes to voting laws in

Michigan are indicative of a powerful thread that ran throughout the 2012 election. Whether successful or not in passing changes to electoral laws, the voter ID movement, viewed by some as anti-immigrant, posed important questions about voting, what it means to register to vote, and who could participate in the process of increasing voter engagement. Some nonprofit organizations confronted this movement with a sharp rebuke and more aggressive work, while others made a more cautious decision to steer clear of controversy.

For immigrant-serving nonprofits in Michigan, they faced a dual threat to participating in the election. Not only was there an atmosphere of distrust of immigrant voting; there were also purposeful efforts to limit organizations from taking part in the election. For an organization that might already be hesitant to participate, these new threats made any kind of electoral activity in Michigan even less attractive.

Illinois

Across other parts of the Midwest, several races exposed even deeper hostilities and more palpable anti-immigrant sentiments. In Minnesota, Congresswoman Michele Bachmann accused Huma Abedin, the wife of former congressman from New York Anthony Weiner, of working in the interest of the Egyptian-based Muslim Brotherhood organization from her position at the State Department (Sherman 2012). The accusation stemmed from alleged connections Abedin's family had to Muslim nonprofit organizations and charities. Few took Bachmann's statements seriously, but the furor caused by the accusations harked back for many to the Red Scare era of Senator Joseph McCarthy. Bachmann made similar claims about fellow Minnesota congressman Keith Ellison, an African American Muslim: "He has a long record of being associated with CAIR [the Council on American-Islamic Relations] and with the Muslim Brotherhood" (Sommerhauser 2012). CAIR was formed as a nonprofit organization in 1994 and seeks to protect the civil liberties of Muslims in the United States through a central Washington office and dozens of regional chapters. CAIR has been active in elections through voter registration drives sponsored by these regional chapters, including in the Pascrell-Rothman race in New Jersey.

In Illinois, a similar confrontation brewed around CAIR. As Grace Meng carved new ground for Asian American women in New York, so too did candidate Tammy Duckworth in Illinois. The Eighth Congressional District of Illinois was home to a large and diverse Asian American population, 12 percent of the district, with a considerable new South Asian Muslim immigrant community. Duckworth, who had served as a high-ranking Obama appointee in the Veterans Administration, was born in Thailand (her father was American) and had immigrated with her family to the United States. She came out strongly for the DREAM Act and other immigration reform, and linked her policy views to her family's own immigrant story: "My father's family came to America before the Revolution and fought for Independence, but my mother is an immigrant who became a citizen in her 50s. My mother and millions of other legal immigrants have followed the rules. Their hard work and love of this country made us the strong, diverse nation we are today."[16] Duckworth ran in part on her identity as an injured veteran, as well as her identity as an immigrant.

Duckworth was pitted against Republican congressman Joe Walsh, who because of 2010 redistricting had lost the Sixth District seat in Congress that he held. Walsh had a background in public policy and advocacy, having worked as policy director of the Heartland Institute before founding the Lead Foundation.[17] During his first term in Congress, he was active on small business and defense issues, and—not ironically—introduced HR 5971, which aimed to "require voters to present a government-issued photo ID at the polls."[18]

Walsh, famous for his outbursts, infuriated Muslim Americans and others with his comments about what he described as "radical Islam" and CAIR. In a town hall talk during the campaign, Walsh explained that he believed there were terrorism threats growing in the suburbs of Illinois. Duckworth's campaign and CAIR resisted responding to these incendiary claims, but Walsh continued in a subsequent speech, "It's important to know that the Department of Homeland Security and the FBI have severed all ties with CAIR because of their ties to terrorism. Let me be clear, bowing down to political correctness has and will get Americans killed. . . . While the overwhelming majority of Muslim Americans are as peace-loving as everyone else, there are radical Islamists right here in the United States trying to kill Americans and destroy this country" (Tafoya 2012). Walsh positioned this nonprofit organization, and by extension the Duckworth campaign, squarely on the side of terrorist threats to the country.

In defending CAIR, Duckworth helped Walsh unearth underlying conflicts in the district that could work to his advantage. Gerald Hankerson, CAIR-Chicago outreach coordinator, said that "within a week [of Walsh's comments], there were attacks on Muslim schools and mosques in his district, and desecration of Muslim graves."[19] New groups also formed, and others began to mobilize in response, reflecting differences within the South Asian community (Kurien 2001). A local businessman named Shalli Kuman, founder of Indian Americans for Freedom, launched the Indian American "super PAC"—a political organization permitted to raise and spend unlimited money to support candidates as long as that support is not coordinated with the candidate's campaign team—to support Walsh. A fact not lost on the community was that Duckworth, in her Democratic primary, had defeated Raja Krishnamoorthi, who was born in India before immigrating to the United States as a child and then graduating from Princeton and Harvard. The new super PAC paid for television ads linking Duckworth with CAIR; the ads included images of the candidate at an Islamic center wearing a hijab, with a soundtrack of Middle Eastern music. The advertisement concluded with the statement: "Ms. Duckworth, you should know better!"(Lester and Peterson 2012). Whereas in New Jersey a close relationship to the Arab American community and attendance at mosque events were seen as assets for Pascrell, Duckworth's organizational connections were portrayed as a liability. Less subtle than Grayson's ads in Florida against John Quiñones, the super-PAC ad nevertheless communicated a similar message: don't trust a candidate with such ethnic affiliations. Duckworth also stepped into divisions within the Asian American community in the district. Geopolitical, religious, and ethnic conflicts that had their home far away from the Eighth District of Illinois came rushing into this contest. Despite the large number of Asian American residents in her district, Duckworth could not count on consensus to support her candidacy.

Other organizations also got into the campaign. The Asian American Institute (Chicago Branch) distributed a candidate questionnaire that queried Duckworth and Walsh about their policy views on Asian American issues: Do you support those sections of the Voting Rights Act that apply to limited-English-proficient citizens? What economic policies would you support to help the Asian American community as a whole? Do you support the federal DREAM Act and creating a road map to citizenship for all undocumented immigrants? Duckworth answered affirmatively to each question. Walsh did not reply to the questionnaire, but his views were largely known, and he had already opposed the president's DACA executive order on immigration.

Duckworth ultimately benefited greatly from her access to President Obama. She had served as an appointee at the Department Veterans Affairs and was invited to speak at the Democratic National Convention in September 2012. Perhaps most importantly, Duckworth received twice as many campaign contributions as Walsh. Emily's List, the pro-women PAC, donated $84,347; J Street PAC, a pro-Israel group, donated nearly $50,000; and labor unions provided a quarter of a million dollars. National super PACs provided some of the most substantial support for her campaign, pouring in millions to combat spending to support Walsh's campaign from two of the major conservative super PACs: FreedomWorks for America ($1.8 million) and Now or Never PAC ($2.1 million). Few congressional races in the country received so much attention and money. But the role of Duckworth's ethnic identity and the contested identity of organizations in this changing district shaped how the two candidates positioned their views and rallied support.

North Carolina

Duckworth and fellow Democrats headed to Charlotte, North Carolina, in early September 2012 for their party convention. With a sitting, unchallenged president in the White House, the convention was less about the practical counting of votes from state delegates and more about rallying the party behind the candidate.

Charlotte and the state of North Carolina had been a compelling choice for the party convention. Barack Obama had narrowly won this southern state in 2008, and in 2012 it remained a toss-up. The state's changing demographics meant that its politics were also in flux. For the president, winning in 2012 could come down to North Carolina and turning out voters, including many first-time Hispanic American voters, in the state as well as in neighboring Virginia.

Much as the Republicans had done weeks earlier, the Democrats placed speakers from a variety of backgrounds front and center. Those speakers included Duckworth, along with California's Congressman Xavier Becerra and Congresswoman Judy Chu, Congresswoman Nydia Velázquez of New York, Secretary of the Interior Ken Salazar, and Secretary of Veterans Affairs Eric Shinseki. On Tuesday, San Antonio's Mayor Julian Castro boomed: "My grandmother didn't live to see us begin our lives in public service. But she probably would've thought it extraordinary that just two generations after she arrived in San Antonio, one grandson would be the mayor and the other would be on his way—the good people of San Antonio willing—to the United States Congress!"[20]

These speakers reflected the diversity of talent that the party could turn to in a national contest for the presidency, but none of the Hispanic or Asian American speakers were from North Carolina. Heading into the 2012 election cycle, all the North Carolina congressional delegation was either white or African American. Though Hispanics were a small portion of the state's registered voters (3 percent), their numbers had doubled between 2008 and 2012, and this influx of immigration established the state as a new southern immigrant gateway. Yet, in 2012, none of the major challengers in the congressional races in the state, Democrat or Republican, were Hispanic or Asian American. Immigrant voters in North Carolina confronted many candidates offering to cater to their needs, yet no candidates for Congress came out of their own ethnic communities. The nonprofits that represented immigrants could mobilize immigrant voters, but none of the candidates courting those voters were from the same communities.

North Carolina showed that despite the gains and the enthusiasm shown for Hispanic and Asian American candidates elsewhere, the major political parties are slow to change, and gains in the number of elected officials from an immigrant community tend to lag years behind gains in population. An important consideration in understanding the mobilization of immigrants is the very slow pace of change in American politics. Even for immigrant groups that now make up a considerable part of a district, it takes even more organizing, infrastructure building, and resources to run candidates in new gateway states like North Carolina.

Conclusion

Much of the interest in U.S. elections focuses at the top of the ticket, often at who is running for president. Immigration and the immigrant story are often aspects of presidential campaigns, but down-ticket congressional races across the country elaborate subplots of that story and are often the most important for immigrant-serving nonprofits. Just as demographic and organizational contexts shape the participation of immigrant-serving nonprofits in politics, so does the local campaign context. Organizations participated in very different ways in each state, and we can learn from these differences.

In just the six states that serve as the focus of this book, key campaign and electoral themes can be gleaned. I have suggested at least six themes that are central to this book: (1) the importance of demographic change and redistricting for elections; (2) the varying ways immigrant candidates confront electoral politics; (3) the policy and campaign threats for immigrants and the groups that serve them; (4) the importance of partisan, inter-immigrant conflict; (5) the role of media and technology; and (6) the importance of money and resources. I use these themes to generate and test theories about the electoral process in the next three chapters.

The first thing this chapter showed was that these six states demonstrate the way demographic change and redistricting—the demographic context—can expose intra-party conflicts and divide a party along ethnic lines during the candidate-selection phase of an election. For Arab American organizations in New Jersey, because of the size of the community's population in the newly drawn district, the primary election energized them to be much more actively involved in mobilizing the community to vote. Demographic change in Queens, New York, brought new Asian American organizations into the electoral fold, while in North Carolina, despite a growing Hispanic American population, immigrant issues remained relatively dormant. The second thing that the chapter showed was that inter- and intra-immigrant group differences, such as those in Illinois and Florida, can shape a campaign narrative about immigration and immigrants. The campaign context in some cases will embolden organizations to participate; in other cases it will discourage participation. In Illinois, the anti-Muslim campaign rhetoric drew Muslim American organizations into the race, but it also attracted organizations representing other immigrant communities, specifically Indian Americans, that also believed they had a stake in the race.

Third, this chapter highlighted the importance of organizing, technology, and money—the organizational context. The low cost of digital media and access to voter databases permitted a variety of organizations in New Jersey to participate in the election in a way that they could not have in the past. Finally, policy change in electoral laws directly and indirectly affected immigrant voting. Efforts to tighten election procedures through more stringent identification requirements and regulations (including on nonprofits)—strategies that have long histories in the United States—may have decreased immigrant voting in some districts while increasing it others following heightened awareness and mobilization. A similar effect may have driven immigrant-serving organizations either into or away from the election, based on details of new state voting laws. The effect was likely different in each community in the country, but was a defining characteristic of the 2012 electoral cycle. Whether it was the subtle choices of ethnic garb, such as those in Florida and Illinois, or the explicit claims made against organizations linked to Bill Pascrell or Tammy Duckworth, the campaign context shapes the immigrant story and affects the composition of immigrant organizations at the heart of many key campaigns.

The lessons that can be learned from these local political campaigns can be expressed in a theoretical framework. That framework—introduced briefly in the introductory chapter of the book—may better explain why an immigrant-serving nonprofit organization in general might engage in some aspect of a campaign. These organizations fit into a policy process that is larger than just their own operations. As we saw in the last chapter, starting in the early 2000s, national philanthropic foundations set out to greatly shape the public policy agenda and direct policy change through major giving related to immigrants, immigration, and voting. *How did organizations opt to participate in this effort to mobilize voters? How do we define the multifaceted context in which immigrant-serving nonprofits make electoral choices?* The next chapter presents a grounded theory—reflective electoral representation—to better explain these choices.

A MODEL OF IMMIGRANT-SERVING ENGAGEMENT

4

The MinKwon Center, introduced at the beginning of the book, was less than thirty years old in 2012, yet its electoral sophistication suggested a much longer legacy and a substantially larger electoral budget. Formed in 1984, the organization has been devoted to providing a variety of social services to the Korean American community in the Flushing neighborhood of Queens. It provided these nonpolitical services for much of its first decade in operation. But it was the Los Angeles riots in 1992 and anti-immigrant animosity in New York City in the early 1990s that, according to Steve Choi, the organization's executive director, "really drove home the message that as Korean immigrants we had very little political power."[1] Though the community had long lacked political power in the city, according to MinKwon's coordinator of civic engagement, James Hong, it boomed in the 2000s: "The Asian American population has grown 32 percent over the last ten years; the [New York] City population overall has grown less than 2 percent."[2] Drawing on these two forces, political threats and demographic opportunities, the organization transitioned from a strictly service-oriented nonprofit to something new. MinKwon has rapidly developed the infrastructure to address political inequities through policy advocacy and a comprehensive three-step process to voter engagement: registration, education, and mobilization. Not only was its strategy voter focused; it was also publicly focused, aimed at drawing wide attention and support throughout the city.

MinKwon's Three-Step Process

Residents of New York City cannot vote if they are not officially registered, and they cannot cast an informed vote without information on candidates and issues. MinKwon ties its voter-focused strategy to this process of voting. It breaks the process of voting into three steps, which its staff and volunteers execute.

The first step for MinKwon is voter registration. MinKwon began the 2012 electoral cycle—one with a prominent Asian American candidate, Grace Meng, seeking office—with a thorough process to get a large portion of the community registered to vote. It helped citizens register to vote individually and also held larger registration drives at community meeting places and local events. As a result, MinKwon registered over ten thousand new voters.

The second step is voter education. Once a potential voter is registered, according to Steve Choi, "education is critical as well; we want them to learn about the races." This is in part because of what Hong discovered about the community: "We have found that people in the limited English proficient, new immigrant [category] . . . they lack information. We say 'We would like you to vote' . . . and many answer, 'Who's running?' . . . They lack basic information." For this reason, the organization developed bilingual voter guides, get-out-the-vote flyers, and regularly held public candidate forums: "We make a big deal out of [candidate forums]. Everything is translated or interpreted, real time interpretation for anyone in the audience that needs that. . . . You can see [candidates] actually responding to questions about significant problems." MinKwon believes that these forums provide the community a chance to size up the candidates and also compel candidates to become more aware of community needs.

The third step is voter mobilization. "The next step after education is mobilization," said Choi. "Now get those voters to the polls!" Technology was central to MinKwon's mobilization strategy in 2012, but not in the way Voto Latino used technology. The Korean American population in Queens, unlike the Hispanic American population nationally, was on average older, and this demographic factor shaped strategy. Choi explained: "Social media is not a big part of our work. At the end of the day, we are trying to get as diverse a group voting [as possible]; the fact of the matter is older people are disproportionately voters. . . . For now the profile of a Korean American voter is going to be middle-age to old and going to be primarily immigrant, foreign-born, not a great command of English."

Instead of social media, the MinKwon Center has used databases provided by State Voices, the organization described in chapter 2. In the past, Choi said,

MinKwon relied on "raw voter data, and we would cull out the Korean names," a laborious and time-consuming process. In 2012, through national and state coalitions, which had previously been funded by philanthropic foundations, MinKwon gained access to the VAN. The developers of the VAN program had already gone through and marked names by ethnicity—possibly more effectively for Korean names than for Arabic or Muslim names in New Jersey, as described in chapter 3. This meant, according to Choi, that while using the predictive-dialer software used to do phone-based mobilization, MinKwon volunteers would "have in front of [them] the information about the other household residents . . . how often they voted, likely voters." The VAN also permitted more effective in-person mobilization. Choi could send out bilingual staff and volunteers with a specific list of Korean Americans' addresses, and, much as in northern New Jersey, "the community was remarkably responsive that people were knocking and talking to them in their language."

MinKwon completed the circle on its voter engagement efforts by actually studying whether the strategy worked. Choi said the organization had "particular metrics for persons phone-banked and pieces of mail mailed out." In 2010, according to Hong, they analyzed a quasi-experiment and found that the 2010 turnout among the Korean Americans they had reached by mail (letters sent to around five thousand names), phone (calls made to around twenty-five hundred numbers), or door knocking (a small portion of the total) was a remarkable 54 percent, nearly double the rate for Korean Americans citywide whom it had not contacted. In 2012, Choi aimed even higher. "We want to reach twenty thousand folks. . . . We are anticipating knocking on about fifteen thousand doors, phone-banking fourteen thousand persons, and registering another five thousand people." This data-driven and technological approach to its work extended MinKwon's small budget and devoted staff to their limits.

The MinKwon Center, much like other examples provided throughout this book, exemplifies a comprehensive strategy for electoral work. The multi-tactic strategy depends on leadership committed to the electoral aspect of the organization's mission, a community that is eager and supportive of the strategy, and a staff capable of executing the strategy. As with Voto Latino's targeting of the increasing numbers of young voters, MinKwon's success is linked to Queens's burgeoning population of Korean Americans, a community growing in affluence as well as numbers. But MinKwon's work also must be traced back to the founding of the organization. Local leaders formed the organization to address a community need that was exacerbated by a citywide crisis. Immigrant-owned businesses were targeted for boycotts and violence in cities across the country, and, in part because they voted in relatively low numbers, immigrants had little institutional or political power to respond. The transformation of this nonprofit organization sought to address that urgent demand and enhance the political voice of the Korean American community.

Differences in Identity

Just sixty miles away, in Princeton, New Jersey, resides another enclave of Korean Americans. The community has been growing and increasingly successful in numerous professional arenas, with many Korean Americans employed in the pharmaceutical and engineering companies of central New Jersey. Long after the turmoil of the late 1980s and early 1990s that emboldened MinKwon, the Princeton-based community formed its own organization in 2007, called the Korean American Community Center of Princeton (KCCP), and it now operates in the surrounding lush New Jersey suburbs. I interviewed one of the organization's leaders, Young Lee, who explained that KCCP had a mission focused mainly on providing cultural services. The group's mission states: "We are building the nucleus to which the Korean community will gather around, provoking serious conversations on common community concerns and issues."[3] The organization had committees set up for discussing personal health issues, women's issues, and issues for younger members.

When it comes to politics, however, the organization usually remains inactive. Lee said: "We come across [politics] during an election year. . . . Different leaders will come asking for our vote, but [politics] isn't what we do."[4] Despite a community with ample resources, connections to universities, corporations, and likely even elected officials, KCCP remains distant from politics, and this is not because there was another organization already focused on electoral mobilization. Lee suggested that the explanation of this decision had to do with the identity of the Korean American community. He said that "it is not the numbers; the numbers are starting to grow, a majority in some towns. . . . It's more cultural, not a learned behavior; the older generation doesn't put a premium on politics as much as other [professional] fields." He continued: "Korean Americans tend to be a little more conservative, but for some individuals, politics generates some more interest. . . . The next generation is more assimilated than their parents, and they are growing more interested in politics." For the time being, KCCP remains focused on its identity as a service-oriented nonprofit, eschewing a political identity and the electoral tactics of an interest group.

In this chapter, I provide a theoretical explanation as to why these two seemingly similar organizations approach electoral politics in such different ways. I argue that in order to understand the electoral engagement activities of the MinKwon Center, or any immigrant-serving nonprofit organization, it is critical to examine the organization's particular identity, mission, and resources, as well as the relative power and politics of the community in local, state, or national affairs. Organizations such as the MinKwon Center and KCCP represent similar communities in terms of nationality, but they formulate an organizational identity in substantially different ways, reflecting the differences between an urban and a suburban immigrant community, the immigrant status of candidates for local office, and when each organization was founded. In short, the demographic, organizational, and campaign contexts have shaped each organization differently.

This chapter builds on the case of the MinKwon Center and KCCP to develop a new theoretical explanation of immigrant-serving nonprofit electoral engagement. The theoretical model draws heavily on the literature from interest group and nonprofit studies, as well as the practical insights gleaned from interviews with nearly seventy-five executive directors and other leaders of immigrant-serving nonprofits. By combining the theoretical and the practical, the model is both inductive and deductive in nature, an approach that produces a grounded theory of action. I begin by developing a theoretical model of immigrant-serving nonprofit electoral engagement—reflective electoral representation—and then explain how specific dimensions of this theory help predict electoral strategies. I end with an examination of the electoral tactics and strategies available to immigrant-serving nonprofits that are interested in participating in elections.

A Theoretical Explanation

In the introductory chapter, I briefly outlined the theoretical argument of what explains immigrant-serving nonprofit electoral activity. The central contention made here is that identity, mission, and political context drive decision making about electoral participation. Facing limited resources and the legal regulations on lobbying, the leaders of an immigrant-serving nonprofit organization make strategic decisions based on the unique identity and mission of their organization. In this way, each immigrant-serving nonprofit organization faces a very different decision about electoral activity, and this decision is prone to change depending on the demographic characteristics of the immigrant community (chapter 1), the availability of new resources and technology (chapter 2), and the characteristics of each election campaign (chapter 3). Building on the foundation established in the previous three chapters, the theory presented here suggests that identity, mission, and context matter, and that they likely matter to different aspects of the various decisions to engage in electoral work. In the end, an immigrant-serving nonprofit attempts to authentically reflect the desires of the community it serves. When this process relates to elections and campaigns, I label this *reflective electoral representation*. When an immigrant-serving non-profit looks to the relative political power of and threats to its constituents in deciding where to focus its electoral work, I label this *electoral venue choice*.

Why Does Mission Matter?

Theory and evidence have long argued that organizational capacity dictates norms of group behavior and also constrains strategy (Mosley 2014). These organizational capacity factors, according to resource dependence theorists, are often the resources necessary to permit certain political and nonpolitical activities and prohibit others (McCarthy and Zald 2001). For example, Pekkanen and Smith (2014) found a significant relationship between the size of a nonprofit's budget and general political advocacy. For electoral work, resources might equate to a budget sufficient to hire voter registration experts, pay for voter mobilization software, and rent space large enough to house election volunteers. Capacity may also be more qualitative and less monetary, such as the type of education and training that organizational leaders possess. A nonprofit operated by an executive director with a deep background in social movements will likely have the capacity to participate in politics to a greater extent than one led by an executive director with a more clinical or issue expertise. Resources certainly are integral to any organization's success, and immigrant-serving nonprofits are no different. I have shown how philanthropic foundations have long provided resources to nonprofits, including some of the funding and technical assistance necessary to expand electoral activities. Winning a grant from a foundation might be the difference between participating and not participating in electoral politics for certain nonprofit organizations. Foundations are not the only source of funding, but when it comes to elections, foundations often have a degree of discretion not given to government sources of financial support for nonprofits. Regulations strictly limit what kind of political activities can be funded by government grants. Irrespective of source, resources must be considered in conceptualizing immigrant-serving nonprofit operations, particularly those operations related to elections. Since foundations generally prefer to support pan-immigrant and pan-ethnic organizations (see chapter 2), it may be that grant resources will disproportionately support certain immigrant-serving organizations and not others.

Holding resources constant, what matters most to a nonprofit organization is its identity, usually reflected in its mission. Gioia and colleagues (2010) argued that through an iterative process of feedback with internal and external audiences, nonprofits construct an identity. Similarly, Halpin (2014) argued in his work on interest groups that "internal organizational agents . . . decide and set out what an organization 'is about' or 'stands for' and this becomes its organizational identity" (46). But Halpin also theorized that identity is constructed from the outside in. He wrote, "While organizations themselves seek to define their own identities, organizations are also evaluated by external audiences. . . . An audience decides on the identity of a given organization, regardless of (or despite) the attempts of organizational insiders" (47). Organizational insiders or leaders who do not appreciate the multidirectional nature of identity formation risk losing the support of external audiences or the community they serve. Thus, identity formation must reflect certain aspects of the community out of which the organization was formed.

Explicit and Implicit Organizational Identity

An organization's identity may change and evolve after formation, as was the case for ACCESS and NICE, mentioned at the start of the book. Those changes in identity are embodied in the mission of the organization. Mission is essentially an abstract notion of beliefs, values, and identity, both about the ideal structure of the organization and about what the organization should do. Out of this abstraction, organizational leaders write—and periodically revise—a statement of mission. The mission statement guides how the organization will function, make decisions, and allocate resources (Vaughn and Arsneault 2014; Pekkanen and Smith 2014). The mission statement should explicitly signal to the executive director what actions should be taken to advance the organization and those the organization represents. For example, the mission statement of the Oregon-based Immigration and Refugee Community Organization (IRCO) is "to promote the integration of refugees, immigrants, and the community at large into a self-sufficient, healthy, and inclusive multiethnic society."[5] IRCO serves the Asian Pacific Islander community in the state, primarily those in the country as political refugees. The organization provides refugees athletics, interpretation, and translation programs. IRCO delivers primarily educational and social services in order to fulfill its mission and reflect its identity. To engage in an election could risk inauthentically reflecting the expectations and desires of the community the organization serves and possibly losing legitimacy in that community.

The Coalition for Humane Immigrant Rights of Los Angeles (CHIRLA), on the other hand, explains its mission: "As a multiethnic coalition of community organizations and individuals, CHIRLA aims to foster greater understanding of the issues that affect immigrant communities, provide a neutral forum for discussion, and unite immigrant groups to more effectively advocate for positive change."[6] Advocacy is explicitly written into the mission of CHIRLA, and its leaders then can look to political action as consistent with the mission and an authentic reflection of the identity of the pan-immigrant community. CHIRLA is clearly an advocacy organization or a type of interest group. CHIRLA and IRCO both serve immigrant communities, but they have adopted very different missions to do so.

Much like CHIRLA, some immigrant-serving nonprofits *explicitly* include political and voter engagement as a part of their mission, while for others politics can be *implicitly* read into the words of the mission or encouraged by conversations with organizational stakeholders (LeRoux 2011). For example, when I interviewed Jerry Clarito, executive director of the Chicago-based Alliance of Filipinos for Immigrant Rights and Empowerment (AFIRE), he said: "Civic engagement *is an interpretation of our mission* [emphasis added]; our mission is a little bit broad: build the capacity of the Filipino American community . . . through grassroots education, action, research, and services. . . . So those three things fit with civic engagement." AFIRE launched "Rock the Balut"—a play on the term for the Filipino tradition of eating a fertilized embryo in its shell—to register and turn out Filipino American voters in the November 2012 election. For AFIRE, electoral participation was implicit in its core nonprofit mission. So even though AFIRE is not a traditional interest group, Clarito increasingly sees the organization's identity, and has adopted certain tactics, in ways that now resemble those of an interest group. AFIRE has transitioned to become more of a hybrid organization, rather than a purely service-oriented nonprofit, like IRCO.

Type and Variety of Organizational Identity

To be sure, there is a complex relationship between mission and electoral participation. The formal mission of the organization will open access points to the political realm, even if politics are not explicitly or implicitly a part of the mission. For example, nonprofit organizations that provide services that are linked with government entities are going to have a relationship to politics different from that of organizations whose operations are distant from government. For example, one would imagine that an organization that has a mission to serve the health needs of an immigrant community will be highly attuned to federal and state Medicaid, Medicare, and other health-care programs and regulations. It is likely to have expertise in how these programs and laws work and regular interaction with public officials charged with delivering and administering them. In some cases, the nonprofit may even be a partner with government, helping to deliver services through a government grant. In any given electoral cycle, those same government services may be up for public debate about appropriate levels of funding or eligibility requirements for immigrants. In the 1990s, for instance, immigrant-serving nonprofits that focused on education were drawn into policy debates about whether the children of undocumented immigrants should pay in-state tuition to attend public universities. During an election in a state or locality that is considering this type of legislation, an immigrant-serving nonprofit may be compelled to share its views with candidates and the public at large. Given that each election campaign will have some but not all issues actively debated, which immigrant-serving nonprofits have their mission or key issues at stake will vary, thereby regularly altering the calculus for electoral participation.

Immigrant-serving nonprofit organizations, however, are also not always narrowly focused; many groups provide a host of different services or start with just one service and grow over time. Breadth of mission has been associated in other research with certain advocacy decisions. For instance, the decision to join a political coalition seems to be related to the diversity of mission (Costain 1981). A group with a varied mission may not have the resources to pursue all the policy objectives contained in its mission; therefore finding common cause with other organizations can reduce the need to prioritize one area over another.

For those groups with a varied, broad, or multifaceted mission, it stands to reason that electoral campaigns will more often trigger an issue that aligns with the organization's mission. If the immigrant-serving organization provides health-care access, English language, naturalization, and cultural services, one would expect that at least one of these areas will be salient during most elections, either as an issue of debate by candidates or up for vote through a state ballot initiative or amendment to the state's constitution. These multifaceted nonprofits are more likely to act like interest groups during an election cycle and adopt an electoral strategy. Over time, these organizations are likely to begin to look like hybrid organizations. On the contrary, other organizations with a narrow focus on primarily one issue, such as financial literacy for recently arrived immigrants, may wait several electoral cycles before that issue rises in electoral importance, and thus these nonprofits are rarely likely to adopt the electoral tactics of an interest group, and likely will never transition to become a hybrid organization. Moreover, since a specific issue may arise in a campaign in one part of a state, but never enter into the campaign debate in other parts, only some organizations may be energized. We know that campaigns differ greatly from district to district and community to community, so organizations, even in a single state, will confront vastly different campaign contexts. In general, then, a varied or multifaceted mission should align more frequently with the issues up for debate in political campaigns, and lead to more electoral activity.

Variation in Immigrant Community Identity

Even though commonalities exist among immigrants in the United States, immigrant-serving nonprofits do not all serve individuals with the same characteristics or identities. Immigrant communities vary greatly, and the particular cultural norms and socioeconomic characteristics of the immigrant community that a nonprofit serves will be reflected in the mission of that nonprofit and drive its decisions about electoral activities. It is important to be clear that my argument here is different from that of some recent interest group scholars who downplay the importance of the characteristics of those whom an organization serves. Hahrie Han (2014) found that the characteristics of members of civic associations do not predict advocacy strategy: whom a civic association serves does not seem to relate to which strategy it employs. This may be the case for civic associations and other explicitly political organizations, because by definition the members of those organizations have already consented to the political mission of the organization. As noted in chapter 2, this is the essential definition of a membership-based political association or interest group. On the contrary, for nonprofits, the relationship between the organization and those who receive benefits from the organization is not the same thing as membership. Nonprofits provide services to the public either for a fee or for free; most of the individuals who receive services have not opted to join the organization, and thus have not affirmatively endorsed political action. The relationship between the nonprofit and those it serves is much looser than it is for associations. It is for this reason that nonprofits have to thoroughly interpret and attempt to mirror the political attitudes and identities of the community they serve.

Since my conceptualization diverges from the approach of many traditional studies of interest groups, it is important to focus on the characteristics of those served by immigrant-serving nonprofit organizations. Some immigrant communities are steeped in a tradition of political activism, whereas others view politics with more ambivalence, or even apathy. Some recent immigrants arrive in the United States from repressive political systems that discourage citizens to express their political voices, while others choose to relocate to a community in the United States because of the opportunity to participate in politics. These differences also exist within a given ethnic group, as immigrants from one time period may have immigrated for political or economic reasons very different from those that motivated immigrants from an earlier or later period. As Ron Schmidt and colleagues (2013) contended, "Immigrants bring with them unique issues and problems that often differ from the priorities of native-born ethnoracial minorities. This diversity creates new pressures, especially for Latinos and Asians, with larger percentages of newcomers, to socialize and mobilize these groups for participation in the political system" (146). For example, Helen Zia (2001), in her examination of the deep racial tensions that emerged in New York City between Korean Americans and African (and Caribbean) Americans in the late 1980s, noted that Korean Americans arrived in New York in large numbers much later than Chinese, Japanese, and other Asian Americans. Protests that ensued after a series of racial conflicts around Korean American–owned businesses—the same events that transformed the MinKwon Center—exposed a lack of unity between these Asian American communities: the older, established communities displayed ambivalence about Korean newcomers that prevented them from reaching consensus and coming to a common defense.

When I interviewed nonprofit leaders, many reflected on the varied constituents that they represent and the difficulty of representing a group political identity. John Albert of Taking Your Seat, a New York–based nonprofit focused on the South Asian American community, explained to me that his organization has to "convince people to see themselves as politically South Asian, especially Indo-Caribbean South Asians."[7] The organization needed "this pan-South Asian bloc" in order to gather political power in a largely Hispanic American neighborhood. Certain communities may even have a tradition of political activism but lack the political knowledge of U.S. institutions to fully participate. Navdeep Singh of the Sikh American Legal Defense and Education Fund (SALDEF) described the strong beliefs, within the Sikh faith, in social justice and activism, but the existence of "latent political awareness" among many Sikh Americans.[8] Parents concerned about school bullying, Singh explained, often lack information on the ways lobbying the school board or voting in school board elections can lead to policy change. The community is not ignorant of politics, yet its small numbers and newness in the country have limited the development of an array of nonprofit organizations that can educate and provide the infrastructure for collective action.

For other immigrant communities, their political background is fraught with violence and persecution. Kathleen Fernicola of the Asian American Institute in Chicago said that her group serves some immigrants that come "from countries where the political culture is violent, dysfunctional. . . . Some have family stories that relatives have been dragged out in the night for trying to engage in politics."[9] And Chi-Ser Tran of the Asian American Legal Defense and Education Fund (AALDEF) said that some older Asian Americans worry that they will "get in trouble with the government if they vote, or based on how they vote. . . . [They] don't understand the confidentiality of U.S. elections."[10]

Illustrative of this, Janelle Wong (2006) summarized interviews she had conducted in New York and Los Angeles related to civic participation: "Mexican immigrants were much more likely than their Chinese American counterparts to have belonged to local organizations or clubs" (48) prior to arriving in the United States. And de Leon and colleagues (2009) explained another disparity in politically oriented immigrant nonprofits: "Many African and Asian immigrants come from countries that do not encourage citizen participation, with some having lived through repressive regimes that instilled fear and distrust of government and its representatives" (24).

To be clear, many individual Chinese Americans arrive in the United States eager and prepared to participate in a variety of political ways, and many Mexican American immigrants have little interest in political activism. Further, some large sending countries in Asia are free and transparent democracies—for example, South Korea—and some countries in Latin America, including Cuba, are not bastions of political liberties. The point here is not that every immigrant arriving from Asia has suffered from political repression, nor does every immigrant from a given country share the exact same political legacy. Rather, the argument is that immigrant communities share identities, and those identities are greatly shaped by the political experiences in the home country and the common and often difficult path to the United States. For an immigrant-serving nonprofit that serves these various communities, it will be difficult to pursue an electoral strategy involving a community with relatively lower levels of political trust, efficacy, and identity, because the community may be unsupportive, wary, or even hostile to vigorous action. The community's identity may simply be incompatible with political action and electioneering.

For other nonprofits, even those with no explicit part of their mission focused on politics, their inclination to be active may be related to other aspects of the political position and characteristics of their constituents. Those constituents may be so numerous—perhaps because the organization has a mission to serve a pan-immigrant community—that mobilizing the community to vote can make the difference in an electoral outcome. Or it may be that, though the community is small in number, the stature or personal financial resources of key members of the organization translate to political influence. For example, in southwest Virginia, primarily Indian American hotel and convenience store owners came together in 2007 to provide a voice in local business and public affairs. They had grown frustrated with the lack of representation of Indian Americans in local business associations and saw growing financial resources in their community as a source of power. In an interview, members of the organization's board recounted how they asked: "Why don't we have a voice? . . . Every community had a representative. . . . Before 2007, there would be zero [Indian Americans] on community boards."[11] A group of these business leaders agreed that "if we can create our own identity, we can show that to the community" and can gain representation. They formed the Roanoke Valley Asian American Business Owners

Association, later broadened to the Asian American Business Owners Association (AABOA) to encompass members who lived in other parts of Virginia. With great pride, current leaders shared how the organization had grown more professional, expanded its membership, and adhered to a strict set of bylaws in making decisions. They argued that these characteristics of the organization reflected the culture and identity of the Indian American community, and any departure from that identity would be met with a sharp rebuke from the community. Candidates for public office now regularly appear at AABOA events, seeking out the support of the growing Asian American community that the organization now represents.

A galvanizing event might also mobilize and embolden an entire community. In 2006, anti-immigrant federal legislation led to major protests in Chicago, New York, Los Angeles, and many other cities. Hundreds of thousands of immigrants, many of them Hispanic Americans, rallied to oppose the proposed policy changes. The 2006 protests energized the Hispanic American community, and to a lesser extent other immigrant communities, around a common political narrative of protest and resistance. For this reason, we might expect these types of events to drive pan-immigrant organizations toward politics faster than organizations that serve just a single immigrant community.

On top of factors such as the large size of the community, affluence, or recent mobilization, it is the political attitudes of a community that shape and drive representation, either of the *descriptive* variety (that is, the makeup and views of those holding elected office), or of the *institutional* variety (the array of political and nonpolitical nonprofit organizations).

At the national level, the work of Matt Grossmann (2012) on political representation in Washington—what he dubbed *behavioral pluralism*—showed that a community's affluence, political efficacy, and level of civic membership were all related to representation in interest groups. Grossmann demonstrated that if a segment of the population views itself as politically efficacious—capable of affecting political outcomes—more interest groups form to represent that segment's views. In the case of immigrant communities, political attitudes and participation vary greatly. In particular, Hispanic Americans have relatively high levels of political efficacy, and Asian Americans have on average lower levels (Hero and Tolbert 2004; DeSipio 2006; Lien, Conway, and Wong 2004). It is important to note that political efficacy is different from political knowledge or interest. Asian Americans have high levels of interest in politics, but low levels of efficacy. Interest and knowledge of politics are different from efficacy (Lien, Conway, and Wong 2004). Individuals may be knowledgeable about electoral candidates or policy proposals yet also believe their vote or their viewpoint will have little impact on political outcomes.

I argue here that these varying attitudes toward politics will be transferred to immigrant-serving nonprofit organizations. Immigrant-serving nonprofits serve as a mirror of the identity of the community in which they are based: they reflect the political beliefs, values, and attitudes of their immigrant constituents. I call this process *reflective electoral representation*. Evidence of this can be found from research that shows different immigrant communities have developed different types of organizations, and those differences relate to what the community expects from the political activities of those organizations (de Leon et al. 2009; Hung and Ong 2012). Hispanic Americans have the most representation in Washington, at least in part explained by the community's higher-on-average level of political efficacy, while Asian Americans and Arab Americans have had much weaker Washington representation (Grossmann 2011). Asian American and sub-Saharan African American nonprofits have been less politically active than Hispanic American organizations, a difference attributed to typical differences in organizational age, resources, and leadership (de Leon et al. 2009). And finally, Asian Americans have tended to form social movements along ethnic rather than pan-ethnic lines, suggesting different political preferences and values. Schmidt and colleagues (2013) argued in reference to Asian Americans that "the increased diversity and relative newness to the country have made panethnic organizing more difficult and more complicated" (143), particularly in respect to the more pan-ethnic organizing tradition among Hispanic Americans. The multitude of languages Asian Americans speak is another explanation for why pan-Asian unity has been more limited than pan-Hispanic unity. Finally, given the preferences of philanthropic foundations noted earlier in the book for pan-immigrant mobilization, the tendency within the Asian American community to form organizations along ethnic as opposed to racial lines might stymie efforts to win grants to support electoral work.

Cultural norms and group beliefs about politics also open doors to particular electoral tactics. In an interview, Alan Kaplan, a representative of the New York Immigrant Coalition, argued that different immigrant communities permit different tactics: "Russian [immigrants] are the hardest to mobilize because of the huge cynicism, but they do respond to door knocking and phone calling. . . . Chinese Americans [are] also hard to mobilize. . . . [They] don't open the door [to strangers] or answer the phone."[12] Experimental research corroborates Kaplan's assertions about differences in how easy it is to contact different ethnicities by phone (Ramírez and Wong 2012). Cognizant of these differences, which are shaped by very different political experiences in their country of origin, Kaplan's coalition helped each immigrant-serving nonprofit design specific mobilization campaigns for its community. "Being a service provider, [the nonprofits] really are aware of what it takes," Kaplan said, "so every time they would explain we have a holiday—Ramadan, for example—it is pointless to get people out" to a civic event. Kaplan built on that local knowledge and experience that only a local immigrant-serving nonprofit possesses. And even within a single community, organizations may adjust their strategies. Leticia De La Vara of One Arizona, a coalition of immigrant-serving nonprofits, said that it targeted voter engagement work by age group: "If [voter interest] is a mainstream Latino pop artist, our communication is going to be more mainstream American. . . . If we are canvassing at a grocery store, it is more Spanish language, [because] we are on the ground."[13]

The argument made here is that by understanding certain dimensions of an organization's mission and whom the organization serves, you can predict the level and type of electoral engagement. Organizations that have an explicitly political mission or that have a mission with numerous connections to government and politics are much more likely to be motivated to participate in elections than organizations with few direct links to politics. Organizations that represent immigrants who are eager for political representation, comfortable with advocacy and civic engagement, will be pushed by the community into electioneering. Immigrant-serving nonprofits reflect these higher levels of political ambition and expectations with an electoral strategy that is deemed appropriate by and reflective of the community.

In making this argument, I am not suggesting there are no immigrant-serving nonprofits that view their role as leading or inspiring the community to change attitudes. Dara Strolovitch (2006) claimed that "advocacy organizations also use frames to try to influence the ways in which their constituents think about issues and more broadly to signal to them which issues are relevant to their interests" (60). Some nonprofits are acutely aware of the latent political excitement in their community and go about changing those cultural norms, not by acting as a mirror of existing attitudes, but rather as an amplifier to model, motivate, and inspire. Recent research, in fact, shows how certain labor union leaders have enhanced the political efficacy of members and transformed beliefs about collective action (Ahlquist and Levi 2013). And Han (2014) showed how an "organizing" strategy can build the capacity of community leaders and then transform the political identity of members.

Also, there may be a relationship between how open an organization is to the community and the attitudes of those in the community toward politics. An organization that is operated in a democratic fashion, with active participation of the local community in decision making, may see the community respond accordingly. For example, opening places on the board of directors for community members may empower the larger community in other ways, including a growing interest in democratic politics and support for electoral advocacy (Pekkanen and Smith 2014).

Thus, the internal structures of a nonprofit reflect—and also shape—those the organization serves. On average immigrant-serving nonprofits will orient their decisions about voting and election work to best reflect and represent the values and attitudes of their community. As these attitudes and conditions change, onetime service-oriented nonprofits will become hybrid organizations and possibly later adopt a full array of electoral tactics and look like an interest group. As Hasan Jaber, executive director of ACCESS, explained about the advice he gives other nonprofits: "The one thing we tell them is [advocacy] has to be organic, has to be driven by the community, it has to be relevant to the community. Don't try to copy any model; really figure out what works as a community."[14]

Electoral Venue Choice

Mission must be understood along with and in the context of power and politics, particularly the relative power of the local immigrant community. In order to represent the interests of a community, in this case the interests of immigrants, a nonprofit organization has to understand the power dynamics of local, state, and national politics, both supportive and hostile. Chapter 3 showed how the very different power dynamics of political races in different parts of the country shaped what immigrant-serving organizations could or could not do. Redistricting in 2010 created new political contexts that forced organizations to use different strategies and confront different political opposition. Immigrant-serving nonprofits absorb and seek to understand their political context. This understanding relates somewhat to the decision of whether or not to engage in an election, but more profoundly it drives the decision of *where* to engage. I approach this as Jill Nicholson-Crotty (2009) has done for health nonprofits. She argued that health nonprofits first decide whether to engage in advocacy, and then choose among available tactics. Similarly, I contend that once an immigrant-serving nonprofit decides it will participate in an election, a second decision has to be made as to whether the focus of that work will be at the local level, the state level, or nationwide. Political scientists have conceptualized this type of decision making as *venue choice* or *venue shopping*: an effort to seek out the most worthwhile place to emphasize advocacy (Schattschneider 1960). Venue shopping can occur vertically among levels of the federal system or horizontally across the legislative, judicial, or executive branches of government, but essentially it involves strategic choices. When these choices occur during an election or campaign, I refer to this as *electoral venue choice*.

In a period of stasis, there may be no natural push for any nonprofit, not motivated by its underlying politically oriented mission, to step into the fray of electoral politics. This work can be expensive and messy, potentially risking an accusation of meddling and the creation of enemies who perceive electoral work as inherently partisan, though it need not be. As LeRoux (2011) showed for social service nonprofits, if immigrant-serving nonprofits are assimilated into the practices of other nonprofit organizations and the political norms of state politics, they may behave in the same ways that the larger political environment permits. Daniel Elazar (1966) famously claimed that each state has a dominant state political culture, either traditionalistic, moralistic, or individualistic. The dominance of the state's political culture may invite or spurn the voice and participation of outside groups, particularly those that represent often marginalized immigrants. For nonprofits operating in traditionalistic states, there may be great resistance to their expressing a loud political voice outside the small, local community in which they operate. Advocacy at the statehouse or governor's mansion may be the purview only of established elites and trade associations, not the domain of nonprofits. A similar dynamic may be in place for electoral work: a traditionalistic state political culture may push nonprofits to make an electoral venue choice to focus at the local, rather than the state level.

Yet states also differ greatly in terms of the composition and size of their immigrant communities, what I called the demographic context. Some immigrant-serving nonprofits operate in isolated communities with small numbers of immigrants. Others work in communities such as Chicago, Miami, and New York, with large and diverse communities of immigrants. The relative size of the immigrant community might act to counterbalance the dominant state political culture. A large immigrant community could embolden an immigrant-serving nonprofit to engage in policy debates outside the locality, voice an opinion on statewide issues, and find a place in a national election. The size of the immigrant community then will affect the electoral venue in which the nonprofit seeks to engage in an election.

State political culture and even demographics change slowly, often imperceptibly, but on occasion power dynamics and politics change rapidly, and new conditions greatly alter the electoral calculation for a nonprofit organization. Sociologist David Meyer (1993), one of the foremost scholars on social movements, explained that movements and countermovements often form in response to political opportunities such as critical events like the Three Mile Island nuclear accident. Similarly, agenda-setting scholars, such as Cobb and Elder (1983), Kingdon (1995), Baumgartner and Jones (1993), and Birkland (1997), suggested that focusing or triggering events, unexpected and often dramatic events that increase public awareness of problems or new policy frames, can stimulate policy change from the status quo.

More recently, Michael Franz's study (2008) of traditional interest groups and electioneering argued that national-level political polarization related to interest

groups engaging in much more electoral work than in the past. For less traditional interest groups, in this case immigrant-serving nonprofits, the electoral
impetus might not be so nationally focused but rather relate to a particularly
polarized issue or perceived threats in the locality or state (de Graauw 2008). For
instance, AFIRE was formed in opposition to the anti-immigration legislation
introduced by Illinois congressman James Sensenbrenner and to support immigration alternatives sponsored by Senators Ted Kennedy of Massachusetts and
John McCain of Arizona. Sensenbrenner was active in the federal push to restrict
states from issuing driver's licenses to undocumented immigrants, called the Real
ID Act (Fraga 2009). Jerry Clarito, executive director of AFIRE, said: "The census says we are second [in size of population] to the Indian community . . . but
there are no Filipino Americans elected at the county or state level in Illinois."
His organization was formed in order to ameliorate this situation in response to
the anti-immigration law and also in recognition of the size of the community.[15]
In Dearborn, Michigan, Helen Samhan, AAI board member, argued that the es-
tablishment of ACCESS, the Arab American organization formed in the early
1970s, "had to do with complaints to the city that the Arab immigrants cook out
on laws, very stupid things . . . but it got people angry, brought AAI into town,
made it a national issue."[16] And in Arizona, site of the anti-immigration policy
associated with Governor Jan Brewer, Leticia De La Vara said the new SB 1070
law served as a "wake-up call" and that the formation of her organization was a
"response to SB 1070; each different group was doing different aspects of voter
mobilization, but there was a need to mobilize in a long-term strategy. . . . There
was a real interest in engaging voters who do not vote."

These external shocks to the status quo for immigrant communities spur the
formation of representative nonprofits and then push them toward political activism. These shocks may have a primarily local character, as was the case in
Dearborn, be statewide, as in Arizona, or be nationwide events, as was the case
with the introduction of the federally sponsored Real ID Act. Whether an event
is local, statewide, or nationally focused will depend on many factors, but elected
officials in corresponding jurisdictions will be held most accountable for redress.
If local police harass immigrants, it will be mayors or mayoral candidates who
will face questions, as has been the case with the "stop and frisk" policy in New
York City, or the treatment of Muslim Americans. Those seeking a seat on the
local school board will be targeted if bullying of immigrant students is a problem
at a public school. The geographic characteristics of the event, then, will drive
immigrant-serving nonprofit electoral venue choice.

Therefore, in addition to the importance of the *mission* and process of reflective electoral representation, the peculiar politics and power dynamics surrounding an immigrant-serving organization will affect the strategy behind electoral

venue choice. Some organizations may never even be aware that these political dynamics are driving them toward electoral engagement in a specific venue; the changes may be so subtle that the adoption of new strategies may come as a natural part of the evolution of an organization, rather than a conscious response to political change. The decision to engage in a particular venue may also never be made in such a formal manner—directed by an official dictum from a board of directors, for example—as alluded to here. Nevertheless, by carefully understanding that each organization engages in certain activities, be they the result of strategic decision making or simple organizational reflex, and also that each operates in a different political environment, we can better predict electoral behaviors and understand how immigrants are represented and served.

The Tactical Toolbox

Nonprofit organizations choose to participate or to not participate in elections, and then the way they wish to participate. They can engage in a variety of electoral tactics, including monitoring campaigns and elections; registering voters; mobilizing voters; translating election information into non-English languages; providing information to the public about policy issues; and joining coalitions with other nonprofit organizations. An additional tactic, the use of technology, may or may not be employed in conjunction with all these other tactics. For example, information about voter registration might be sent via traditional newsletter in the U.S. mail or via a website or social media application. It is worth noting that in a nonelectoral context, some of these tactics might also be labeled as *civic engagement* tactics, others as *lobbying* tactics. The tactics I label here as *electoral* are a subset of these two other broad political umbrellas but are unique because they are so closely tied to the months leading up to an election.

The choice to use each of these tactics involves different considerations. Each tactic varies in acceptability, feasibility, and cost (see table 4.1). Additionally, tactics can be studied individually, and they can also be combined to reveal a strategy. Jack Walker argued that interest group tactics can be grouped according to whether they are *inside* (lobbying, giving testimony, petitioning the courts) or *outside* (protesting, mobilizing grassroots activism, and working with the media). Walker deemed electioneering an inside tactic. The inside/outside dichotomy allowed Walker and others who have followed his approach to observe an underlying political strategy to the tactics used by interest groups. I make a similar, though not identical, distinction that within the category of electioneering there are several important dimensions along which a nonprofit might pursue its work. These dimensions, publicly versus privately focused, and voter focused

TABLE 4.1   Nonprofit electoral toolbox

	VOTER FOCUSED	ISSUE FOCUSED
Publicly focused	· Holding a voter registration event · Conducting phone banks for GOTV · Organizing candidate forums · Endorsing a state ballot initiative · Forming a political action committee (PAC) to give donations · Joining a voter mobilization coalition · Using website / social media to publicize voting issues	· Issuing policy recommendations · Writing an opinion editorial for local newspaper · Joining an immigration-focused coalition
Privately focused	· Sharing election information through an organizational newsletter · Translating voter information for constituents · Displaying voting information in the organization's lobby or common space · Registering organizational staff and employees to vote	· Monitoring campaign news · Meeting individually with candidates for office to discuss immigrant issues

versus issue focused, provide a way to understand the underlying strategies that are reflected in individual tactical choices.

Private Focus and Public Focus

First, there are a set of tactics that an organization can use that are oriented inward or focused on those close to the organization. These tactics may be directed at the internal staff of the organization or leaders of the organization's board of advisers. If an organization has a distinct group of constituents or specific individuals it provides services to, then these too may be a part of the internal audience for the electoral tactic. In each case, the focus is private, rather than public. The mechanism of the tactic may also be private, such that only those with access to the organization's building or a closed virtual network can easily consume the information provided by the tactic. A private meeting with candidates for office might also fit within this strategy, since the conversation will be limited to just those invited to attend. I group these tactics together as privately focused, to reflect the fact that the target of the tactic is within the private circle of the organization.

Conversely, other tactics are targeted at external audiences or publicly focused. These electoral tactics may broadly target those running for office or immigrants as a group, rather than just those who receive services from the organization. Or the tactic may rely on a mechanism that cannot be kept limited, such as an advertisement broadcast on local radio or posted on a highway billboard. Based on the mechanism and the target of these tactics, I group them together as publicly focused.

Different organizations will opt for a strategy that is primarily publicly focused, primarily privately focused, or a balance of private and public, depending on the organization's political identity, characteristics, and other contextual factors. Publicly focused tactics can open the organization to scrutiny from those outside the scope of the organization, including the media and hostile opponents. This may be deemed an acceptable risk by some organizations that are comfortable with electoral politics, but for others—including those new to politics—this scrutiny may be discomforting.

Voter-Focused and Issue-Focused Strategies

In addition to privately focused or publicly focused, tactics can also be focused on voters or focused on issues. A voter-focused strategy will rely on tactics that target individuals, primarily individuals who are eligible to vote in an election. As such, the procedures of voting (eligibility, registration, and turnout on Election Day) fall within this strategy.

An issue-focused strategy, on the other hand, will also address an upcoming election but focus on providing information about issues up for debate, tracking how an issue might harm or benefit the organization's community, or informing candidates for office. An issue-focused strategy, what Han (2014) called a "lone wolf" strategy, might never address voter and voting issues at all, preferring instead to address underlying issues and policy. An issue-focused strategy will often rely on research and statistics, necessitating an organizational staff with sufficient expertise to analyze data. Conversely, a voter-focused strategy may be more compatible with an organization that represents a large or growing immigrant community.

Organizations opt for a strategy that is voter focused, issue focused, or both, depending on their identity, organizational resources, and other factors. These are not neat categories and may in practice blend together, depending on how each tactic is applied. But these groupings provide a way to think about electoral strategy.

Monitoring Campaign and Election News

Perhaps the easiest tactic for any nonprofit to employ related to elections is simply to keep abreast of news about various campaigns. Daily reading of the local or state newspaper or watching television campaign coverage costs little and can be done with only minor effort. Immigrant-serving nonprofits could use monitoring of the news to track whether different candidates have expressed policy views on immigration or other issues that are critical to the immigrants that the organization represents. For this reason, I categorize this as an issue-focused tactic.

Today, with the aid of the Internet, this tactic is even easier to execute, especially for a nonprofit with a small staff or operated mainly by volunteers. Also, monitoring can occur without the awareness of external audiences. Donors, policy makers, and even constituents of the nonprofit organization might never know whether the executive staff of the nonprofit has employed this tactic. For a nonprofit that is unsure about whether to dip into politics, this anonymity or privacy may prove advantageous. I categorize this tactic as privately focused for that reason. One would expect if an immigrant-serving nonprofit did nothing else related to an election, monitoring would be the tactic it would use.

Registering Voters

Beyond simply monitoring, the foundation of any electoral engagement project often rests with registering voters. This may be an interest of any nonprofit organization, but it is a particularly important priority for immigrant-serving nonprofits. Because some members of the immigrant community will be newly naturalized citizens, these nonprofit organizations—which may also provide naturalization classes—will have a greater demand for registration services than nonprofits in the health or environmental areas. For example, one New York–based group, Latino Justice (formerly the Puerto Rican Legal Defense and Education Fund), used naturalization ceremonies to encourage voter registration. The organization relied on pre-law students to volunteer to staff registration tables near New York's City Hall to encourage those who had just gained citizenship to then register to vote.[17] For these reasons, I categorize this tactic as voter focused, since it is targeted at voting-eligible citizens.

Unlike monitoring voting information, however, which can be done privately, registering new voters often requires a public demonstration of the nonprofit's commitment to electoral engagement. Like Latino Justice, the organization might set up a registration table at a naturalization event, or it might use a community event, parade, or celebration to invite people to register to vote. In all these cases, the nonprofit must step into the public sphere and risk offending those in their community, or in other communities, who may believe electoral engagement is not consistent with the organization's mission. For these reasons, I also categorize this tactic as publicly focused.

Ironically, federal law passed in 1993 (the National Voter Registration Act) encouraged nonprofits to engage in voter registration in order to increase turnout

(LeRoux and Krawczyk 2013). Registering new voters, though, is not a tactic appropriate to all organizations. As mentioned at the start of the book, the New Immigrant Community Empowerment (NICE) served primarily undocumented workers in Queens, New York. Because most of its constituents were not naturalized citizens or even likely to be eligible in the foreseeable future, NICE shied away from voter registration as an electoral strategy. Within the related realm of advocacy for immigrant rights, organizations that focus on undocumented workers use strategies different from those that serve other categories of immigrants (Gleeson 2012).

Translating Voter Information

The peculiar characteristics of the constituents of an immigrant-serving nonprofit affect other tactical choices. Many immigrant communities that are largely first-generation or recently naturalized citizens have language issues as a chief barrier to engagement in politics. The federal Voting Rights Act requires translated voting information to be made available to voters on Election Day, but the languages are limited to communities that meet a 5 percent (or numeric) threshold of the local population.[18] For individuals who speak a language that does not meet this threshold, the law does not mandate that election material be translated for them, and they cannot rely on government language aid. Moreover, as recounted earlier in the book, major political parties may provide translated information on occasion, but rarely in any language other than Spanish, and often, even then, in a weak attempt at providing accurate and authentic wording. For these reasons, translation of campaign and electoral information is another potential tactic, and one I categorize as voter focused, since it is usually focused on providing language-accessible information to potential voters. Priya Murthy, an adviser for South Asian Americans Leading Together (SAALT), explained that "our organization and local organizations make sure folks know that even if you don't speak English you can still vote, you will have interpreters and language materials."[19] Murthy continued: "Our local partners know people locally who can do translation" in different languages. And Navdeep Singh, a policy adviser to the Sikh American Legal Defense and Education Fund (SALDEF), expanded on the importance of good language translation: "Messaging in Punjabi, even events like the [candidates'] town hall . . . instead of word-by-word translation, you can use Google, but it won't be a proper translation."[20] Nonprofit organizations can use their access to a multilingual staff, community members, and trained volunteers to provide translated voting information in a host of languages. In many cases, this tactic is privately focused, since the translated information is shared directly with those whom the organization serves. This is particularly the case if the translated language is spoken by only a small subset of the population, and those outside the nonprofit's service area would not benefit. In some other cases, the translating tactic can be oriented toward the public. For example, as MinKwon has successfully done, an organization can hold public forums where candidates have their campaign pledges and answers to questions translated immediately for the non-English-speaking audience members. In general, though, this tactic is categorized as privately focused.

Mobilizing Voters

Actual voting is what drives the need to register eligible citizens and translate electoral information. For many groups, all bound to remain nonpartisan in their activities, Election Day provides the opportunity to take months and even years of effort and translate it to action. As the examples provided throughout the book have demonstrated, organizations may approach voter mobilization through old-fashioned door knocking, phone calling, or public rallies held in community centers or religious venues. These tactics are almost always publicly focused and voter focused. For example, Taz Ahmed, voter engagement manager of the Asian Pacific American Legal Center (APALC), explained how members of her organization infuse authenticity into their neighborhood door knocking. After they map a neighborhood using the VAN database, they choose volunteers with specific language abilities. Volunteers then go door to door and tell voters: "Your vote matters. . . . I'm Chinese and my vote matters. . . . I am Cambodian and my vote matters." According to Ahmed, APALC has been involved in research projects (such as those presented by García Bedolla and Michelson in *Mobilizing Inclusion* [2012]) that show the value of "having someone of [the voter's] language speaking in a culturally appropriate way."[21] But mobilization may also be as routine as responding to a phone call. Remziya Suleyman, of the Tennessee-based American Center for Outreach, said that "on a regular basis I get requests from folks as simple as where do I go to vote, to something more difficult like [providing information on the] redistricting process that our state has gone through."

All these approaches to voter mobilization are driven by the goal to turn out as many individuals as possible to demonstrate that the immigrant community can have an impact on electoral outcomes. A community that actually votes in high numbers can demand the attention of policy makers, even if the community is split along partisan lines. Elected officials are likely to be more responsive to requests from a nonprofit organization that represents a community that is actively engaged. Seema Agnani, executive director of Chhaya CDC, said that in the Hispanic American–dominated part of New York where her organization operates, "South Asian voices are drowned out because we can't bring out the numbers." Agnani's organization has increasingly turned to social media to aid its outreach: "More and more so, Chhaya CDC works with a lot of younger families. We are using Facebook more and more so . . . anything cell phone related; text messaging is very big, we are using that technology." By reaching individuals more effectively, Agnani can better mobilize a community that has not turned out in large numbers in the past. Mobilization means many different things, and each immigrant-serving nonprofit adopts the tactics that it views as authentic, appropriate, and hopefully effective.

To be sure, many approaches to voter mobilization are expensive. It is costly to purchase the technology to do so-called robo calls—using a computer program to automatically dial a list of phone numbers and play a recorded message about an election—and it takes a lot of time to send volunteers to knock on each door in a neighborhood. One of the most innovative, but expensive, tactics used by the Asian American Legal Advocacy Center of Georgia was to rent a billboard with the slogan "Nov. 6—Vote for Our Future—It's Up to You" and photographs of four local children (Silver 2012). Eleven percent of the population of Gwinnett County, Georgia, where the billboard stood, were Asian Americans, and the organization hoped to mobilize these voters and inform them of Election Day—certainly a unique, but also expensive, approach to voter mobilization. As Donald Green and Alan Gerber (2008) wrote in their seminal guide to voter mobilization: "Direct mail, phone calls, and precinct walking all sound like good campaign tactics, and a campaign with an infinite supply of time and money would use them all. But here on planet earth campaigns face budget constraints" (12). Even an eager and willing immigrant-serving nonprofit will face decisions about what it can and cannot afford during an election, likely weighing what other services it might have to forgo if it devotes volunteer hours to mobilization rather than other aspects of its mission.

Providing Policy Information

Voter registration, translation services, and voter mobilization are tactics directed at constituents, but other tactics, such as providing policy information, may be directed externally at candidates or parties—what I categorize as issue focused. For a marginalized community, data and information about the plight faced by its members may be of particular value to candidates for office. A nonprofit organization may not have the resources to hire economists, statisticians, and policy analysts, but the existing staff may themselves be issue experts. The deep knowledge and access to a local community may mean that a local nonprofit can easily collect information and report about social problems. In communities that may be largely invisible to local or state government because of their small numbers, the information collected by a nonprofit may be the only reliable information available on the struggles of an immigrant group. Nonprofits can share this information with policy makers. Scholars of interest groups refer to this as "legislative subsidy": how interest groups work cooperatively with friendly legislators to subsidize issue research and analysis (Esterling 2007; Hall and Deardorff 2006). Interest groups align with favorable legislators who then rely on the group for information, ideas, and recommendations. A similar dynamic may be at play for nonprofits operating far from Washington. Berry and Arons (2003) wrote: "The entrée that [ethnic] nonprofits have with their funders at city and state agencies also gives them the opportunity to educate officials about the unique culture of their constituents and of the misunderstandings and stereotypes that harm them" (120).

The practice of educating elected officials may transfer to election season when challengers may face a particular deficit in knowledge about certain immigrant communities. In my own interviews, I found certain nonprofits filling this niche. For example, according to Ami Gandhi of SAAPRI, a Chicago-based nonprofit, the group was "founded in 2001 to serve South Asian Americans in the Chicago area through research that informs policy recommendations.... The four academic founders were feeling that there was a critical information gap in the community.... [There] wasn't good communication of lessons learned, and everyone was operating without data."[22] SAAPRI did not focus on traditional voter registration or mobilization; rather it collected data, including extensive exit polling research and an "updated demographic profile of the [South Asian American] community in Illinois." Gandhi's group also linked this work to traditional print media because the South Asian community in Chicago did not "have radio or TV stations like you would see in New York or New Jersey." For SAAPRI, this tactic was publicly focused, since the information it collected was being shared with the general public. In other cases, policy reports are shared in a more private or direct manner with individual candidates or other organizations seeking to advocate for particular policy alternatives during an election.

Utilizing Technology

The use of technology has been a theme in recent nonprofit research (McNutt and Boland 1999; Suárez 2009). Voto Latino, the MinKwon Center, and others have integrated technology into electoral work. The ubiquity of technology in modern life suggests that perhaps it is not itself a tactical choice, but simply a part of the operations of any organization. However, for some organizations, the particular application of technology has permitted the expansion and increased effectiveness of other electoral tactics. Navdeep Singh from SALDEF claimed "technology is one of the biggest reasons we can do what we do. It has transformed advocacy. We now have the ability to send targeted e-mails, web-stream the town hall, webinars on training for voter education and registration—we would have not been able to do [all this] just a few years ago." As has been the case for SALDEF, certain technologies can multiply the opportunities for a nonprofit with a small staff to reach thousands of potential voters without the need to employ hundreds of volunteers.

Technology, of course, and social media in particular, is not for every group, particularly those that serve communities not attuned to new media. For example, Ali Najmi, cofounder of the New York–based nonprofits SEVA-NY and Desi Vote, said that "social media does not work well; you have a whole generation of people who aren't on Facebook or Twitter. All the young people are, but those in the voter pool aren't young."[23] Najmi's organization focuses on "old-school canvassing, door to door, ethnic media outreach, creating events and a buzz on the ground." Ami Gandhi described something very similar about the South Asian population in Chicago: "A lot of the eligible new voters in the South Asian community are seniors, particularly limited English, less likely to use technology."[24] In short, as they do with other tactics, immigrant-serving nonprofits have to adjust their use of technology to their constituents.

For other organizations, technology offers the chance to reach many more potential voters and a wider audience. While resources do not seem to limit nonprofit use of technology for advocacy (Suárez 2009), staffing does. One of the keys to effectively using technology is an organizational decision to create a staff person charged with those responsibilities. David Castillo of the National Council of La Raza, one of the most prominent national Hispanic American organizations, said that he was hired specifically to manage the social media work of the organization. He said that his was a "relatively new position," since in the past social media had been done with an "ad hoc approach—several different people were charged with social media. . . . There were people with different responsibilities. . . . [It was] not viewed as a priority."[25] As a result, until Castillo took over social media, "it could go days between tweets." When Castillo consulted with other immigrant-serving organizations, many of them local affiliates of NCLR, he recommended that "if they really want to invest time in social media, then they are going to have to make it a priority, even if that is an hour or thirty minutes a day. . . . They have to prioritize it on a daily basis."

Social media technology can be used to communicate with an organization's internal constituents and also with external audiences. Social media integrates messages that are both verbal and nonverbal, including photos and videos. Castillo of NCLR described how his organization used online blog posts about what voters might face in Florida in light of the new voter ID law. The blog post included a link to a web video with advice on what types of identification to bring to the polls. On Election Day 2012, NCLR publicized the "hash tag" #mobilize2vote—the title of its 2012 voter mobilization project—to collect Twitter photographs of Florida voters waiting on long lines.

One of the most important factors in internal communication, and another theme that has run throughout this book, is the authenticity of the communication. According to Hoda Elshishtawy of the Muslim Public Affairs Council, MPAC aimed to "make the message sound as organic as possible."[26] Similarly, Jazmin Garcia of Latino Justice said that they faced a decision about whether to use formal or informal language in their social media. Ultimately they chose informal and to switch between Spanish and English because their audience, younger Hispanic voters, is often bilingual or English only. Before posting on Facebook or Twitter, they ask themselves: "Would I want to receive that message?" and "Are we harping too much?"[27]

Joining Electoral Coalitions

Many of the electoral tactics described above are used by nonprofits independently of other organizations, yet, as chapter 2 showed, cooperation has become important for many immigrant organizations. Coalition work, joint lobbying, and cooperative advocacy are all terms used for a related tactic that permits the merging of forces and coalescence around a central political or policy objective. Coalitions are sometimes formed on an ad hoc or as-needed basis, in order to link organizations together for a single pursuit, such as an election campaign. In other cases, the coalition becomes more formalized for an ongoing or a more general pursuit, such as a regular effort to increase funding for a policy area. Power in numbers is one of the main benefits of using a coalition. Research suggests that coalitions also tend to build on each other: immigrant-serving organizations that collaborate in one coalition are likely to work together again in the future (Cordero-Guzmán et al. 2008).

Coalitions can also provide small organizations with the opportunity to greatly expand the reach of their electoral work. Amrita Singh of SALDEF, an organization with only three full-time staff members, explained that "because we are so small . . . we often rely on other organizations . . . often work with ACLU, SAALT, NAACP, and Human Rights Coalition."[28] Similarly, Gregory Cendana, executive director of the Asian Pacific American Labor Alliance (APALA), related that coalitions may be particularly useful around a single tactic: "We try to do our best to make [translated materials] accessible," but owing to limited resources, "[we] try to connect with different ethnic organizations, figure out how to partner."[29] Because of the wide variety of languages spoken by Asian immigrants,

APALA relies on ethnic-specific partner organizations that have unique language expertise.

Ad hoc partnerships also allow small organizations, those with limited capacity to pursue electoral work, to support voting-focused organizations. For example, the Latino Advocacy Coalition (LAC)—a coalition in name only established in 1998—operates a community center for many undocumented Latino immigrants in Henderson County, North Carolina. North Carolina has a growing but still small immigrant community and, as a result, a limited set of nonprofit organizations established to provide electoral services. Carolina McCready, the co–executive director of LAC, said that, with the exception of citizenship classes, the organization did "very little in the traditional sense of civic engagement."[30] But with its professional staff of fewer than five, LAC provided a host of services for the local immigrant community with which other organizations could partner. McCready said: "If we organize the Children's Day festival for three to four thousand families, the League of Women Voters will want to know if they can send bilingual volunteers" to register new voters. Although LAC does not participate actively in elections itself, the relationships and partnerships it has formed with other organizations allow for the immigrant community it serves to receive voting services. In Virginia, also a growing center of immigration, the Virginia Caribbean American Cultural Association (VCACA) had few resources to spend on politics. The Caribbean population in the Tidewater section of the state is small and relatively new, meaning that few candidates for office seek out its support, and the association focuses most of its attention on education and the arts. But at its annual CaribFest in August, VCACA invited outside organizations, such as student groups at Norfolk State University, to register voters.[31] These are examples of an informal coalition or partnership helping to meet the needs of a nonprofit that lacks resources.

For a coalition to work effectively, it often takes a lead organization to establish the space for common cause to be found. Alan Kaplan with the New York Immigration Coalition (NYIC) described the combined effort of three groups, the Illinois Coalition for Immigrant and Refugee Rights (ICIRR), the Coalition for Humane Immigrant Rights of Los Angeles (CHIRLA), and his own group to form a coalition of dozens of New York–based immigrant groups. Kaplan said: "Three groups came together in the 1990s after welfare reform"—the bipartisan move to change welfare laws, which had a disproportionate impact on immigrants—"as service providers that realized they needed a coherent voice because they were getting *screwed*."[32] Kaplan explained that the formation of this coalition in New York was "a little different than other parts of the country. In other parts of the country it is more ideology focused; [in New York] they've tried to keep it very nonpartisan, give groups the chance to participate how they want." Kaplan traced this back to the long history many immigrant-serving organizations have in the city, and the varying and sometimes conflicted ideologies held by different immigrant communities.

To be sure, coalition and common cause are not as easy as they may appear. Organizations that compete over government and foundation funding may view other organizations with suspicion. Deeply held divisions across ethnic or religious lines may present a barrier to working together on common interests. Coalitions provide an attractive alternative to meet organizational goals, but to join a coalition in the context of an election presumes an interest in working with other organizations and often requires a history of doing so prior to the election.

Coalitions vary greatly in what they seek to accomplish during election season. An immigrant-serving coalition might focus on voters, on policy issues, or on both. Because the type of coalition varies greatly, the factors that relate to an immigrant-serving nonprofit joining one will also vary greatly.

Developing an Electoral Strategy

While mission and power are likely related in complicated ways to each individual tactic in an electoral strategy, each tactic also relates to the choice of an array of tactics, or doing nothing at all. Some groups will pick and choose, while others will opt for multiple tactics. We can think of these choices resulting in a continuum of electoral engagement that ranges from no engagement to intense engagement. Remziya Suleyman gives one example: "We are a political advocacy organization. . . . We provide everything from civics trainings, to how to vote, phone-banking, how to speak to the media, to anything else that we can do." Organizations such Steve Choi's MinKwon Center in Queens, New York, or Salah Mustafa's loose coalition of Muslim Americans in Paterson, New Jersey, utilize each and every opportunity they have to engage the community in an election and to engage candidates as well. A "do it all" electoral engagement strategy characterizes their approach. This expansive view of electoral participation is particularly important for organizations that represent immigrants who cannot yet vote. Priya Murthy of SAALT said "a lot of folks in our community are not eligible to vote," but she contended that "anyone can attend a candidate forum, anyone can write an op-ed. We try to have a mix" of tactics that invites noneligible legal immigrants to participate. One can think of the strategy behind this comprehensive approach as decidedly aggressive in its tone and public in its orientation.

Other organizations, such as LAC in North Carolina, take more limited approaches. David Heinen, executive director of North Carolina Nonprofits, a coalition of nonprofits in the state, reassured his members—some that represent immigrants—"that there is a lot you can do, but you don't have to do it all.

A poster with information is better than nothing; it is cheap and easy."[33] Heinen's view of voter engagement, one shared by the national organization Nonprofit Vote, encouraged individual organizations to build certain tactics into existing operations, rather than think of voter engagement as a totally separate endeavor. He said: "Our approach is to make sure nonprofits know they can do it, then integrate it into what they are doing . . . as a part of their intake process, part of their regular work, [an] assumption that people are coming to the nonprofit as a trusted resource," and use that as a basis to encourage individuals to participate in elections.

In Michigan, Nadia Tonova of NNAAC proposed a similar approach. Her organization coordinated with twenty-three local groups focused on various issues in the Arab American community. Many of these nonprofits were hesitant to engage in voter mobilization. She explained to me in an interview: "We have had to do a lot of work with our members; many needed a lot of work to explain to them it is allowable, what is allowable, what isn't."[34] Over time, many came around to the desirability of mobilization work, but NNAAC still lacked the staff and resources to know exactly what it could do. Tonova continued: "One of the things we really try to emphasize is easy ways to get involved. Some of our members might just focus on registering their clients and doing get-out-the-vote just of those clients . . . reaching out to the people they see every day." Others hung small election posters in their waiting rooms, placed voter registration forms in social service intake packets, or incorporated voting into English as a Second Language classes. As opposed to the aggressive and public orientation mentioned earlier, the strategy behind this approach is much more limited and private in its focus.

The theoretical model presented above argued exactly this point: organizational identity, mission, and political context will be particularly strong predictors of the number of electoral tactics a nonprofit will employ or the intensity of electoral activity, including the choice of not doing anything at all or simply employing a few tactics. Certain immigrant-serving nonprofits will feel comfortable only with engaging in a small set of privately focused tactics, while others will pursue a wide range of publicly focused tactics. Which exact factors are related to which strategic approach is the focus of the next chapter.

Conclusion

So why has the MinKwon Center expended so many resources on voter engagement and electoral work? For an organization with thousands of constituents who have educational, family, and health needs, what explains the organization's decision to prioritize voter registration, education, and mobilization? And why has the Korean American Community Center of Princeton opted for the exact opposite approach to fulfilling its mission? The answer to the first two questions seems to lie in the particular politics, demographic trends, and dramatic events that led to the founding of the MinKwon Center in the 1980s, and its transformation in the late 1990s. MinKwon was pushed and pulled into electoral politics through its mission, its members, and the conditions of the city in which it is located. A major foundation grant to support these activities also helped, of course. And despite the relative newness of the Korean community in New York, MinKwon is located in a city that has been one of the major immigrant hubs for over two hundred years.

But what about the answer to the other question? Why has the Korean American Community Center of Princeton opted for the exact opposite approach? Organizations such as the KCCP in central New Jersey and the LAC in North Carolina face a very different immigrant community and a larger political context that may not be as friendly to newcomers. LAC has adopted a much more limited electoral strategy that is sensitive to the growing yet still young immigrant community in its part of the state. Lacking the institutional resources and traditions of New York, LAC has avoided direct electoral engagement, but partners with other organizations in order to help register voters.

This chapter grounded the cases of MinKwon in New York, KCCP in New Jersey, AFIRE in Illinois, and LAC in North Carolina in a theory of immigrant-serving nonprofit electoral activity—reflective electoral representation—based on existing scholarship and on interviews with nonprofit leaders. Because immigrants share interests, some of them political, the nonprofits that serve those various interests can act in political and nonpolitical ways to advance a mission and best reflect the community. This is what makes understanding nonprofits different from understanding traditional interest groups that are established to pursue politics and therefore never face the same type of question of identity. Why some nonprofits choose an exclusively nonpolitical path and others incorporate electoral politics and voter advocacy is the focus of the chapters to come.

5

FROM MISSION TO ELECTORAL STRATEGY

"We are a purely 'cultural' group, [we] do not involve in politics at ALL," declared one immigrant-serving nonprofit leader in response to the fall 2012 survey. Another wrote: "We help prepare individuals for citizenship but we don't take a stand on who they should support. We also don't actively advocate on political issues, as we are a non-profit, and other than contacting legislatures about questions our clients have or reporting on how state money is spent we keep a low profile." Others followed with consistent statements about the incongruity of politics and their nonprofit status: "Our agency is a not-for-profit organization, we are not allowed to do political activities"; "As a 501(c)(3) nonprofit organization, we do not participate in political issues"; "As a cultural institution, we need to remain non-political or lose our not-for profit status"; "We are a 501(c)(3) purely cultural and humanitarian organization so we are specifically barred from engaging in any political activities." Right or wrong, many groups were concerned about losing their protected status.

During interviews with immigrant-serving nonprofit leaders, I heard similar explanations of why their organizations had opted not to participate in elections. For example, Dale Asis, executive director of the Coalition of African, Arab, Asian, European and Latino Immigrants of Illinois (CAAAEII), said: "In 2012, CAAAELII has redirected its efforts in doing health-care organizing and organizational capacity building for small ethnic organizations. CAAAELII is currently not doing any active get-out-the-vote campaigns at this time."[1] Asis's organization shifted from a hybrid nonprofit with a small number of election-related activities to one that is almost exclusively service oriented. In Virginia, Chaitali Roy, the president of the Greater Richmond Bengali Association (GRBA), described how a candidate for local office asked the GRBA to e-mail its members and encourage them to turn out to vote. The GRBA board met and "were debating about sending the e-mail. [Some board members] said 'why not? . . . we can definitely support him,' but . . . some of our members may feel offended because some are Democrats and some are Republicans. We have a mission that it is clearly stated that it is for cultural activities. We had a two- or three-minute discussion; then we voted who wanted to support the e-mail. A majority said no."[2]

In each of these cases, the nonprofit organization interpreted its mission, and the germane regulations, as prohibiting it from doing anything related to the election. And research confirms that this is not an anomaly: most nonprofit organizations do not view politics or advocacy as a priority, and many steer clear of politics as inconsistent or at odds with identity, mission, and goals (Child and Grønbjerg 2007; McAdam and Tarrow 2010).

Despite such perceptions, practically the only prohibited electoral tactics for a 501(c)(3) nonprofit organization are explicitly endorsing candidates for office and contributing campaign funds. And with the exception of exclusively focusing on lobbying, nearly every other political, advocacy, or election-related activity that is done on a nonpartisan basis is permitted. So why are so many immigrant-serving nonprofits opting out? Given what was presented in chapters 2 and 3, suggesting a groundswell of attention and new resources for immigrant rights and voter engagement for nonprofits, why did so many respondents to the survey and individuals whom I interviewed decide not to participate in the 2012 election? And, just as important, what explains which ones did?

The previous chapter established a grounded theoretical model, built on the demographic, organizational, and campaign contexts, focused on explaining how identity, mission, and power are strongly related to the decisions immigrant-serving nonprofit organizations make regarding electoral engagement. This chapter operationalizes that grounded theory with empirical measurement of those various factors. Specifically, I operationalize the first half of the theory related to mission—reflective electoral representation—with quantitative measures. I then connect those independent variables to the actual decisions about electoral tactics and strategies that nonprofits made during the 2012 election. The data are drawn primarily from an original survey of immigrant-serving nonprofits in six states, and I use original interviews to contextualize and explain the analytical findings. I begin by describing the way the data were collected, the measurement of the key dependent variables, and then demonstrate the relationship to each independent factor.

Measuring Electoral Tactics

In the analysis the electoral activities of nonprofits, survey methods permit a close examination of organizational decisions. Survey methods are particularly useful in collecting data across a large number of organizations in a relatively short period and an efficient fashion. Unlike much of the research on immigrant-serving organizations that has used primarily case study analysis for an in-depth examination of specific organizations, survey methods allow for breadth and greater potential to generalize from the research findings.

Since the study was of electoral activities, and elections are most numerous at the state and local levels, I chose nonprofits based on the state in which they operated. Because much of the existing literature has focused on California, I opted to leave California out of the study, despite the reality that it is the home of large, diverse, and well-organized immigrant communities. I sought out diversity of immigrant community by choosing states that varied in terms of the percentage of major immigrant groups. As demonstrated in chapter 1, the six states chosen (Florida, Illinois, Michigan, New Jersey, New York, and North Carolina) all have large numbers of immigrants, as well as substantial variation between each state in the composition of the immigrant community. North Carolina—a new gateway for immigrants—has a younger and newer immigrant population, primarily from Mexico, whereas Michigan has an older and more established immigrant population and one of the largest Arab American communities in the country. Florida is home to the largest Cuban American population and a growing Caribbean and Puerto Rican community, while Illinois, New York, and New Jersey stand near the top of nearly every category of immigrants.

These states also differed in terms of their electoral position in 2012. At the national level, Florida and North Carolina—and to a lesser extent Michigan—were closely contested by President Obama and Mitt Romney as "battleground states," while Illinois, New York, and New Jersey saw little action in the presidential contest. At the state and local levels, there were numerous competitive party primary campaigns and later general election campaigns, which make the mobilization of immigrants critical to understand, even if the state's Electoral College votes were never disputed. And recall that Florida enacted some of the strictest changes to its electoral laws in 2011, presenting voters and nonprofits with new challenges not encountered in the other states. But because this is a nonrandom selection of states, generalizing from these results to other states should be done with caution, care, and attention to whether the characteristics of these six states align with others. Generalizing to non-immigrant-serving nonprofits also must weigh the relative similarity of the populations those organizations serve and the importance of identity to how they develop and pursue their missions.

The survey was distributed to the full population of immigrant-serving non-profit organizations in all six states, and I conducted follow-up through e-mail and phone calls to encourage completion by nonrespondents. Twenty-two percent of those that were sent a survey ultimately completed the questionnaire, a response rate that was lower than one would expect for individual surveys but on par with other survey research on nonprofits where published findings typically range from the low teens to approximately 50 percent. Further, by comparing respondents to nonrespondents along organizational variables obtained from IRS data, such as budget and age, I found little evidence of survey response bias. A full description of the survey methods can be found in the technical appendix at the end of the book.

Measuring the Dependent Variables

As described in the previous chapter, electoral participation can be conceptualized as (1) a series of individual tactical choices; (2) a continuum from strong ("do it all") to weak ("do nothing") that combines a series of tactical choices; or (3) an underlying strategy that assembles various tactics (publicly focused / privately focused, voter focused / issue focused). The survey instrument queried each immigrant-serving nonprofit about whether it had or had not used each tactic (see figure A.1 in technical appendix). I then look to how each organization responded as an indication of the ways that each participated in the election in 2012.

The first important finding from the survey was that nearly 60 percent of respondents did not use a single electoral tactic. In line with the qualitative findings presented at the start of this chapter, many nonprofits did not include electoral activities in the way they met their mission, either because of concerns about the IRS, limited resources, or other worries about mission. Further, just over 40 percent of respondents used "at least one" electoral tactic. For these organizations, while the extent of engagement varied from just a single tactic to the choice to use all the possible tactics, each decided that the election mattered in meeting its mission to serve immigrants.

Second, in regard to particular tactics, over a quarter (26 percent), the largest percentage of respondents, chose to use the tactic of monitoring the news about the campaign (see figure 5.1). Given that this is arguably the least costly and least public tactic, this finding is not surprising. Nearly a fifth (19 percent) of respondents were involved with voter registration, and 13 percent with voter mobilization. Each of these tactics is relatively costly in terms of time and resources, and also is a public demonstration of how engaged the nonprofit is in the election. Smaller percentages of respondents provided electoral information

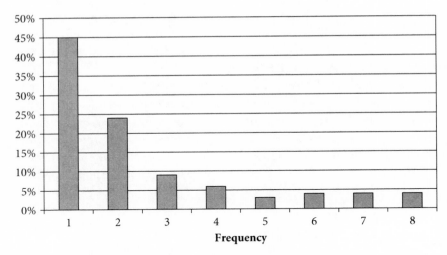

FIGURE 5.1. Of those participating in 2012 campaign, percent of respondents using each electoral tactic
Source: Author.

to the community (10 percent) and translated voting information (6 percent). Also, only a few respondents provided information to candidates about local issues (6 percent) or foreign policy issues (4 percent) (because of the small numbers, I combined these to create a single measure of "policy reports" in the analysis below). The smallest number of nonprofits, just 3 percent, joined a national coalition, and 6 percent joined a local electoral coalition (I combined these two tactics into a single "coalition joining" tactic in the analysis below). In general, these responses show that immigrant-serving nonprofits used a variety of tactics, but no single tactic was used by a majority of respondents overall.

Third, individual tactics also may be combined to form a single continuous measure or index. Where a nonprofit falls along that continuum may indicate the intensity or comprehensiveness of its electoral work.[3] I combined all the individual tactics into a simple eight-item measure, *electoral index.* As demonstrated above, a majority of nonprofits did not use a single tactic, but 40 percent used at least one. Of those, 45 percent used *just* one tactic, 24 percent used two, and 31 percent used more than two (figure 5.2). A small number, just 4 percent of the respondents, used eight tactics.[4]

Finally, tactics can be grouped together to demonstrate a strategic focus. In the last chapter, I argued that electoral strategy might see a nonprofit concentrate on a publicly focused strategy (one oriented outward to the community and the larger political arena) or privately focused (one oriented inward, toward the

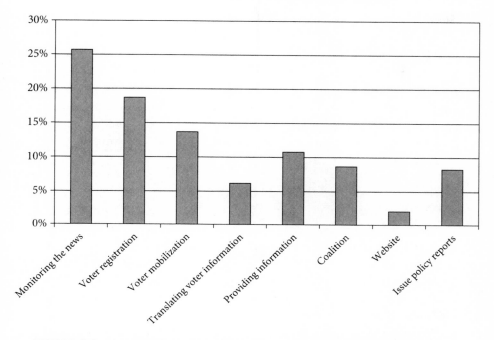

FIGURE 5.2.   Percent of all respondents using number of electoral tactics
Source: Author.

organization itself, community insiders, and supporters). Accordingly, I grouped tactics into two measures: publicly focused strategy and privately focused strategy. The measure of publicly focused strategy combined five tactics, while the measure of privately focused strategy combined three tactics.[5] Slightly more than a quarter (26 percent) of respondents used the publicly focused strategy, and nearly a third (29 percent) used the privately focused approach. Given the concerns raised about losing the protected 501(c)(3) status and potential incompatibility between nonprofit mission and politics, it stands to reason that a larger percentage would use the privately focused strategy, which draws less attention to the organization.

The second way to organize the tactics is by examining whether a nonprofit focuses its electoral work on voters (that is, on individuals eligible to vote and their needs for information, education, and mobilization) or on issues (that is, on campaign debates about ideas and salient policies that affect immigrant communities). An immigrant-serving nonprofit might choose to focus on voters, on issues, or it might pursue both. The measure of a voter-focused strategy combined five questions, while the measure of an issue-focused strategy combined two of the survey questions.[6] Using these two measures of strategy, I found that a larger portion (28 percent) used the issue-focused strategy than used the voter-focused strategy (25 percent), though the difference is fairly small and not statistically significant. One possible reason for this small difference is that an issue-focused strategy may fit with other activities that persist long after elections are done. For example, a statistical report for a grant proposal could also be used to inform candidates about local problems. The tactics underlying a voter-focused strategy, however, would likely be difficult to reuse until the next election. This may explain why slightly more respondents appeared to use the issue-focused strategy compared to the voter-focused strategy.

Differences by State

The most obvious difference in the operations of each survey respondent was the state in which it was located. The six survey states vary widely in terms of the size of immigrant populations, the history of immigration, and policies regarding elections. In general, there were few differences in how electorally engaged nonprofits were, based on state. With the exception of those nonprofits in New Jersey, where only a third (35 percent) used at least one tactic, in the other five states a little less than half used at least one tactic. These consistent patterns generally hold for individual tactics. However, the percentage of nonprofits using the tactic of voter registration was statistically much lower for Florida (5 percent) and somewhat lower for Michigan (17 percent) than in the other states, where around a fifth used that tactic (the difference was statistically significant at the .05 alpha level for Florida but not for Michigan) (see table 5.1). Recall from chapter 3 that Florida passed a new voting law that required third-party organizations to comply with new regulations, including heavy fines and possible prison sentences if individuals were found submitting false registrations. The Michigan legislature

TABLE 5.1 Percent of all respondents using each tactic, by state

	MONITOR-ING THE NEWS	VOTER REGIS-TRATION	VOTER MOBILI-ZATION	PROVIDING INFOR-MATION	COALITION	TRANS-LATING	POLICY REPORTS	CHANGES TO WEBSITE
Florida	31	5**	11	8	2	2	0*	2
Illinois	31	21	23	19	21	6	14	6*
Michigan	31	17	17	6	10	6	20	0
New Jersey	17	21	11	9	3	11	5	1
New York	28	28	8	14	5	5	5	0
North Carolina	36	21	10	5	10	5	5	0

* p value < .10

** < .05

*** < .01 indicates statistical differences for each compared with all other states for each bivariate chi-square test.

passed a similar law, but the governor later vetoed the change. It stands to reason that the limited use of the voter registration tactic by immigrant-serving non-profits in these two states related to the imposition of these actual or threatened new regulations.

Also worthy of note, immigrant-serving nonprofits in Illinois stood out for their stronger likelihood of using voter mobilization (23 percent); in the rest of the states, fewer than 15 percent used this tactic. Chicago was the headquarters of the president's reelection operations in 2012, so there may have been heightened awareness concerning the mobilizing of voters in Illinois compared with other states. If nonprofits were working too closely with the Democratic Party, they would be violating nonprofit and election law, but there was no evidence that 501(c)(3) nonprofits were engaged in partisan mobilization in support of the Democratic or Republican Parties. Instead, it may be that the political environment encouraged more electoral activity in Illinois than it did in the other states.

With those differences noted, it did not appear that there were systematic differences in the bivariate relationship between state and electoral engagement. It may have been that local, city, or county factors were more strongly related to nonprofit decision making. The subsequent multivariate analysis controls for some of those local political factors.

Differences in Resources

Another focus in the literature on interest groups and nonprofits is the importance of resources and money. Chapter 2 showed how certain nonprofits have been supported by grants from philanthropic foundations. Foundations increased funding of immigrant issues and nonprofits that focus on integrating immigrants, yet most nonprofits received no new funding during election time. Insufficient resources may dampen the willingness of immigrant-serving non-profits to engage in electoral activities. Resources have been associated with the number of political tactics, policy successes, and sustainability of interest groups and other nonprofits (Mahoney 2008; Grossmann 2012; Hung and Ong 2012).

In order to investigate whether resources explained differences in immigrant-serving electoral activity, I compared respondents that used at least one tactic with those that had not, based on a measure of the organization's total revenue. Total revenue combines various sources of revenue, including the support from philanthropic foundation grants; but because philanthropic grants may be for nonelectoral purposes, I chose not to isolate grant funding and simply used total revenue as a proxy for resources. The average size of revenue for a respondent that had used at least one electoral tactic was $68,000, compared to only $31,000 for others, a statistically significant difference (at the .05 alpha level). Respondents that employed the voter-focused strategy and the publicly focused strategy were also significantly larger in revenue than others (at the .05 alpha level), but no different in regard to those that employed the privately focused and issue-focused strategies. It seems that the relationship between revenue and electoral strategy is different for different strategies. Berry and Arons (2003) reached similar conclusions about the ability of nonprofits to contact government: the size of revenues and staff did not predict contact, but having a dedicated research staff that increased the "capacity to conduct research" did statistically relate to government contact. A similar dynamic may be in place for electoral tactics. There may be fixed technology and expertise costs that even medium-size nonprofits cannot afford; therefore those nonprofits cannot adopt certain electoral tactics to any greater extent than small-resource nonprofits.[7] These findings suggest that getting a grant to expand organizational resources may be an important step in participating in certain aspects of electoral politics, but not all. Organizations that fail to apply for or fail to win a grant may not have the discretionary resources available to move beyond pursuing a social mission or a limited array of low-cost tactics.

Relevance of Organizational Mission

Organizational resources may relate to certain operational decisions, but they do not relate directly to an organization's determining of its mission or whom it serves. Resources may be better thought of as controls that might drive electoral decision making in any type of nonprofit, not just immigrant-serving nonprofits. To address the key theoretical argument presented in the last chapter—defined as *reflective electoral representation*—I operationalized those factors specific to the mission and identity of immigrant-serving nonprofits, including political orientation, the range of issues, and the immigrant community served.

Politically Oriented / Not Politically Oriented

As explained earlier, some immigrant-serving nonprofit organizations have an explicitly political identity, reflected in their mission statement, while others have politics implicit in their mission, or absent altogether. Nonprofits that include politics in their mission might be described as advocacy organizations; but even without politics in the mission, an organization may still provide political services and thus resemble what I called a hybrid organization. We would expect these organizations to be more involved in any number of political realms, including elections. Rather than reading and coding each mission statement according to its wording in this respect, I used a variable from the survey that reads: "Does your organization devote substantial resources to providing any of the following services to the community? (choose all that apply)." I labeled each respondent as politically oriented (I combined "government advisory" and "political" to come up with a total of 14 percent of the respondents) or not politically oriented (86 percent). Parenthetically, one concern about doing survey research among nonprofits is that respondents will overrepresent the phenomenon the researcher is studying: one might be worried that only politically oriented nonprofits would respond to a survey about electoral politics. The small minority of politically oriented that responded to this survey, merely 14 percent, suggests that survey respondents were not simply those interested only in politics: the majority of respondents expended very few resources on politics compared to other nonpolitical activities. Thus, most remained service-oriented nonprofits, not fully transitioned to the hybrid or interest group type of organization.

In comparison, politically oriented immigrant-serving nonprofits were much more likely than other immigrant-serving nonprofits to employ at least one electoral tactic: 87 percent versus only 36 percent. The differences were particularly true for monitoring the news, voter registration, and voter mobilization, where around half of politically oriented nonprofits chose each tactic. These respondents were also more likely to use the voter-focused and publicly focused strategies. These finding adhere very closely to expectations and confirm that this dimension of an immigrant-serving nonprofit organization's mission matters for electoral engagement.

Multifaceted Mission / Simple Mission

The next aspect of the theory proposed in the last chapter suggests that the more multifaceted or complex the services provided by an immigrant-serving organization, the more likely it will be that an election campaign will focus on some organizational priority. This will then pull organizations with multifaceted missions into electoral politics. In order to examine this, I coded respondents based on the number of issues on which they "expended substantial resources" (see appendix table A.2). Respondents provided a variety of services, with education by far the most common, followed by health and food services. Each respondent could check as many of the services as they provided. An organization that chose only one issue area—45 percent of the respondents—was labeled as *simple mission*, and the rest as *multifaceted mission*.

Using this new variable, I found that more than half (53 percent) of immigrant-serving nonprofits with a multifaceted mission used at least one electoral tactic, versus only a quarter (26 percent) of those with a simple, single-issue mission, a statistically significant difference (at the alpha level of less than .05). This pattern also held for each individual tactic, though not always statistically so, and also for publicly focused strategy.

Overall, the theoretical expectations were met that immigrant-serving nonprofits with more multi-issue missions would be more likely to engage in electoral activities and to employ more electoral tactics. Using these bivariate comparisons, the survey results suggest that the particular aspects of an immigrant-serving nonprofit organization's mission that are related to elections—political orientation and multifaceted mission—both seem to be related to greater engagement in the election.

Inter-Immigrant Community Differences

The final mission factor suggested by the theoretical model, and perhaps the most important for this study, was the political culture and efficacy of the immigrant-serving nonprofit's constituents. The higher the level of politically efficacy of the constituents, and the stronger the belief in group political identity, I argue, the more electorally active the immigrant-serving nonprofit will be. This is a difficult factor to measure in a systematic way, as different immigrant communities have different political experiences and identities. For example, evidence from California suggests that compared to white and African Americans, Hispanic Americans and Asian Americans have lower levels of political efficacy, and that Asian Americans have been on average the least efficacious group (Michelson 2003; Lien, Conway, and Wong 2004). Hispanic Americans have a longer history of collective political organizing and a stronger sense of group identity than Asian Americans (Schmidt et al. 2013). Finally, Masuoka and Junn (2013) found that Asian Americans have lower levels of shared identity with other Asian Americans, compared to shared identity within the Hispanic American community. But grouping ethnicities together poses some of the problems raised earlier in the book. In reality, efficacy varies within these Hispanic and Asian pan-ethnic umbrellas. In an ideal world, we could fully disaggregate nonprofits by each ethnicity served and have a more micro-level understanding of the identities of each ethnicity. The limitations of survey data methods prevent this fine-grained approach; thus grouping by pan-ethnic categories provides a widely used proxy but admittedly second-best approach to test relationships across immigrant communities.

In order to investigate this aspect of the theory, I compared nonprofits representing Hispanic Americans to those representing Asian Americans (including Indian Americans), Middle-Eastern Americans (including North African Americans), and those that represent other communities (including immigrants generally). I expected that the large number of Hispanic Americans and more established history of activism in the Hispanic American community would lead Hispanic American nonprofits to be more active than Asian American and other nonprofits. For those groups representing individuals from Middle Eastern countries, it was less clear what to expect. This is in part because there is great heterogeneity among those immigrants from Middle Eastern countries. Some are Arabs, though many are not. Some are Muslims, but others are Christians or Jews. Some have ties to Africa, others to Asia, and still others to Europe. Even the term "Middle Eastern" is subject to criticism as excessively Eurocentric (Jamal and Naber 2008). In part because of this diversity, and also the smaller relative size of the community in the U.S. population, we know less about the political participation of Middle-Eastern Americans than other groups. However, leaders of Middle-Eastern American nonprofit organizations whom I interviewed repeatedly mentioned the importance that the 9/11 attacks played in mobilizing the community. The aftermath of September 11, 2001, politicized the lives of Arab, Muslim, and other Middle-Eastern Americans, and it is reasonable to suspect that nonprofits responded accordingly. On the contrary, there is also reason to believe that the persecution and hostility borne by many Middle-Eastern Americans could have discouraged nonprofits from being politically assertive, in an effort to avoid drawing attention to the community (Howell and Shryock 2003).

With these cautions noted, the evidence from the survey generally supports the hypothesis about interethnic differences, though the results are complicated (table 5.2). The bivariate statistics suggest that Hispanic American organizations were much more active in electoral politics than organizations representing other immigrant communities. Nearly two-thirds (62 percent) of nonprofits that serve Hispanic Americans used at least one tactic. This compared to more than a third (38 percent) of Asian American nonprofits that used at least one, half of Middle-Eastern American nonprofits, and 32 percent of nonprofits representing other communities. These differences are also notable in terms of the average number of tactics used. Middle-Eastern American nonprofits used on average 1.77 tactics, statistically more than the .97 average for the comparison group "other" (at the .10 alpha level). This compares to 1.20 for Hispanic American and 1.25 for Asian American nonprofits, neither statistically different from "other." As such, nonprofits representing Americans from various Middle Eastern countries, interestingly, stand out for their level of participation in the election. These organizations were also the most active in nearly every category except translating, though not statistically different. The examples presented throughout this book from Paterson, New Jersey, Dearborn, Michigan, and elsewhere, related to the deep concerns and resentment felt after 9/11 by many from these communities,

TABLE 5.2 Percent of all respondents using each tactic, by immigrant-serving category

	AT LEAST ONE TACTIC	MONITORING THE NEWS	VOTER REGISTRATION	VOTER MOBILIZATION	PROVIDING INFORMATION	COALITION JOINING	TRANSLATING	POLICY REPORTS	CHANGES TO WEBSITE
Hispanic American	62***	31	25	15	16	9	11	4	4
Asian American	38	26	23	20	12	10	10	13	3
Middle-Eastern American	50	39	28	22	17	22	0	22**	6
Other	32	21	10	7	8	6	3	5	1

* p value < .10

** < .05

*** < .01 indicates statistical differences for each category compared with all other respondents for each bivariate chi-square test.

may explain this high level of activism. Representative organizations, acting as a mirror of the political attitudes of those they serve, may be responding to these sentiments with full electoral engagement.

The findings for strategic choices are equally interesting. The higher levels of political efficacy in the Hispanic American community should invite an electoral focus on public tactics and tactics focused on voters. Conversely, if Asian American organizations reflect the comparatively lower levels of political efficacy in their communities, we would expect less of a focus on the public tactics and less of a focus on voter tactics. Again, Middle-Eastern American nonprofits remain a mystery as to what strategies they might pursue.

In table 5.3 one can see that a larger portion of Hispanic American nonprofits used the publicly focused strategy (39 percent compared to only 16 percent for other) and a larger portion used the privately focused strategy (41 percent compared to only 22 percent for all others), both statistically significant differences (at the alpha level of .05). Middle-Eastern American nonprofits were no different in terms of privately focused strategy, but a notably larger percent used the publicly focused strategy (38 percent), though not a statistically significant difference. Asian American nonprofits were no different from others for both of the two measures. This finding reinforces what was found earlier for the active role played by Hispanic and Middle-Eastern American organizations.

I found a similar pattern for the voter-focused strategy. Hispanic American nonprofits were the most active in pursuing this approach (and statistically so), but no different in terms of issue-focused strategy. The other notable difference was for Middle-Eastern American nonprofits that used the issue-focused approach much more so (44 percent), though again this was not a statistically significant difference.

TABLE 5.3 Percent of all respondents, by immigrant-serving category, using each electoral strategy—publicly v. privately focused / voter focused v. issue focused

	PUBLICLY FOCUSED STRATEGY	PRIVATELY FOCUSED STRATEGY	VOTER-FOCUSED STRATEGY	ISSUE-FOCUSED STRATEGY
Hispanic American	34**	31**	40***	33
Asian American	29	27	28	29
Middle-Eastern American	38	38	33	44
Other	17***	23*	15***	23

* *p* value < .10
** < .05
*** < .01 indicates statistical differences for each category compared with all other respondents for each bivariate chi-square test.

Because of how central this finding is to the conclusions that can be drawn from the survey results, I sought out another measure of organizational advocacy outside the survey. In order to verify and check the reliability of the survey results, I examined whether these differences between immigrant communities still appear when we look at other aspects of how each organization engages the public. Social media usage is one way to compare these organizations. Researchers such as Melissa Merry (2010) have increasingly turned to organizational websites to study nonprofit organizations. While social media can be used to do many things for an organization, from publicizing upcoming events to sharing the successes of community members, it is increasingly incorporated into advocacy and political engagement. Suárez (2009) found that environmental and rights-based organizations were particularly likely to use their websites to promote civic engagement and advocacy. With help of a graduate student, we coded each of the survey respondent's websites for the use of Facebook and Twitter, the two most common social media applications in 2012.[8] Using an archive of websites, we also collected data on each organization's website in 2010 and 2011 in order to see which organizations had adopted social media earliest. Using the coding scheme, I compared respondents that had integrated social media on their websites versus those that had not.

Based on the evidence presented above about differences between organizations representing different communities, the findings about social media usage support the reflective electoral representation theory. In 2010, less than a quarter of all the categories of immigrant-serving nonprofits had integrated social media, yet Hispanic American nonprofits stand out, as do particular nonprofits from other communities (see figure 5.3). Hispanic American nonprofits were the most active: over twice as many, as compared to Asian American nonprofits, used social media. Over time, all four categories increased their use of social media, but Hispanic American nonprofits continued to be more likely to use social media. In 2012, a small majority (52 percent) of respondents had integrated Twitter or Facebook, significantly more than all the other categories. These findings gel with the theory developed earlier and differences between immigrant communities. As Voto Latino demonstrated, the particular demographics of the Hispanic community have pushed organizations to respond, and we see Hispanic American organizations integrating technology into their public engagement activities at a high rate. Conversely, as some leaders in the Asian American community have noted, the older population and lower levels of political efficacy may combine to place only weak pressure on Asian American organizations to integrate social media into their operations.

What has been presented thus far supports the reflective electoral representation theory. The bivariate comparisons show that mission and organizational

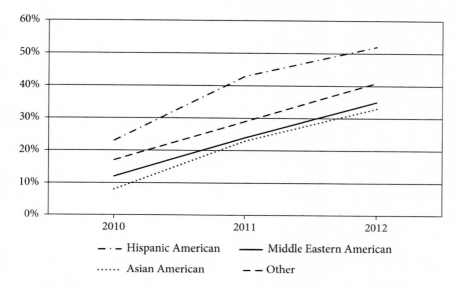

FIGURE 5.3.   Percent of all respondents using social media (Facebook and Twitter), by immigrant-serving category
Source: Author.

identity matter a lot. Immigrant-serving nonprofits with multifaceted missions and missions that focus on politics were more likely to be involved in electoral work. And differences within the immigrant community also related to different levels of electoral and public engagement. However, bivariate comparisons provide only some information about key relationships. Multivariate statistical techniques allow for other related factors to be statistically controlled for and for deeper conclusions to be reached.

Other Contextual Variables

In order to probe these relationships more deeply, I developed a series of multivariate statistical models that use the various measures of electoral engagement as dependent variables. I linked these dependent measures to the independent variables presented above for various aspects of each respondent's mission and a series of statistical controls (institutionalization, age, and revenue) that are widely used by other researchers in studies of nonprofits and interest groups. I also controlled for the potential effect of new state voting regulations, with a dummy variable that compares respondents based in Florida to those in the five other states, demographic context, and campaign context. I briefly explain the operationalization of these statistical controls, then the findings from multivariate analyses in order.

Organizational Context

INSTITUTIONALIZATION

In order to describe a full model, the statistical analysis must control for other relevant organizational factors raised in previous research, including institutionalization, resources, and organization age. Institutionalization is a concept used to describe the process through which organizations formalize their operations and make their practices routine. For many immigrant-serving groups that start as informal collectives, the first step in institutionalization involves submitting paperwork to get 501(c)(3) status from the IRS. For others, hiring a professional staff, rather than operating with just volunteers, is an additional step toward institutionalization. Institutionalization is a complex process that may mean different things for different groups, but it has been shown to relate to politics (Grossmann 2012; Mosley 2011). I operationalized institutionalization in this study based on the number of professional employees. Many nonprofits operate with only volunteers, so the number of professional employees can serve as a proxy for the institutionalization of the nonprofit. One would expect more-institutionalized immigrant-serving nonprofits to be more engaged in electoral activity than those that are not institutionalized. In fact, one survey respondent wrote: "We would be interested in advocacy for international health related issues, but are limited by size (all volunteer) and resources."

RESOURCES

Thus a related factor to control for is available resources. Chapter 2 showed the rising amount of philanthropic support for immigrant-serving nonprofit organizations during the 2000s. But it is not always clear how additional resources relate to political decision making (Caldeira, Hojnacki, and Wright 2000; Hojnacki and Kimball 1998). I argued in chapter 4 that monitoring campaign information is a low-cost tactic, one with which resources may not be strongly correlated. Others, such as voter mobilization, will likely require a substantial budget; therefore one would expect a stronger relationship between resources and organizations that use the voter-focused strategy. Similarly, research suggests that providing policy information and research is an expensive endeavor for organizations (Esterling 2007; Schlozman and Tierney 1986). Resources will greatly determine whether an organization can hire a staff of policy experts and analysts, how large that staff will be, and whether the organization can contract for external expert research

(Robbins 2010; Wright 1996). The same may be true for immigrant-serving non-profit organizations pursuing an issue-focused strategy.

AGE

Organizations vary in terms of how long they have been in operation. Organizational age may matter to tactical decisions, because older organizations will have experienced more elections and observed the benefits and costs of participating. As I have noted, a nonprofit might evolve its identity over time, transitioning from a primarily service-oriented organization to a hybrid organization with a stronger emphasis on electoral politics. However, newer organizations may be more open to certain tactics, less aware of the potential pitfalls of experimentation. There is an uncertain relationship between organization age and electoral strategy. Age in this statistical model was included with a variable (converted to its log form) based on the number of years between 2012 and the year the organization was legally incorporated. Some of these organizations may have been in existence prior to this date in an informal manner, but the incorporation date is the most reliable and easily accessible measure of age.

LOCAL AND PAN-IMMIGRANT FOCUS

In chapter 2 I showed that the nationwide movement to support immigrant integration focused on supporting pan-ethnic and pan-immigrant organizations. Organizations that serve just a single immigrant community appeared to receive less-robust support. Thus, it is important to control for organizations that represent immigrants in general. There is also evidence suggesting that organizations that descriptively represent the community—such as an executive director who is from the immigrant neighborhood—are more likely to engage in advocacy (LeRoux 2011). These organizations may be viewed as more democratic by their constituents, and thus those constituents may support other forms of democratic participation, such as during elections (Pekkanen and Smith 2014). In lieu of a direct measure of descriptive representation, I use a proxy for how tied the organization is to its locality. I argue that an organization that is focused on delivering services at the international or national levels will not be viewed in the same way as an organization with a local focus. The locally focused immigrant-serving nonprofit will be viewed as more of a reflection of the community in a way that is analogous to an organization that is clearly representative of those living in the neighborhood, and this is likely to be related to electoral participation.

DEMOGRAPHIC CONTEXT

As was shown in chapter 1, demographic characteristics of immigrant communities vary greatly. There are a number of ways to operationalize this factor, but the most straightforward is the percentage of the population that is foreign-born and naturalized citizens. It would be reasonable to assume that as this percentage goes up, immigrant-serving nonprofits are more likely to participate in elections, and to do so in a public fashion.

CAMPAIGN CONTEXT

The campaigns I described in chapter 3 illustrate how competitive primary races in New Jersey and New York brought immigrant-serving organizations and co-alitions into the campaign. And tight general election races in Illinois and Florida featured immigrant issues and immigrant organizations. Because of the importance of the campaign context, I included a control variable to capture this factor.

Multivariate Models and Dependent Variables

In order to test the theoretical expectations about reflective electoral representation, I constructed a series of statistical models based on the factors described above (see the technical appendix for a full explanation of how each variable was operationalized). Statistical models allow researchers to isolate the relationship between an independent and a dependent variable, holding other important factors constant. The research hypotheses can then be tested in a more rigorous way than just using bivariate comparisons in which other factors cannot be accounted for (see table 5.4). The first statistical model uses a dichotomous dependent variable for "at least one electoral tactic." The dichotomous dependent variable takes on a value of zero if no tactics were chosen by a respondent and 1 if the respondent chose at least one tactic. Since this is a dichotomous variable, I used binary logistic regression to analyze the multivariate relationships. The second statistical model uses a dependent variable measured with a count equal to the number of tactics each respondent chose. This variable ranges from zero, meaning no tactics chosen, to eight, meaning the respondent chose all eight options provided on the survey. Because of the count nature of the dependent variable, standard ordinary least squares is not well suited, so I used the preferred Poisson distribution to analyze the model.

At Least One Tactic

The first model provides support for the major hypothesis. Holding the other variables constant, Hispanic-serving nonprofits were more likely to use "at least one tactic" than were nonprofits serving other immigrant communities, though the difference was not statistically significant. Asian American and Middle-Eastern American nonprofits were also statistically no different from other immigrant-serving nonprofits. However, organizations that serve more than just one immigrant

TABLE 5.4 Models of electoral participation

	VARIABLE	AT LEAST ONE TACTIC ODDS RATIO (STANDARD ERROR)	NUMBER OF TACTICS POISSON (STANDARD ERROR)
Mission	Serve pan-immigrant community (compared to other)	2.31* (.91)	.24 (.18)
	Hispanic American (compared to other)	1.77 (.80)	.15 (.21)
	Middle-Eastern American (compared to other)	.88 (.55)	.23 (.25)
	Asian American (compared to other)	1.18 (.48)	.52*** (.20)
	Multifaceted (compared to single issue)	2.79*** (.84)	.69*** (.18)
	Politically oriented (compared to other)	9.70*** (7.95)	.98*** (.16)
	Locally focused (compared to state or nationally focused)	1.18 (.39)	−.07 (.14)
Organizational context	Revenue (log)	.85 (.10)	−.04 (.04)
	Institutionalized (based on number of employees)	2.48*** (1.60)	.81*** (.17)
	Age (log of years since formed)	1.23 (.21)	−.17* (.08)
Demographic context	Percent foreign-born in county (log)	1.16 (.30)	.31** (.14)
Campaign and political context	Based in Florida (compared to not based in Florida)	.92 (.41)	−.48** (.22)
	Competitive campaign county (compared to not competitive)	1.40 (.53)	.48*** (.15)
	Constant	.35 (.853)	−.96 (.65)
Pseudo R^2 or adjusted R^2		.19	.21
N		215	215
LR chi^2		55.85	158.99

* p value < .10
** < .05
*** < .0

group—pan-immigrant—are statistically more likely to use at least one tactic. Further, immigrant-serving nonprofits that have a political orientation to their mission were also much more likely than those without a political orientation to use "at least one tactic." And those immigrant-serving nonprofits with a multifaceted mission were more likely to use "at least one tactic" than those with simpler missions.

The variables that were not significant also provide some interesting information. Resources and age were not statistically related to the use of "at least one tactic," while institutionalization was. This suggests that nonprofits with small budgets or short histories are not shut out of electoral engagement, but those with only volunteers may be. Professional staff, what the institutionalization variable captures, appears to be a strong predictor of electoral engagement. A final important finding was that the dummy variable for Florida was not significant. Immigrant-serving nonprofits based in Florida were no more likely to engage in even a single electoral tactic compared to those operating in the five other states. Also, the size of the immigrant population was not significantly related to electoral participation, nor was the electoral competitiveness of the county. This suggests that the larger demographic and campaign context in which the nonprofit operates is not as important as internal organizational factors and identity.

Predicted probabilities provide a clearer way than odds ratios to interpret the findings related to "at least one tactic." This statistical calculation shows the probability of a respondent using "at least one tactic" holding the other variables at their mean or modal value. For example, the predicted probability of using "at least one tactic" for immigrant-serving nonprofits with a politically oriented mission was 93 percent, compared to 38 percent for other immigrant-serving nonprofits. For those with a multifaceted mission, there was a predicted probability of 61 percent of using "at least one tactic," compared to 27 percent for those with a simple mission. And nonprofits that serve pan-immigrant constituents had a 66 percent predicted probability of using "at least one tactic," compared to 33 percent for those serving a single immigrant group. Moreover, if we compare nonprofits that serve a pan-immigrant community and that do *not* have a politically oriented mission to those *with* a politically oriented mission, the predicted probability of using "at least one tactic" goes from 54 percent to 95 percent. Finally, if we compare nonprofits with simple missions that serve a pan-immigrant community to those with multifaceted missions, the predicted probability goes from 43 percent to 80 percent. These predicted probability values suggest that the differences were not just statistically significant, but also of a large magnitude.

Electoral Engagement Index

The second model using the count-dependent variable and Poisson regression provides more support for the key hypotheses, but with somewhat less clarity. Immigrant-serving nonprofits that had a politically oriented mission were associated with using more tactics compared to those that were not politically oriented. Those with a multifaceted mission were significantly associated with using more tactics than those with a simple mission. What is interesting is that while pan-immigrant organizations were more likely to use "at least one" tactic, they were no different in terms of the number of tactics—similar to Hispanic and Middle Eastern organizations. Asian American organizations, though, were statistically different in terms of the number of tactics. This runs somewhat counter to expectations but sheds interesting light on the strategy used by some Asian American organizations. Given the finding from the previous statistical model, this difference is worthy of further interpretation later in this chapter.

The significant and negative direction of the dummy variable coefficient for Florida (–48) suggests that the new third-party voter regulation penalties may have had a discouraging effect for immigrant-serving nonprofits based in the state. What this shows is that those respondents based in Florida used a smaller number of tactics as compared with those in other states. However, without additional evidence, it may be that Florida nonprofits were simply less interested in electoral engagement, possibly because the state was a "battleground" state and the two major parties expended so much time and money there. If this was the case, then we would also expect to find no difference in the choice of the voter-focused or public-focused strategy for respondents based in Florida versus the other states.

Interestingly, while the variable for the size of the immigrant community was not significant in the first model, it is a significant predictor of the number of tactics in the second model. An organization may first look inward to decide whether or not to participate as a reflection of its identity but then, once it has opted in, look outward to decide just how aggressively to participate. A larger immigrant community may open more avenues and opportunities for electoral participation. For example, a larger population may mean a wider range of younger and older immigrants, first-time immigrant voters, and immigrant candidates, each of which invites more and varied tactics.

A similar pattern may occur related to the competitiveness of the campaign. Holding all other factors constant, those respondents in counties with a competitive contest between President Obama and Mitt Romney used more tactics than those in counties where the campaign was not competitive.

Publicly versus Privately Focused Strategy

In the interest of space, the full statistical tables for the following analysis can be found in the technical appendix. The findings from those analyses show similar patterns, though not identical. First, I used a dichotomous variable equal to 1 if the respondent used at least one publicly focused electoral tactic, and zero otherwise. Second, I used a dichotomous variable equal to 1 if the respondent used at least one privately focused electoral tactic, and zero otherwise. In both models, I used logistic regression. As predicted, Hispanic-serving nonprofits were significantly more likely to use the publicly focused strategy (see appendix table A.4), whereas Asian and Middle-Eastern American nonprofits were no different from the comparison category. Pan-immigrant organizations were also no different

TABLE 5.5 Predicted probabilities of using publicly and voter-focused strategy (percentage)

	PUBLICLY FOCUSED STRATEGY	VOTER-FOCUSED STRATEGY
Hispanic American	39	38
Other nonprofit	21	17
Based in Florida	13	11
Not based in Florida	28	25

from others. If we compare the predicted probability values, holding the other variables at their mean and modal value, the probability of pursuing the publicly focused electoral strategy goes up from 21 percent for other nonprofits to 39 percent for Hispanic American–serving nonprofits (table 5.5). Conversely, Hispanic American nonprofits were no different in terms of pursuing a privately focused strategy. This adheres to theoretical expectations explained earlier.

Some of the other key variables, though, remained significant and in the positive direction. Those immigrant-serving nonprofits with a politically oriented mission were more likely to use both the public and the private strategy. Those with a politically oriented mission have a predicted probability of using the publicly focused strategy of 76 percent, compared to only 21 percent for those without a politically oriented mission.

The finding on the relationship between Florida and "publicly focused" strategy aligns with expectations (note that the coefficient value less than 1.0 indicates a negative relationship). If the new voter law in Florida had a discouraging effect on nonprofits, it is reasonable to assume that it would be observed more in the open and publicly focused strategic approach, rather than in the privately focused strategy. Being located in Florida results in a predicted probability value of 13 percent for using the publicly focused strategy, compared to 28 percent for those in the other states, demonstrating that the relationship is significant and of a large magnitude (see table 5.5). For Hispanic organizations, their predicted probability of using the publicly focused strategy goes down from 51 percent when operating in one of the five states other than Florida, to 17 percent in Florida. However, respondents based in Florida were no different from those in other states in using the privately focused strategy, an indication that the effect of the policy was primarily for publicly focused tactics, as expected.

Voter-Focused versus Issue-Focused Strategy

The second dimension of the strategic choice made by immigrant-serving nonprofits involved a voter-focused strategy or an issue-focused strategy (see appendix table A.5). In this model, to code the voter-focused strategy, I used a dichotomous measure of whether each respondent used at least one voter-focused tactic (coded as 1) or did not use a single voter-focused tactic (coded as zero). I did the same with issue-focused tactics. For this reason, the logistic regression model was again used as above.

The findings largely support the theories presented earlier. As has run through all the analyses thus far, politically oriented respondents were more likely than nonpolitically oriented respondents to use both the voter- and issue-focused strategies. Politically oriented respondents simply do more of everything related to elections, a consistent finding that verifies expectations. More interestingly, the bivariate results above suggest, as expected, that Hispanic American nonprofits were statistically more likely to use a voter-focused strategy, but not more likely to use an issue-focused strategy. The multivariate results presented in the technical appendix provide some support for this finding. In particular, holding all other variables constant, Hispanic American nonprofit respondents were statistically more likely to use the voter-focused strategy, but were no different from other respondents in terms of issue-focused strategy. Interestingly, Asian American groups were also more likely to use the voter-focused strategy. The predicted probability of using the voter-focused strategy goes from 17 percent to 38 percent for Hispanic American organizations, but from just 20 percent to 24 percent for Asian American organizations (based on author calculation not presented in the table).

In each case, most of the evidence supports the major components of the reflective electoral engagement theory. By carefully measuring the political orientation, variety of issues addressed by the organization's mission, and differences across the immigrant community, the model predicts various levels of electoral engagement. What is also deeply intriguing about the evidence is the lack of statistical significance for the controls for resources and organizational age, two frequently cited measures of organization capacity, often linked to advocacy decisions. Based on these data, it appears as though an organization's size and age do not predict its decision to engage in electoral activities, though extent of institutionalization does. The size of the immigrant community is also not consistently significant. Rather, it is primarily features of the mission that draw an immigrant-serving nonprofit into or away from electoral work.

In regard to the situation in Florida, the evidence supports the argument that the voter registration policy change had an effect on nonprofits. Respondents based in Florida were statistically less likely to use the voter-focused strategy, yet not statistically different for the issue-focused strategy. Since the new Florida law addressed only third-party voter registration but did not result in new regulations on writing policy reports or circulating information about the election, it makes sense that the significant difference would be observed for the voter-focused strategy alone. The predicted probability of using the voter-focused strategy decreased from 25 percent for all other respondents to 11 percent for those based in Florida.

The electoral competitiveness of the county was also significantly related to a respondent using the voter-focused strategy, but not the issue-focused strategy. The predicted probability of participating in a voter-focused strategy went up from 20 percent, for those in a noncompetitive county, to 25 percent, for those in a competitive county. This suggests that organizations may respond to the increased attention to the campaign by focusing on voters, but that attention does not draw them to focusing as much on issues. Finally, whereas revenues were not significant in the other models, revenues were significant, yet in the opposite direction from what would be expected, for the voter-focused strategy. This poses a real challenge to interpretation, since it appeared as though voter-focused tactics would be more expensive and thus would be associated with higher revenue, not less.

Making Sense of the Findings

While these findings largely support the reflective electoral representation theory presented in the last chapter, they also must be discussed in the broader study of immigrant politics and nonprofit electoral advocacy. These findings support the supposition that aspects of the mission of an immigrant-serving organization are related to the propensity to engage in electoral work, in general, and also in particular strategic ways. In other words, if you want to figure out whether a nonprofit will register and mobilize voters, look to what its mission explicitly and implicitly states. Nonprofits that pursue a politically oriented mission, those we might label "advocacy organizations," are in fact more likely to engage in nearly every type of electoral activity. This is not a surprise. But holding this factor constant, how multifaceted the immigrant-serving nonprofit's mission is also almost always increases the probability that the nonprofit will be engaged in electioneering. This supports the argument that a varied mission will open more frequent electoral access points for the organization, thereby inviting more frequent electoral engagement.

Another interesting discovery is the non-finding related to certain organizational characteristics. Revenue and organizational age, two factors that are often linked with organizational behavior, did not predict electoral engagement in most of the statistical models. This may be because many of the electoral tactics in question are relatively inexpensive and have been made even more convenient through new technologies. The privately focused tactics do not necessitate a large, dedicated budget, and therefore resources may not be the deciding factor for an organization considering whether or not to employ this strategy. It may also be that the pan-immigrant organizations capture some of the influence of philanthropic foundations demonstrated in chapter 2. Pan-immigrant organizations had on average $81,000 in revenue, while those organizations serving a single immigrant community had on average $26,500 in revenue.

There was one exception that showed, holding other factors constant, that fewer resources were associated with a voter-focused strategy. This finding runs counter to what previous scholarship and some interviewees told me. For example, I learned from Juan Alfaro, of Latin Americans United for Progress (LAUP), that he credited its electoral work to funding provided by a foundation to another group and then subgranted to his organization. LAUP had a mission to educate and celebrate Latin Americans in Hope, Michigan, in a semirural part of the state. No part of LAUP's mission was clearly connected to politics or elections. Nevertheless, Alfaro said, "we did a voter registration drive . . . and got a grant from a Michigan nonprofit association; they sent a small grant" to support the organization's new electoral activity.[9] He said that the funding "allowed me to grab a couple of volunteers and give them a stipend to do house-to-house work, making phone calls, data entry." Money seemed to matter to LAUP.

In Chicago, Jerry Clarito of AFIRE told a similar story. He said that in "late 2008, we were able to get a grant from the Illinois Coalition for Immigrant and Refugee Rights to do an information campaign on public benefits, therefore we were able to get a part-time campaign worker, and a program worker part time, [which] gave us the ability to learn the tricks of fieldwork and running a skeletal office." Out of this funding grew other opportunities for AFIRE to partner with Latino newspapers, coordinate volunteers to translate information for the community, and ultimately launch the Rock the Balut campaign. While resources did not consistently matter for other electoral strategies, in the case of the voter-focused strategy, illustrated by the examples of LAUP and AFIRE, a new grant might permit an organization to engage in electoral work for the first time or expand its electoral activities. Thus, this contradictory statistical finding does not quite make intuitive sense, and is worthy of further exploration in the future.

The characteristics of whom the immigrant-serving nonprofit serves also matter a lot. The consistent finding is that those nonprofits that serve Hispanic Americans are more likely to engage in electoral work, and in several particular ways. Hispanic American nonprofits were more likely to engage voters directly and to do so in a public fashion. I argued earlier that this is likely a result of the different political attitudes, values, and beliefs about collective action held within the Hispanic American community that are receptive, supportive, and inviting of these approaches. Hispanic American–serving nonprofits reflect these attitudes in the electoral decisions they make.

Illustrative of this was what I learned from an interview with Lindolfo Carballo of Casa in Action, a nonprofit organization operating in Virginia. While Virginia was not in the survey, organizations in the state face circumstances similar to those in neighboring North Carolina, and thus the story of Casa in Action can shed light on these findings.[10] Virginia, particularly the northern section of the state, has a rapidly growing Hispanic American population. Carballo explained that when Casa in Action (which had previously been focused mainly in the state of Maryland) was first established in Virginia, the community's reaction was immediate and enthusiastic. He said that "people knew about Casa de Maryland—the reaction was very powerful." His strategy was to form what he called "brigades" in counties across Northern Virginia to help coordinate local canvassing. "I organized around twelve to fifteen active leaders, held the first leadership meeting, and had ninety-three come to our first leadership meeting in February." The huge turnout showed Carballo how eager the community was for political representation and "interested in being part of a grassroots [movement]." Casa in Action Virginia formed based on this community support, participated in political rallies, and then moved to "registering and mobilizing voters in Virginia." Carballo's comments showed how his organization saw the growing population in a part of the state as a reason to form, and then used the groundswell of support for political activism as a signal to quickly adopt a range of political and electoral strategies, thereby transitioning to the hybrid type of organization.

It is important to note that this is not to suggest that every Hispanic American organization is highly involved in elections. I interviewed Diana Mejia of Wind of the Spirit, based in Morristown, New Jersey, an organization that focuses on mobilizing the Hispanic American community, especially younger residents of the state. But Mejia cautioned that they "do not focus on voting" because, as the coordinator of youth activities, Ana Bonilla Martinez, explained, "most of our members can't vote, so it isn't a priority."[11] Instead, Wind of the Spirit focuses on rallying the community to oppose anti-immigration legislation and advocate for the state's version of the DREAM Act. Despite representing Hispanic Americans, Wind of the Spirit is directed away from electoral engagement by the identity of its constituents. And Wind of the Spirit was not alone. Based on the bivariate findings presented at the start of the chapter, many Hispanic-serving nonprofits did not engage in any electoral tactics. Nevertheless, the consistent conclusion that can be drawn from these statistical models is that Hispanic American nonprofits engaged in the 2012 elections and used the electoral strategies predicted by the theories presented here to a greater extent than organizations representing immigrants in general.

For Asian American nonprofits, the evidence runs somewhat counter to expectations. Asian American organizations resemble Hispanic American organizations in certain tactics, specifically the propensity to use the voter-focused strategy, and were more likely to use a wide array of tactics. Asian American organizations were not statistically different from others in terms of the other strategies. This is an interesting finding and suggests two very different types of nonprofits representing Asian Americans—those that are not involved at all in elections, and those that are highly engaged. The recent and rapid growth in Asian American immigrants may explain this less clear pattern for Asian American nonprofits: the attitudes of various new Asian American communities may be more in flux than others, and nonprofits are responding in similarly varied ways. Certain segments of the Asian American community are experiencing great financial and social success, whereas others are suffering. Dr. Joy Cherian recounted to me how in the mid-1980s he helped form a coalition of over ten Asian American organizations, the Asian American Voters Coalition (AAVC). In rallying support, he said, he told the community "we are doctors, engineers, technologists, accountants; we are opinion makers.... That is the philosophy that the Asian American coalition adopted."[12] It was this identity as a community made up of professionals that ultimately shaped the identity of the AAVC. Of course, not all Asian Americans hold such prestigious jobs. The diversity of professions and experiences may produce greater variation in the types of nonprofits that represent Asian Americans than exists in other communities.

Middle-Eastern American nonprofits, conversely, were not more likely than other immigrant-serving organizations to pursue electoral work, and also no different from other immigrant-serving nonprofits in each particular strategy. Middle-Eastern American nonprofits, whose community has been under such close scrutiny and subject to great hostility since 9/11 and in the wake of more recent events, may too be receiving mixed messages about electoral engagement: from some a call for more direct action, and from others a desire for peace and quiet. In the interviews I conducted, many organizational leaders spoke of the complexity of reflecting the identity of different immigrant communities. Hasan Jaber of ACCESS in Dearborn, Michigan, described the way the Arab American residents associated with his organization debated how to respond to 9/11. He said: "We've seen a shift after September 11. There was really a conversation going on in the Arab American community about the community agenda; before 9/11 most activism was focused on foreign policy and the situation in the Middle East. But that focus almost instantly changed after 9/11. There was a strong desire to put energy [into relations with] and open dialogue with non–Arab Americans, to build institutions, to sustain institutions." Ever since, ACCESS has been increasingly involved in registering and mobilizing voters at all electoral levels.

But the Arab American community in Dearborn is large and established, in part the result of several decades of work by ACCESS. In other regions, the situation is very different. I interviewed Remziya Suleyman of the American Center for Outreach in Tennessee,[13] an organization that has a mission to "inform, educate and empower Muslims to become engaged in society by providing the assistance they need to become productive citizens."[14] She said that her work is more restrained because most of those in her community are "newer immigrants that are here rebuilding, and the last thing on their mind is being politically active. . . . There is a mistrust of government, a psychological issue that you have to take into consideration when you are an organizer talking about politics." Suleyman's organization reflects the identity of this Tennessee community with a more limited approach to political engagement.

To be clear, these findings do not suggest that every nonprofit sits down prior to an election and examines its mission, reflects on priorities, and decides whether or not to participate. Decision making is likely much less linear and rational. For some nonprofits, participating in an election may be so deeply embedded in their organizational soul and identity that explicit decisions are never made. For others—as the quotes presented at the start of the chapter suggest—the mission may be interpreted as so incompatible with electoral work that a meeting of the board of advisers or senior staff may never be necessary. In both these cases, however, even though a formal decision may never be taken, it is those deep aspects of the mission, captured in the variables above, that are related to opting in or out of an election.

Finally, one of the most important findings from this chapter is the potentially negative effect state law can have on immigrant-serving nonprofit electoral engagement. Nonprofits based in Florida were less likely to be involved in the election in the exact ways one would expect and in ways that the interviews corroborated. The bivariate findings suggested that only a small percentage, just over 5 percent of Florida-based nonprofits, registered voters. And in the statistical models for using the voter-focused and publicly focused strategies, those respondents in Florida were significantly less likely than others to use these strategies. Interviewees corroborated these statistical findings. For example, Joy Bruce, the president of the Asian American Federation of Florida (AAFF), recounted AAFF's decision not to register voters: "We were initially planning to, but decided not to do voter registration ourselves in 2012 because of the voter suppression act that severely limited the deadline for reporting to forty-eight hours instead of ten days. . . . [We] didn't think that we could afford to pay the $1,000 penalty if we did not meet the deadline. Also we did not have enough volunteers to comply with the limited time. All we did was voter education, encouraging people to register to vote."[15] In states where legislators enacted no new third-party policies and nonprofits did not confront the potential penalties faced by AAFF, organizations were more likely to employ a publicly focused and voter-focused electoral strategy. It is unclear whether the authors of the policy change in Florida had this in mind: they probably argued that they simply intended to make sure cases of voter fraud were minimized and punished when violations occurred. They likely would contend that nothing in the new law forbade nonprofits from registering voters or using any other legal electoral tactic. Nevertheless, given the fact that a state court dismissed major parts of the new law at the tail end of the campaign, these arguments are dubious at best. The discouraging effect of the new policy could not have come as a surprise to the conservative nonprofit organizations—such as True the Vote—that lobbied for the law, the lawmakers who voted for it, or the Florida governor who signed it into law.

It is important to note, though, that despite this significant and alarming finding, generalizing from it to other states should be done with caution. The survey was of a subset of nonprofits, and it is unclear whether the effect in Florida on immigrant-serving nonprofits would be the same for nonprofits in other sectors. Also, it is unclear whether the same regulations adopted in other states would have the same effect as they had in Florida. To be sure, there were other political differences between Florida and the five other states in the study. Generalizing these finding, thus, must be done with these important caveats in mind.

While that Florida law seemed to dampen support for participating in the election, the size of the immigrant population did not consistently increase participation. With the exception of the significant finding for the number of tactics used, in the other models, there was no relationship between the size of the immigrant population and electoral participation in general, or participation with one of the particular electoral strategies. What this suggests is that internal organizational context may matter more to an immigrant-serving nonprofit than external political and demographic factors. In many ways, this further supports the theory of reflective electoral representation. Immigrant-serving nonprofits must be understood in terms of how each develops its unique identity, not simply as generic organizations responding to contextual cues. The consistent and predictable statistical relationships between mission and electoral strategy support this contention.

Conclusion

Previous chapters in the book established the importance of the demographic, organizational, and campaign context for immigrant-serving nonprofit organizations. In chapter 4 I theorized that we must control for those factors in order to isolate the importance of mission and identity in determining electoral participation. This chapter took that theory and operationalized the various contextual factors and organizational mission variables and linked them to measures of electoral participation or nonparticipation.

Controlling for certain aspects related to demographic, organizational, and campaign context, this first examination of the data comports with the broad theory presented in the previous chapter. The reflective electoral representation theory shows promise in predicting the decision to engage in electoral activity of immigrant-serving nonprofit organizations. Three aspects of an organization's mission are statistically related to the decision to use "at least one" tactic. Immigrant-serving nonprofits that have more multifaceted missions and those with a politically oriented mission were more likely to use "at least one tactic" and to use more tactics. This suggests that nonprofits that most resemble interest groups also participate in elections as many interest groups do. This is not surprising but does build on existing research from other segments of the nonprofit universe. Further, Hispanic American nonprofits, those predicted to be most involved in electoral activities because of the relatively high levels of political efficacy in the Hispanic American community, were in fact more likely to use the voter-focused and publicly focused strategies. Finally, state policy had the anticipated, whether or not intended, effect of limiting voter registration activities of nonprofits in Florida. Nonprofits do not respond to all external contexts but do seem to respond to this type of policy change. Interviews with immigrant-serving nonprofit leaders support many of these statistical findings, and also reveal more nuance and detail as to how these electoral decisions are made.

These findings suggest organizational identity matters to certain aspects of electoral strategy. An additional factor must also be considered. Given the federal system of elections in the United States, do immigrant-serving nonprofits consider venue when they engage in an election? Where did those nonprofits that did engage in the 2012 election place their focus: at the federal, state, or local level? And, if venue choices were made, what explains those choices? The second half of the theory presented in the last chapter argues that once an immigrant-serving nonprofit opts to participate in electoral activities, political factors drive the choice of venue. The following chapter explores that aspect of the theory with additional statistical analysis.

6

CHOOSING WHERE TO FOCUS

On August 4, in the midst of the 2012 campaign, Wade Michael Page walked into a Sikh *gurdwara* (temple) in Oak Creek, Wisconsin, and shot and killed six worshippers. As tragic and as senseless as these murders were, it appeared that the location and targets were not chosen at random. Estimates of the Sikh American population in the United States range from two hundred thousand to five hundred thousand; a large number of first-generation immigrants from India reside in California and in the New York City area.[1] Sikh Americans made up a small but important portion of the suburban Wisconsin community of Oak Creek.

By August 6, the front-page headline in the local newspaper, the *Milwaukee Journal Sentinel,* said what many already suspected: "Sikh temple gunman linked to hate groups."[2] The paper reported that Page was a member of Volksfront—a white supremacist organization initially formed as a prison gang in the 1990s—and he was active in the associated racist music scene. According to the Anti-Defamation League, members of Volksfront had been convicted of brutal crimes against Jewish and African Americans in Washington State and Oregon.

Many of the crimes committed by members of Volksfront and associated organizations were officially classified by the Department of Justice (DOJ) as hate crimes, but at the time of the Wisconsin murders, the DOJ did not specifically label hate crimes committed against Sikh, Hindu, or Arab victims; these hate crimes would be labeled as "other."[3] As a result, it was very difficult to know the extent to which the Oak Creek crime was a tragic anomaly or a part of a larger trend to target Sikh Americans. In either case, considerable public attention was drawn both to the victims and to the ethnic and religious community in which they lived.

Amid the grieving, and as the criminal investigation proceeded by local and state officials, Sikh American nonprofit organizations focused and collaborated on a response. A number of national groups worked together on media and communications strategy, concerned that these types of tragedies had not been addressed properly in the past. The cofounder of the Sikh Coalition, Amardeep Singh (quoted in Hoffman 2013), explained: "We were on CNN and other national outlets helping to address the message and constantly issuing press releases. As a result, we helped to shape the government's response. By that Friday, the attorney general had declared the incident a hate crime."

The strategy to focus advocacy on national figures, such as Attorney General Eric Holder, fit with the characteristics of this tragic event. It is the federal government that has primary authority to classify hate crimes, and crimes labeled as such compel a much more complete federal response than otherwise. Without the rapid work of the Sikh Coalition and others, the federal government might not have classified the crime as potentially motivated by hatred and then added their investigative resources to the case as quickly as they did.

Sikh advocacy organizations also had a longer-term policy aim. As noted earlier, the Justice Department did not at the time specifically label hate crimes committed against Sikh Americans, resulting in the failure to fully measure and address this issue. By quickly focusing their policy response on national officials, advocacy organizations could also pursue longer-term policy change with the Justice Department and advance the interests of Sikh Americans nationwide. Without the work of Sikh American organizations to advocate for a policy response from the federal government, the persistent violence directed at their community might continue to marginalize and intimidate Sikh Americans. In June 2013, following Senate hearings and debates within the Federal Bureau of Investigation's Criminal Justice Information Services Advisory Policy Board, the Sikh Coalition could report: "Victory! 10 Months after Oak Creek, FBI Group Votes to Track Sikh Hate Crimes."[4]

Wisconsin was not alone in witnessing ethnic, racial, or religious-based hostilities during the run-up to the 2012 election. The Pew Institute found that, in 2012, fifty-three proposed mosques and Islamic centers faced organized opposition, some based on fierce anti-Islamic sentiments. One of the most notable was in Naperville, Illinois, a suburb of Chicago (Swasko and Gregory 2011). In 2011, the Islamic Center of Naperville sought to purchase land on 248th Avenue from the United Church of Christ—whose congregation was moving to a new location—in order to house administrative offices and possibly a religious building in the future. The parcel of land was not incorporated by DuPage

County and thus could not be served by county water and sewage services. The Islamic Center petitioned the county to annex the land in order to make the land purchase and construction feasible. Before the local planning and zoning commission voted on annexing the land, signs began to appear in front yards and stapled to utility poles that read: "Vote No on Mosque on 248" and "No Ragheads on 248."

Naperville is home to a large and diverse Muslim population, many of them recent immigrants from South Asia. The town was also squarely in the congressional district of the controversial Walsh-versus-Duckworth House race outlined in chapter 3. Though the commission voted in favor of annexing the land, the controversy and animosity directed toward Muslim Americans drew attention to the community and district politics.

Nonprofit organizations responded to these events with focused mobilization. In addition to legal and policy advocacy on the specific mosque issue, nonprofits like CAIR-Chicago directed intense voter mobilization efforts toward the district. Gerald Hankerson, outreach coordinator for CAIR-Chicago, said that Representative Walsh's inflammatory comments about Muslims, together with the Naperville mosque controversy (there were also other mosque issues in the same district), drove his organization toward the Eighth District. Despite its name, CAIR-Chicago was the main CAIR chapter in the state and also served neighboring Muslim American communities across the Midwest.[5] With this wide jurisdiction, CAIR-Chicago could have focused on other races in Cook County or Jackson County, each with equally large populations of Muslim Americans and immigrants, or instead could have focused on the presidential race, yet Hankerson argued, "knowing that the Muslim American community is not always considered [during elections], we know that is something we can change. . . . When we did our GOTV campaign, it was a no-brainer to zero in on that district." Through extensive phone banks staffed by volunteers who had access to the VAN, "we asked registered voters whether they were aware that the incumbent [Walsh] had made these statements" about the Muslim American community and links to terrorism. CAIR-Chicago focused much of its electoral efforts on this district and this controversial campaign. CAIR-Chicago also did electoral work outside the Eighth District, but it is the focus and emphasis it placed on this one race that raise intriguing possibilities for understanding another dimension of nonprofit electoral strategy.

In both these episodes—the temple slayings and the mosque controversy—crime and antagonism directed against largely immigrant communities that occurred during the 2012 campaign compelled immigrant-serving nonprofits to make strategic decisions about where to expend time and energy. In Wisconsin, a vicious hate crime drew national nonprofits such as the Sikh Coalition to the community to develop a nationally focused media and policy strategy in order to best represent and advocate for Sikh Americans. In DuPage County, Illinois, CAIR-Chicago saw the anti-Muslim sentiments and competiveness of the election as a call for them to focus locally on mobilizing South Asian and Muslim American voters in the district to turn out on Election Day. According to leaders of the Sikh Coalition and CAIR-Chicago, these two sets of events directed advocacy and political efforts to specific political venues; but are these two anecdotes generalizable to other organizations and other events? Do dramatic events typically drive nonprofit strategy, particularly electoral strategy? It may be that in attempting to explain a decision to an interviewer, nonprofit leaders impose a post hoc logic that results in the appearance of strategy, while in reality decision making is much less planned and predictable. Nevertheless, it remains a point in need of clarification: Do political factors and dramatic events direct nonprofit advocacy in general, and electoral tactics specifically, toward particular locations and away from others? Or are decisions about where to focus electoral work explained by the same organizational and contextual factors presented in the previous chapter? The answers presented in this chapter suggest that these political factors do indeed focus immigrant-serving nonprofit decisions. That is, once an organization decides to engage in electoral work, a second decision is made regarding electoral venue—*electoral venue choice*—that is greatly shaped by political context and power. Because that nonprofit has opted to take on the characteristics of a hybrid organization or an interest group and utilize political tactics, we can then apply one of the important theoretical perspectives from the field of interest group studies, that of venue shopping, to better understand these patterns.

Choosing an Electoral Venue

The germ of the idea of venue choice or venue shopping can be traced to the pioneering work of E. E. Schattschneider on interest groups. Schattschneider first outlined the broad strokes of the concept in his seminal work *The Semi-Sovereign People* (1960). Schattschneider was primarily interested in how different segments of society were represented by interest groups in the policy process. He differed with David Truman (1951) and others who argued that a pluralistic system provided representation for broad segments of the U.S. population, what many have called Group Theory. Schattschneider summarized his dissent with his oft-quoted line: "The flaw in the pluralist heaven is that the heavenly chorus sings with a strong upper-class accent." He saw a political system that favored some communities over others because they were better organized, had better representation, and had representative interest groups able to strategically win policy debates. Given the evidence from the previous chapter, Schattschneider's adage rings true: there is not equal electoral participation by organizations across immigrant communities.

Schattschneider's argument was more complex than a simple characterization of organizations participating or not participating. Within his conception of American politics, he argued that opposing sides of a policy issue seek to narrow or expand a conflict in order to advance their interests. Strategic manipulation by interest groups of the boundaries of a conflict can help to stabilize, shift, or alter a policy agenda. As such, the scope of a conflict often has many dimensions, including how an issue is framed, who has standing in the policy debate, and who has authority to determine policy outcomes. Interested groups compete over determining scope.

Frank Baumgartner and Bryan Jones (1993) later adapted some of these ideas of venue shopping into the field of public policy. Venue shopping is built on the particular policy characteristics of the U.S. system of government. Policy decisions are highly dispersed in the federal-style government where power is divided between nation and state, and then within states between counties, cities, and other local municipalities. Policy decisions are further dispersed across branches of government, at the national, state, and local levels. Checks and balances provide further safeguards against too much power accumulating in any one of these locations. Each of these locations of policy decision making (such as a local mayor's office, a U.S. Senate committee, or a state bureaucratic agency) acts as a *policy venue*, defined by its own norms, rules, and beliefs.

Building on Schattschneider's concept of issue scope and conflict, Baumgartner and Jones argued that interest groups *shop* for or choose the policy venue where they believe their views will be advanced. If a mayor is more sympathetic than a city council with regard to a group's claims, for example, then advocacy might be directed at the mayor's office while making certain the city council stays out of the picture. If a state legislature is hostile to the group's aims, then lobbying might focus on persuading a federal official to claim authority.

Venue choice has remained a theoretically appealing concept, but empirical evidence has been lacking until recently. Much policy research has focused on a single venue, such as the interesting finding from Steil and Vasi (2014) that the number of pro-immigration associations in a locality is positively correlated with passage of more pro-immigration policies, while the number of anti-immigration associations is not correlated with the passage of more anti-immigration policies. That research did not apply the findings to different venues or to the strategic venue decisions made by pro- and anti-immigration organizations. Some recent scholarship has focused on the venue choice across branches of government, such as the finding of Boehmke, Gailmard, and Patty (2013) that, at the national level, interest groups tend to lobby in multiple venues, rather than simply choose the legislative or the executive exclusively. More germane to this study, Sarah Pralle (2006) used the concept to explain interest group activities in Canada's federal system of environmental policy making. She found that antipesticide advocacy groups, frustrated with their lobbying of national officials, focused instead on municipal venues. Venue choice has also been used to explain the political activities of nonprofit organizations. Holyoke, Brown, and Henig (2012) examined the ways charter schools—typically operated analogously to a nonprofit organization—make venue choices. They found that charter schools with ample resources seek out multiple venues, but when the school's students are residentially concentrated in a small area, the school is more likely to lobby local officials. In that case, the students, though they cannot vote, serve as political capital that the charter school can use to influence local officials. The influence of those students would be diluted if a charter school opted to lobby at the state level. Karch (2013) also applied these ideas to education policy-making in his study of early childhood policy. Rebuffed at the national level by the Nixon White House, early childhood advocates shifted their lobbying to a handful of friendly states, a strategy, Karch noted, that was replicated by advocates of universal preschool two decades later.

The concept of venue shopping has not been widely applied to organizational advocacy and elections, despite the fact that many of the same characteristics of U.S. policy-making venues also apply to U.S. elections. Elections occur at the national, state, and local levels, as well as within the executive, legislative, and sometimes judicial branches of government. Each location of an election may serve as an electoral venue, defined by a different set of eligible voters, a different set of rules, and a different array of potential candidates. As the research on lobbying and venue choice suggests, groups might look to characteristics of various electoral venues as opportunities to focus electoral activities. Some electoral venues may be too crowded with other groups to make a difference, while other venues may be ripe for even a small organization to mobilize enough voters to determine the final vote tally. While there are a host of factors that relate to nonprofit decision making, I argue here that the culture of state politics, the competitiveness of local races, and the types of dramatic political events described above each shape how inviting an electoral venue might appear. Because each of these factors has a particular and important meaning for immigrants, the nonprofits that represent immigrants will pay close attention to how these factors relate to elections. Once an immigrant-serving nonprofit has decided to engage in electoral work, it then weighs these factors in focusing its electoral activities and making electoral venue choices.

Relevance of State Political Culture

Scholars of state politics have long wrestled with describing the cultural differences that exist across states and regions and how those differences relate to public policy. Federalism results in more than just power shared between nation and states; it also has served to incubate different policies and political beliefs. Elazar (1966) established one of the first approaches (and one still widely cited in research and college textbooks) to categorizing states by their common political cultures. Because each state was settled by different groups of immigrants, each aligned with different religious, language, and cultural traditions, very different state political cultures have emerged over the nation's two-hundred-plus-year history. Elazar claimed that certain states, those he labeled "traditionalistic," developed elite-oriented political values that eschewed broad-based participation in politics in favor of small segments of society serving in politics. Elazar, Gray, and Spano wrote in 1999 about the role of government in traditionalistic political cultures: "[Government] functions to confine real political power to a relatively small and self-perpetuating group drawn from an established elite who often inherent their 'right' to govern through family ties or social position. . . . At the same time, those who do not have a definite role to play in politics are not expected to be even minimally active as citizens. In many cases, they are not even expected to vote" (256). These states are mainly in the South and West. Conversely, in the "moralistic" states, a puritanical religious tradition emphasizes the duty of citizens to participate in politics and a strong belief in the common good. These states are primarily in New England and the Great Lakes region. And, finally, "individualistic" states, located mainly in the Northeast and West, are defined by a political culture based on partisanship, competition, and individualism above all else.

Elazar's typology, though introduced decades ago and subject to criticism as empirically thin (Wirt 1991), is still used by researchers. Putnam (2000) found that social capital was correlated with Elazar's typology; Fisher and Pratt (2006) linked the typology to state death penalty policies; and Lieske (2010) validated the typology with county-level data. While it may not capture everything about state culture, and public opinion may add other dimensions to what we know about state politics (Erickson, Wright, and McIver 1993), Elazar's typology does provide a mechanism to categorize states in a way that may influence the political participation of nonprofit groups. Furthermore, other popular measures of state politics, such as Hero and Tolbert's research (1996) that links racial/ethnic diversity to variation in state policies, likely mirrors too closely other control variables presented later in this chapter for the percentage of immigrants in each county, thereby violating the assumption of limited multi-collinearity between independent variables. For these reasons, Elazar's typology of states represents an effective way to conceptualize the political culture in which local nonprofits operate.

Given the marginal position of many immigrants, particularly first-generation and naturalized citizens, I argue that the nonprofits that represent them will capitulate to the dominant state political culture in which they are based. Traditionalistic states are likely to be controlled at the state level by entrenched elites and be dominated by a political culture that offers few invitations to newcomers to participate in policy making. I expect the same for electioneering, such that immigrant-serving nonprofits in traditionalistic states will find local electoral venues much more welcoming and will therefore focus on those venues.

Relevance of Constituent Political Power

Despite the cultural commonalities in a given state, communities within a state vary in terms of the relative prominence of immigrants, what I have referred to generally as the demographic context. Major cities have been the home to new immigrants for centuries, and this concentration has often resulted in growing political power (Dahl 1961). Immigrants have recently settled in novel locations, meaning there are a host of new gateway communities that can claim a significant immigrant presence. Similar to what Holyoke, Brown, and Henig (2012) found for the relationship between the concentration of students and charter school venue choice, the size of the immigrant community in a town, city, or county might lead an immigrant-serving nonprofit to focus at the local level where its constituents are concentrated. A large, relatively unified immigrant community could be the basis of local political clout during election season, assuming that a large portion of constituents are registered and show up to vote. For example, John Albert of Taking Your Seat explained that his South Asian American organization in New York focuses on races based on two factors: the size of the South Asian community, and whether there is a South Asian candidate running. He said: "We are also engaged, but less so, in voter registration as a blanket tactic. We focus on very specific neighborhoods, blocks where the South Asian vote will become critical. We aren't going to just set up shop on the corner in front of a supermarket; we are more likely to go to a community event."[6] This is one reason his organization focused in 2013 on the race for borough president in Queens, the borough where South Asians are most numerous, rather than the more widely followed race for New York City mayor, where South Asians are a much smaller portion of the total population. And even if the South Asian community is small in number, if a South Asian candidate has entered the race, Albert clarified, "we don't promote a candidate, but we do pay attention to the race."

Moreover, constituents may be powerful in ways other than sheer numbers. An economically affluent immigrant community might wield power in state or national politics, even if its numbers are small. Affluence might lead to campaign contributions or simply a number of constituents with a large and established social network that can connect the community to local political elites. Ved Chaudhary, a founder of the Indian American Forum for Political Education, initially a Jersey City, New Jersey–based group, explained that "[Indian Americans] are educated people . . . [and] some of us have good reputations. If we want to meet with the political leaders, they will meet, so that is where we began."[7] Chaudhary's group started working on policy and soon expanded to local elections. He summarized how they focused their early strategy: "In Jersey City we became part of the process of citizenship, then registration, then GOTV. For a new community it takes time to get organized."

Whether measured in numbers or affluence, the position of an immigrant-serving nonprofit's constituents, the demographic context, will likely relate to electoral venue choice. Just as a nonprofit organization looks to its constituents' level of political efficacy to signal whether or not it should participate in electoral activities, the size and power of those constituents will drive where to participate.

It is less clear, however, in which direction organizations will be pushed. It may be that large numbers in a local community will drive a nonprofit to focus electoral work just within the locality, based on the expectation that influence will be greatest at town, district, or county-level elections. It may also be the case that large numbers in the community will embolden the nonprofit to seek out other venues. Size and prominence might push the organization to stake out a position in statewide or national-level contests. In either case, it seems likely that this factor will strongly relate to strategic electoral venue choices.

Relevance of Focusing Events

State political culture and constituent political power are relatively stable factors, especially from one election to the next. Other factors, though, may change the political context rapidly. In her research on venue shopping, Pralle (2006) argued that in addition to resources and the breadth of policy interests, external political opportunities and constraints drive venue-shopping decisions. Public policy scholars have long connected policy change to the type of situation that Pralle called a "political opportunity" and what Kingdon (1995) called an "open policy window." One mechanism to open these windows of opportunity is a "focusing event." Birkland (1997) defined a focusing event as "an event that is sudden, relatively rare, can be reasonably defined as harmful or revealing the possibility of potentially greater future harms, inflicts harms or suggests potential harms that are or could be concentrated on a definable geographical area or community of interest, and that is known to policy makers and the public virtually simultaneously" (12). Hate crimes meet this definition, since they are relatively (and thankfully) rare, do harm to a specific community (if they didn't they would not be classified as hate crimes), and draw sufficient media attention that the public and policy makers will learn of them together. Birkland linked focusing events to advocacy for policy change, such as the relationship the *Exxon Valdez* oil spill had on lobbying for stronger environmental regulations. Hate crimes, as Haider-Markel (2006) showed, have been linked to organized advocacy for policy change. As was the case in Oak Creek, Sikh American organizations first sought to make sure the DOJ pursued the case as a hate crime, not just as murder, and then other policy proposals followed. And in Naperville, though hate crimes did not occur, CAIR-Chicago and other organizations advocated for the planning and zoning commission to grant the Islamic center permission to use the land in the face of heated anti-Muslim sentiments.

Hate crimes, as a type of focusing event, also may spur organizations to focus their electoral work. Because these crimes have a spatial dimension—they are committed against an individual or group of individuals who reside in a specific jurisdiction or neighborhood—hate crimes are likely to sharpen attention on those elections that are most closely connected to the associated community. Even if officials outside the community share responsibilities for addressing the crime, as was the case with the Justice Department in Wisconsin, those public officials most directly affected are local officials, be they city council members or the sheriff. This should be particularly true for electoral venue choice because public sentiment and anger are more closely tied to voting. Unlike policy venues, where unelected bureaucrats may remain distant from the voting public, electoral venue decisions involve candidates seeking popular support. This is clearly the case for those running in local elections, since they are geographically closest to those who suffered from the hate crime. Those candidates will be campaigning in the very neighborhoods where the crimes were committed.

After a hate crime, an immigrant-serving nonprofit may be pushed into a local electoral venue by the community. As Jumana Judeh of the Arab American Women for Obama (AAWO) explained, "Hate crime has been rampant post 9–11 unfortunately. This issue can mobilize the community in a manner that is quick and efficient given that we are just tired of being targeted for things we are not responsible for."[8] Communities thus mobilized may then call on local nonprofits to be more aggressive in their electoral venue. Absent a hate crime, the community may not call for a collective response as vociferously, and the immigrant-serving nonprofit may feel no pressure to focus its electoral agenda.

Another reason for this local electoral focus is related to what Holyoke (2003) concluded about venue choice at the national level (in his case, concerning financial modernization). He found that the expectation of opposition from hostile interests was a predictor of venue choice. Interest groups focused on venues that they believed would be dominated by their opposition if they did not concentrate their efforts. In a similar way, a hate crime will raise attention to the issue of anti-immigrant violence, but may also increase anti-immigrant interests in that locality. In a related way, Remziya Suleyman of the Tennessee-based American Center for Outreach said, "It is important to get into districts where a candidate is against our issues. We have found that in the political climate in Tennessee it is just as important to support allies."[9] Immigrant-serving nonprofits may observe or anticipate organized opposition and make a venue choice accordingly.

For these reason, local elections—whether they are congressional contests, mayoral races, or county sheriff elections—should draw the most public attention following a hate crime or anti-immigrant hostilities. As a result, immigrant-serving nonprofits will likely be drawn to these local election venues when a hate crime occurs. They will focus electoral activities on that venue, potentially to the exclusion of state or national races, hoping to respond to community demands and to have the biggest impact on the election.

Electoral Venue Choice in Practice

Even if electoral venue choice makes sense in theory, how might it actually work in practice? Another example can help demonstrate just this. Four days after Election Day in 2008, Marcelo Lucero, an Ecuadorian immigrant, and a friend walked near the local train station in Patchogue, a town in Suffolk County, Long Island, New York. The two were confronted by a group of teens who began yelling anti-Hispanic slurs. A confrontation ensued, and Lucero was repeatedly stabbed and killed.

Much as in Wisconsin, this was not simply a murder; it was a hate crime. Suffolk County and many other counties in Long Island had seen recent increases in Hispanic population, and a series of attacks against Hispanic Americans preceded the murder of Lucero. As the crime occurred after the 2008 election, concerned organizations planned responses for future elections; but planning was not limited to just those organizations based in the county. Nonprofits from across Long Island created a coalition called the Long Island Civic Engagement Table (LICET) in response to the crime.

LICET adopted a strategy to focus on Suffolk County, rather than pursuing electoral work in each partner organization's own county. The targeting of their voter mobilization activity was also motivated by the county executive, Steve Levy. Levy had made inflammatory comments about "anchor babies" and complained of the detrimental effects of Hispanic immigrants on local public health services (Peters 2010). He also had founded Mayors and Executives for Immigration Reform, an organization with a mission to fight illegal immigration.

The hate crime and the county executive's strident anti-immigrant posture focused the work of LICET and its nonprofit partners. Pat Young, program director of the Central American Refugee Center (CARECEN), based in neighboring Nassau County, said: "CARECEN is working to turn immigrants into the most vital opponents of hate mongers—informed and voting United States citizens. Suffolk officials who try to win votes by scapegoating immigrants will be held accountable by new citizens anxious to move the county forward and help it emerge from its climate of fear."[10] Other organizations with offices across the New York region also joined in the focused electoral mobilization. María Magdalena Flores, a member of Make the Road New York, with offices in New York City and Long Island, said: "Our communities have suffered too much from hate crimes, discrimination, and the irresponsibility of certain politicians in Suffolk County. Now is the time to go to the polls to vote in numbers so that they listen to and respect us."[11]

In October 2011, LICET announced a monthlong series of GOTV activities. First, it held a candidate debate for the upcoming Suffolk County executive election. In a press release, LICET wrote: "By allowing questions in other languages and offering simultaneous translation to those with limited English abilities, the debate will also provide a prototype for a new, inclusive politics in Suffolk County."[12] Second, the coalition recruited volunteers to mobilize voters for the election. And, third, on November 5, LICET held a final press conference to "mark the final stage in a month of action." All these tactics (candidate debates, voter mobilization, and press conferences) were focused squarely on the county in which the hate crime committed against Marcelo Lucero occurred.

What the case of the hate crime in Suffolk County, New York shows is the ways electoral tactics can be focused. To varying degrees, each of the electoral tactics explained in the previous chapter has the potential to be focused in a specific venue or employed more generally. For example, a nonprofit might monitor just local or ethnic newspapers for information about candidate positions on key issues, or it could monitor national papers such as the *New York Times* or *USA Today*. In making this choice, the organization would be choosing a venue in which to employ the monitoring tactic. The organization could also opt to monitor the news in both types of newspaper, thereby making no venue choice decision at all.

Another nonprofit might disseminate policy recommendations on foreign policy issues that affect the community, or focus instead on municipal policy.

According to Dr. M. Zaher Sahloul, president of the Syrian American Medical Society, "Lately, because of the conflict in Syria, there has been more advocacy in [Washington,] DC. [We] push certain policies: at the humanitarian, medical relief, or political level."[13] Conversely, Latino Justice has worked on a campaign to compel New York City to reconsider its "stop and frisk" policing policy because of the disproportionate impact on young Hispanic American males in the city.[14] The Syrian American nonprofit has chosen the national venue, while Latino Justice has chosen the locality in which it is based. To be sure, such decisions are not exclusively electoral; some also involve policy areas where immigrant organizations may not all agree. Vanderkooy and Nawyn (2011) showed that significant policy differences exist between what immigration organizations advocate for at the local versus the national levels. For example, Abdelnasser Rashid of the Chicago-based Illinois Coalition for Immigrant Refugee Rights (ICIRR) said, "We do look at places and try to help communities respond to attacks and bad experiences. Elections are a part but not the only thing we do."[15] ICIRR also works in direct policy advocacy, community organizing, and media, and uses each to deal with hate crimes and other exceptional events that might harm immigrants and refugees. Also, electoral work in one venue does not preclude work in other venues. Nevertheless, given limited nonprofit resources and staff, rarely will a nonprofit be able to disseminate policy recommendations or advocate for policy in numerous electoral venues at the same time.

As Suffolk County showed, this calculus may be no more important than in the resource-intensive area of voter mobilization. Voter mobilization requires a staff, volunteers, and technology. Mobilization also occurs in a short window of time, often just the weeks leading up to Election Day, necessitating strategic choices. For that reason, a nonprofit might opt to prioritize a single congressional district election, as CAIR-Chicago did in Illinois, or instead do phone-banking across the state. If a nonprofit wants to do neighborhood canvassing, where volunteers literally go door to door, venue choices will be especially important. One of the ways to minimize certain mobilization costs—particularly those related to technology—is to form common cause with other nonprofits. This choice may also require a strategic choice of venue. An organization might join a national coalition to advocate in the presidential election, as many did in 2012, or instead join a local coalition voicing opinions on local school board electoral issues or a statewide ballot initiative.

Nonprofits also are sometimes pulled into a particular venue by specific election officials. For example, the mission of the South Asian American Policy and Research Institute (SAAPRI) is to serve South Asian Americans in the Chicago area, mainly through research and policy analysis. Ami Gandhi, executive director, described how they chose to provide policy advice to the election boards in the City of Chicago and Cook County: "We focused on advising the City of Chicago and suburban Cook County clerk's office on their implementation of language assistance during the 2012 elections . . . [after] learning from demographic research and talking to the community that limited English proficiency is a growing concern for South Asian Americans, particularly in the Chicago suburbs; [and] learning from the election boards that they needed information about how to implement language assistance to our community (in other words, we observed that there was a critical information gap)."[16] SAAPRI's specialty in policy analysis could have been directed at providing information to candidates for national office or at statewide immigrant issues, but the organization chose the local venue based on the needs of municipal officials and an opportunity to fill a gap in information.

It is worth noting that the relationship between electoral venue choice and hate crimes also may relate to other aspects of the structure of local government and elections. In cities that appoint a city manager, rather than elect a mayor, or where local officials are not up for election in the immediate aftermath of a hate crime, the electoral venue choice effect may be dampened or altered. Some nonprofits may not have a clear choice between focusing electoral activities at the local, state, or national level. A multitude of electoral distinctions may relate in complex ways with the actual venue choice decisions, which may complicate the general theoretical conception I argue for above.

Notwithstanding these caveats, in the wake of a focusing event that directly affects immigrants, such as a hate crime, and in view of state political culture and constituent power, local nonprofits that have committed themselves to participating in an election face a second decision: whether to focus on the local venue, to focus instead at the state or national level, or to remain unfocused on a single venue.

Data and Analysis

In order to test the theory of electoral venue choice, I relied upon the same survey data presented in chapter 5.[17] Respondents to the survey answered a question regarding whether their organization had focused its electoral work at the local, state, or national level, or whether there was a focus on more than one level (if respondents did not engage in any tactics, they did not respond to the focus question and are excluded from the analysis below).[18] I coded respondents as focused exclusively on the "local venue" if they chose only the local option; coded them for a second variable for "state/national venue" if they chose state or national only; or coded them as focused on no venue otherwise. The respondents showed that there is variation in choice of venue. Around a quarter (23 percent) focused at the local level; most, however, focused at the state or national levels (70 percent).

Again, in order to test the theory of electoral venue choice, I collected data to measure the three factors that drive electoral venue choices. First, I linked each responding nonprofit to its home state and assigned the state political culture category according to Elazar. Two of the six states (Florida and North Carolina) examined in this study were labeled by Elazar as traditionalistic; the other states were labeled as non-traditionalistic.[19] I expected that immigrant-serving nonprofits operating in the traditionalistic states would be more likely to focus electoral work at the local level, knowing that the state political culture would be inhospitable to electioneering at the state level.[20]

Second, I used data from the U.S. Census on the percent of the county population that was naturalized citizens.[21] This serves as a proxy for constituent power. Third, I collected data from the Bureau of Justice Statistics Uniformed Crime Report (UCR) on all hate crimes in 2011—the year before the 2012 election and the latest available data. The 2012 election was the first electoral cycle to observe the effect of the 2011 hate crimes on nonprofit electoral venue choice. In 2011, 720 hate crimes motivated by ethnicity/national origin were reported nationwide, 11.5 percent of the total. The UCR is based on localities reporting to the Department of Justice and is therefore disaggregated in an annual report by city and county. I matched each nonprofit that responded to the survey to its county and then tallied the number of hate crimes in 2011 for the categories of race, ethnicity, and religion. A little more than half (53 percent) of respondents were located in counties that had experienced recent hate crimes.

Other Controls

Because mission drove the choice of whether a respondent did or did not engage electorally, I included these mission-related variables as controls in the model of electoral venue choice. I also included the organizational controls used in the previous chapter. Even though resources and age of organization were not significant predictors of the choice to engage in electioneering, it may be that they relate in some fashion to venue choices. Juan Alfaro, of the Michigan-based nonprofit Latin Americans United for Progress (LAUP), whose organization conducted a voter registration drive and a community forum on several state ballot initiatives, said that "we stay more at the local level, being a small nonprofit."[22] And Ami Gandhi of SAAPRI related that their focus on providing information to the local city clerk's office was possible because they "were able to conduct work in that area because we secured partial funding to do so."[23] For these reasons, I included the same variables for resources as in the previous chapter.

One of the most important controls that I included in the statistical models of electoral venue choice was whether the immigrant-serving nonprofit had an overall mission that was focused on the local level or beyond. It is reasonable to suspect that organizations with a local mission would be more likely to focus electoral work at the local level, and those focused beyond the locality would be correspondingly involved at the state or national level during elections. Bivariate evidence suggests this is partially true, but not to the great extent one might assume. Close to a third (29 percent) of respondents with a local mission focused their electoral work at the local level, while 13 percent of those without a local mission did so—not a statistically significant difference.

Finally, elections, particularly at the national level for the presidency, can be highly competitive in one part of the country and uncompetitive in another, and therefore we might expect that attention to elections will also vary. As McKay (2011) showed for the relationship between the level of conflict in a venue and interest group lobbying, it stands to reason that nonprofits located in a district with a closely contested election will be drawn into that locality, whereas another nonprofit that is located in an uncompetitive district may see no obvious reason to engage locally. In 2012, certain districts were strongly supportive of President Obama and others of Mitt Romney. I used the final vote tally as a measure of competitiveness of the county, as I did in the last chapter.

Understanding the Multivariate Analysis

Because each of the models uses a dichotomous venue choice as a dependent variable, I used logistic regression in both cases. The coefficients then can be interpreted as the odds of the immigrant-serving nonprofit choosing to focus either in the local venue (versus some other focus or no focus at all) or the state/national venue (versus a local focus or no focus at all), given one-unit changes in the independent variables.

The multivariate model largely supports the theory of venue choice presented earlier (see table 6.1).[24] Interestingly, none of the mission variables that were significant in the previous models of electoral choice in chapter 5 were significant here in the models of electoral venue choice. This provides support for the argument that the decision to participate is separate and distinct from the choice of venue. In particular, the lack of significance for the variable "local focus of mission" is noteworthy for the reason mentioned earlier. What this suggests is that venue choice is not simply a reflection of the scope of mission: nonprofits that have a mission focused on just the local community are no more likely to focus their electoral work locally than those with a state, national, or even internationally focused mission. Venue choice, additionally, is not a function of resources or

TABLE 6.1 Electoral venue choice of local focus and state/national focus, logistic regression

	VARIABLE	LOCAL FOCUS ODDS RATIOS (STANDARD ERROR)	STATE/NATIONAL FOCUS ODDS RATIOS (STANDARD ERROR)
Mission	Serve pan-immigrant community (compared to other)	.55 (.62)	.27 (.26)
	Hispanic American (compared to other)	.91 (1.01)	2.26 (1.28)
	Asian American (compared to other)	.12 (.18)	3.01 (3.57)
	Middle-Eastern American (compared to other)	.30 (.46)	1.29 (3.01)
	Multifaceted (compared to single issue)	8.20 (10.90)	.86 (1.05)
	Politically oriented (compared to other)	1.87 (1.79)	1.39 (1.09)
	Locally focused mission (compared to state or nationally focused)	2.27 (2.25)	.33 (.28)
Demographic context	Percent foreign-born in county (log)	.51 (.33)	3.01* (1.80)
Campaign and political context	Hate crime in county (dichotomous)	4.27* (3.86)	.33 (.28)
	Traditionalistic state Elazar (compared to moralistic and individualistic)	4.91* (5.01)	.13** (.12)
	Competitive electoral county (compared to uncompetitive)	1.86 (1.70)	1.38 (1.13)
Organizational context	Revenue (log)	1.03 (.29)	.99 (.24)
	Institutionalized (dichotomous based on number of employees)	1.06 (1.10)	1.31 (1.20)
	Age (log of years since formed)	1.79 (1.33)	.48 (.32)
	Constant	−8.53 (5.164)	4.69 (3.90)
Pseudo-R^2		.24	.20
N		64	64
LR chi^2		16.80	15.82

* p value < .10
** < .05
*** < .01

organizational factors. Institutionalization, such a consistent predictor of tactical choices, does not relate to the strategic choice of venue. Also, the variable for electoral competitiveness was not significant in either model. This political factor that all nonprofits face did not seem to have a particular relationship to immigrant-serving nonprofit venue choices.

Most important, the theory of electoral venue choice is supported by the statistical models. First, as the percentage of naturalized foreign-born in the county went up, immigrant-serving nonprofits were more likely to focus their electoral work at the state or national levels, but not more likely to do so at the local level. In only the state/national model was this variable significant. This partially supports the notion that the relative political power of immigrants—captured here in numbers—emboldens nonprofits to focus beyond just the locality. As the immigrant community grows in number, nonprofits may be seeking out electoral influence at the state and even national level. As the community grows, it may also be the case that statewide officials and candidates increasingly invite immigrant-serving nonprofits into the electoral process. Electoral venue choice may then be the result of a push-and-pull effect on immigrant-serving nonprofits. This is an important potential conclusion about the way immigrant communities can grow in electoral power through the increasingly ambitious activities of the nonprofits that represent their interests. If nonprofits remain only locally focused, the community may never increase influence over wider politics and policy.

Second, immigrant-serving nonprofits in traditionalistic states were more likely to focus at the local level and less likely to focus at the state/national levels—both statistically significant findings. This supports the argument that traditionalistic state political culture creates an uninviting atmosphere for immigrant-serving nonprofits to advocate at the statewide level. Respondents in these traditionalistic states instead focused at the local level, which may have been more hospitable and welcoming to their electoral activities. This is a potentially discouraging finding for immigrants living in traditionalistic states. It suggests there are cultural limits in these states on how politically active immigrant-serving nonprofits will be and, as a result, potential limits on how politically influential immigrants can be in state affairs. For traditionalistic states with increasing immigrant populations, such as North Carolina and Virginia, it remains a question whether there are ways to change this phenomenon. How can states with long traditions of exclusionary politics toward outsiders figure out how to open doors and welcome newcomers? State political culture is so deeply ingrained that it is unlikely to change in the near term, but perhaps new public policies can create opportunities for a wider array of participants to enter into the political conversation (for instance, holding more community forums, experimenting with participatory budgeting, and supporting publicly financed campaigns). In a broader sense, potential policy solutions to open political institutions may also be as important for women and African Americans—two groups frequently excluded from traditionalistic political cultures—as they are for immigrants.

Third, immigrant-serving nonprofits located in counties that had experienced a hate crime were also much more likely to focus electoral work at the local level and less likely to focus at the state or national level, though this finding was statistically significant only for the local level. This provides some support for the theory of focusing events as a trigger for electoral venue choice. It is important to note here that this finding demonstrates a statistical correlation but does not show that there is necessarily a causal relationship between hate crimes and nonprofit venue choice. There may be situations where a long history of advocacy on behalf of immigrants triggers anti-immigrant animosity, as has been the case in states with increasing immigrant populations. The causal mechanism may not always be as clear as anecdotes about a specific hate crime triggering an immediate focus on the local level. Notwithstanding this caveat, the evidence here does support the conclusion that there is a relationship between hate crime and nonprofit strategic choices.

The magnitudes of these regression coefficients are tricky to understand. Predicted probability statistics help tell an illustrative and more interesting story. Predicted probability allows for a closer examination of the change in the probability of an electoral venue choice, given different scenarios. With all other variables set at their mean or modal values, being located in a county that had a hate crime increases the probability of an immigrant-serving nonprofit focusing at the local level from 3 percent to 16 percent. Similarly, if we compare an immigrant-serving nonprofit in a non-traditionalistic state to one in a traditionalistic state, setting all other variables to their mean or modal value, then the probability of focusing at the local level is increased from 2 percent to 19 percent. An immigrant-serving nonprofit located in a county that has had a hate crime and in a state that is traditionalistic increases the probability of focusing electoral work at the local level to 63 percent.

The statistical models presented here are far from perfect. There are many difficulties in properly measuring state political culture, the power of immigrants, and focusing events. The independent variables are proxies of these complex phenomena. These data are also from a single period in time, and therefore the analysis does not gain the advantages of time-series data. Despite these limitations, the significant relationships support the theory of electoral venue choice. Immigrant-serving nonprofits responded to the political context of the 2012 election in predictable ways, seeking out electoral venues to focus their tactics.

Conclusion

Hate crimes are a brutal aspect of modern life and offend just about everyone in the community in which they are committed. These crimes have a particularly harsh effect on immigrants new to the country, often living at the margins of civic life. A hate crime committed because of someone's ethnic background, race, or religion can have the effect of further isolating entire communities of immigrants. It is reasonable to assume that the organizations that represent immigrants would be particularly attuned to when and where hate crimes occur.

The evidence presented in this chapter suggests that the occurrence of a hate crime drives electoral strategy for immigrant-serving nonprofits that are already prepared to engage in an election and have begun to act like an interest group. Hate crimes push nonprofits to focus their electoral program at the local level, perhaps in an attempt to convince local candidates of the significance of these crimes, or perhaps just as a way to demonstrate to community members that they have a voice in local affairs. In either case, the statistical evidence supports a theory of immigrant-serving nonprofit electoral venue choice that extends the earlier theory of reflective electoral representation.

In addition, these organizations appear attuned to other political factors in making venue choices. The nature of the state's political culture may limit electoral work to the local level. Conversely, the size of the immigrant community may push an organization to work beyond the locality at the state level. These relationships hold even when controlling for organizational and mission factors that relate to other electoral decisions. What this suggests is that forces largely out of the control of each organization shape certain aspects of electoral strategy. Whereas an organization can shift its mission and adjust its identity based on changes in priorities, it cannot change two hundred years of political history in a state or greatly alter the overall flow of immigrants into the county. By focusing on local electoral venues, immigrant organizations may gain a voice in city or county affairs but may not extend that voice to state or national affairs. There are serious implications of this for national debates about immigration reform and federal policies toward hate crime. If immigrant-serving nonprofits remain locally focused, policy change that will directly affect their constituents, such as the voter ID laws in Florida or the DOJ regulations on classifying hate crime, may continue to be dominated by the anti-immigration organizations described in chapters 2 and 3. This is not good for immigrant organizations and certainly not good for immigrants.

Overall, this chapter extended the reflective electoral representation theory of immigrant-serving nonprofit participation. It supports the second half of the electoral theory that argues these organizations first look to their mission as a reflection of the characteristics of the community, then look to the political and power position of immigrants to make a strategic decision about where to focus an electoral agenda. There may be other strategic choices that immigrant-serving nonprofits make during elections, and those choices may also relate to politics and power. The evidence provided in this chapter provides a justification to pursue that potentially fruitful line of research with data from future elections and different states.

BOLDLY REPRESENTING IMMIGRANTS IN TOUGH TIMES

When the counting was done, President Barack Obama was reelected, and the press lauded 2012 as a watershed moment for immigrants and ethnic minority voters. Headlines read: "Obama Win Fueled by Latino Voter Muscle, FOX Exit Polls Show"; "Asian-Americans Backed Obama Overwhelmingly"; "Why American Jews and Muslims Backed Obama by Huge Margins" (Lienas 2012; Schneier 2012; Borchers and Wirzbicki 2012). Demographic change is reshaping the country. Electoral politics is changing as well, and immigrants are slowly finding their voice. This is good for the state of democracy in the United States.

Also in the 2012 elections, more than eighty first- and second-generation immigrant candidates ran for federal office, and many prevailed. Four Arab Americans, ten Asian Americans, one Caribbean American, and thirty Hispanic Americans won congressional races. Ted Cruz, a Cuban American newcomer to Texas politics, won the open Senate seat to become the state's first Hispanic American U.S. senator and a future presidential contender. Tammy Duckworth defeated Joe Walsh to win a congressional seat in Illinois. And Bill Pascrell and Alan Grayson also easily won their congressional races in New Jersey and Florida, respectively. Immigrants are now finding a voice, not just in the voting booth, but also in Congress. This is also good for the state of the representative dimension of democracy in the country.

Despite the fears of some Tea Party–affiliated policy advocates, as immigrant voting increased, there was scant evidence of voter fraud. Even in states that had not passed new voter identification laws, there were few cases of voting irregularities and violations of election law, and most Election Day problems were related to malfunctioning equipment and long wait lines (Vielmetti 2013). Thus, as participation in voting has increased, the integrity of voting procedures and the administration of fair elections have not suffered, also on the whole a positive sign.

And following years of advocacy and lobbying by organizations across the country, and the support of millions of dollars from philanthropic foundations, the first steps toward immigration reform were taken during the 2012 campaign. The president announced the new immigration policy called DACA—Deferred Action for Childhood Arrivals—providing a limited mechanism for some younger undocumented residents to remain in the country with legal protections. While full immigration reform remained stalled through the election and into the president's second term in office, DACA was viewed by many as a sign of hope for immigrants and a demonstration of the influence of immigrant-serving nonprofits and advocacy organizations. Certain policy makers are listening to the voice of immigrants and better representing their wishes, two positive indicators of a responsive representative system of government.

Nevertheless, 2012 was not all good news. In New York, Grace Meng defeated her primary challenger for the open congressional seat but then faced a bruising general election campaign, fueled by the potentially harmful role played by new media. On her Republican opponent's campaign Facebook social media website, Dan Halloran posted a picture of himself at a procession at the Ganesha Temple in Flushing, Queens. Halloran stood among the Indian American community members, seeking to rally their support. His strategy was to position Meng as an ethnic opportunist, whose views were hostile to Jewish American and Indian American voters. In an Israeli newspaper, Halloran was critical of Meng's Chinese American background, arguing that she "has been sympathetic to the Chinese, and she's touted her strong Chinese history as being the reason she's the appropriate candidate to represent the Chinese people in New York." He added, "I believe she even has dual citizenship" (Gur 2012). Halloran suggested that China's hostility toward Israel might be advanced by Meng. He also referenced his own faith—he practiced Theodism—which he argued made him an outsider in the district but "has enabled me to reach out to communities which have traditionally been underrepresented, like the Hindu community that has always felt marginalized by the mainstream." Meng eventually won the race, but in doing so she had to confront the all-too-common strategy used by her challenger that questioned her immigrant identity and patriotism.

While 2012 was a shining success for some immigrant candidates, such as Grace Meng and Tammy Duckworth, many of them—along with others who lost their races, such as John Quiñones—had their ethnic affiliations and background used against them for personal distortions and attacks. Even in victory, immigrant candidates had to defend their loyalty to their district and their patriotism to the country. Further, as brutal hate crimes, like those committed on Long Island and in Wisconsin, and anti-immigrant bigotry, such as witnessed in Chicago, shook local communities, for some immigrants the very same type of ethnic, religious, or racial violence and persecution they fled in coming to the United States remained a threat in their new home. The democracy has therefore improved, yet remains subject to barriers to full and free participation by all citizens.

The situation for immigrant-serving nonprofit organizations was just as fraught with turmoil. Despite many organizations working in close harmony, collaborating on plans to register new immigrant voters across ethnic lines, old conflicts persisted in certain parts of the country. In the state of Washington, a dispute between two local leaders in the Vietnamese American community reached the state supreme court and exposed long-standing rifts. According to court documents, the conflict arose between Duc Tan, leader of the Vietnamese American Council of Thurston County, and Norman Le, a member of the Committee against the Viet Cong Flag.[1]

The two were both Vietnamese immigrants, having settled in the southwestern part of Washington in the 1970s. The Vietnamese American Council was one of the prominent community organizations in the region for Vietnamese Americans, and Tan and Le both held leadership positions. The council regularly provided cultural services, hosted community events, and taught language classes to schoolchildren in a rented space at a local private school. That school had classrooms festooned with flags of the world, including the Vietnamese flag, which some, including Le, believed was the flag of the Communists and therefore an affront to Vietnamese Americans. As the council debated the issue, Tan refused Le's demand to remove or alter the flag in this borrowed space. Le accused Tan of Communist sympathies that stemmed from Tan's life in Vietnam. In a series of 2003 newsletters circulated in the community, Le claimed Tan had worn Communist symbols at a local event and was an undercover agent of the Viet Cong, or Vietnamese Communist Party. In response, Tan sued Le for defamation of character. In 2013, following a series of lower court rulings, the state supreme court ruled to reinstate a $300,000 jury award to Duc Tan and the Vietnamese American Council.

Historical context matters to the development of organizations in the United States. History also matters to immigrants, perhaps more so than for the native born. The long and difficult history of Vietnam traveled with those who came to the United States and embedded itself in the identity and organizational politics of newly formed community nonprofits. A dispute like Tan and Le's is not unheard of; other immigrant communities struggle to find common ground in the midst of disputed legacies and long-standing conflicts, thereby limiting many of the benefits that common cause yields during elections. For small immigrant communities, with short histories in the country, a lack of consensus and a strained sense of shared identity send mixed messages to resource-poor non-profit organizations about whether or not to pursue electoral and voter engagement. Many nonprofits reflect these ambiguities and opt out of electoral politics, leaving voter mobilization, translation, and the provision of voting information to other organizations, or not to be done at all.

For those who believe the research that says voter mobilization led by local nonprofits makes a difference in voter turnout and helps encourage residents to register and vote, then the 2012 election and its aftermath suggested as many reasons for concern as for hope. Evidence of the continued problematic state of immigrant voter engagement was easy to find. For one, despite the symbolism at party conventions, many immigrants remained out of reach for the two major political parties and underrepresented in elected office. Hispanic, Arab, and Asian American representation in Congress still remained far below those groups' respective portions of the overall population.

Moreover, the two political parties devoted only minimal effort to persuade immigrants to vote, particularly Asian Americans, the fastest-growing group in the country. In the run-up to the 2012 election, fewer than half (48 percent) of Asian Americans who were registered as Democrats reported that they received a phone call or direct contact from their party, and little more than a third (36 percent) of registered Republican Asian Americans. Fewer than 10 percent of Asian Americans overall reported to pollsters that they had been contacted "a great deal" by either political party. Even more interesting, for Asian American independents—the most highly prized voting bloc during election season and half of the Asian American electorate—nearly 60 percent reported that they had not been contacted at all by Republicans or Democrats. Some of this has to do with where Asian American voters are concentrated: 83 percent of them lived in non-battleground states. According to a postelection poll, those located in battleground states were more likely to be contacted (48 percent) than those in non-battleground states such as California and New York (27 percent).[2] As a result, only a quarter of Indian American voters received any contact at all. While some policy makers were listening, parties remained deaf to the voice of immigrants. Hence, pluralism remains a shallow concept for most immigrants; most are largely ignored by the established interests in the country.

Further, it was true that record numbers of Hispanic and Asian Americans voted in elections across the country. Eleven million Hispanic Americans voted in 2012, over one and a half million more than in 2008. Five hundred thousand more Asian Americans voted in 2012 than in 2008, including 79 percent of those registered. But as a percentage of the eligible pool of voters, the numbers were less impressive. There were a large number of Hispanic and Asian American voters, but still only 48 percent of those eligible and registered to vote turned out (this compared to 65 percent of white and African American voters).[3] Hispanic Americans made up 10.8 percent of the eligible electorate, but only 8.4 percent of those voting. Asian Americans made up 3.8 percent of those eligible, but only 2.9 percent of those voting. These differences limit the full impact of immigrant voting and threaten to perpetuate the underrepresentation of immigrants in the democracy.

Finally, just months after Barack Obama was inaugurated for the second time, the U.S. Supreme Court overturned major parts of the Voting Rights Act. In its *Shelby County v. Holder* decision, the Court stripped many of the federal protections provided to voters in certain states with legacies of violating voting rights that were included in Sections 4 and 5 of the law.[4] Without these provisions, the U.S. Department of Justice would no longer be authorized to rule on changes in voting laws in covered jurisdictions, permitting legislators in those states to enact such changes unencumbered by federal oversight. Almost immediately, legislators in many of those formerly covered states introduced changes to their voting laws. For example, in Texas, Mississippi, and Alabama, state lawmakers quickly worked to pass and enact new voter ID laws. In North Carolina, one of the most vigorous efforts to change voting laws sought to cut the number of early voting days, as well as numerous other proposed changes (Cooper 2013). Evidence from this book suggests that in Florida these types of laws discouraged immigrant-serving nonprofits from registering voters and using other tactics aimed to encourage voter participation. The possibility is real that this same harmful effect will be repeated in the future for states that enact similar electoral provisions.

Immigrant voters and those concerned with their political participation in politics no longer have some of the protections historically provided by the federal government. Though Section 203 language translation assistance provisions of the Voting Rights Act remained, the implementation of those voter language translation services seemed tenuous. In the heavily South Asian part of Queens, New York, Indian and Bangladeshi American voters looked forward to the promise of Bengali language assistance on Election Day. The Department of Justice found evidence from the 2010 census that the number of Bengali speakers was sufficiently large in some parts of the country to mandate Section 203 coverage. But in 2012, despite assurances from the City of New York, Bengali speakers had none of the assistance that the federal government had mandated the city to provide. Chhaya CDC and AALDEF later sued the city for violating the 2011 federal decision and for providing insufficient numbers of Bengali translators (Hu 2013).

So while the 2012 election may have been the "Year of the Immigrant Voter," there were as many troubling aspects regarding the status of immigrant voters as there were positive signs. New policies, lingering nativism and violence, and poor implementation of existing laws all restricted the full expression of immigrant political power and limited the continued maturation of the democracy in the United States. Immigrant-serving nonprofits confronted many of the same barriers imposed on individual voters. Some overcame these barriers with the assistance of philanthropic foundations, partnerships with electoral coalitions, and the integration of new technology. Others, spooked by the rise of advocacy aimed at their constituents and at their own efforts to register new voters, opted to remain far from electoral politics, thereby sacrificing many of the benefits associated with nonprofit electoral engagement and further limiting the extent to which pluralism can represent vast segments of the population.

Findings from the Book

In this book, I sought the answer to three questions: (1) Which contexts shape how nonprofit organizations represent immigrants? (2) What drives some immigrant-serving nonprofits to engage in complex and technologically sophisticated electoral strategies and others to opt out of even the most basic electoral action? And, (3) Once an immigrant-serving nonprofit decides to participate in electoral politics, what factors relate to its choice of electoral strategy and electoral venue? In order to answer these questions, I argued for a theory of reflective electoral representation to explain the ways immigrant-serving nonprofits make decisions about electoral participation. I pursued this theory because much of the existing research on immigrants has omitted the organizational dimension of their politics. And despite their growing interest concerning the intersection of interest groups and nonprofit organizations, researchers have not sufficiently examined the particular political position of immigrants. I drew on the existing research of political behavior and interest group scholars in formulating my theoretical perspective. The model I developed rests on three important contexts: demographic, organizational, and campaign.

To answer research question 1, the first three chapters of the book examined how each context relates to the position and political circumstance of immigrants and the organizations that serve them. We cannot detach organizations from the demographic characteristics and change occurring among those they serve, nor can we divorce immigrant-serving organizations operating in the twenty-first century from the involvement of philanthropic foundations that have been operating since the early 1900s. Organizations also confront the localized politics of political campaigns that feature immigrants in different ways, including as key blocs of voters and campaign donors; as powerful positive and negative images used in campaign advertising; and increasingly as candidates for office. I hope that future researchers will continue to build on this more contextual understanding of what shapes immigrant politics. Every day, new immigrants arrive in the United States, but their political lives do not start anew upon arrival. We must connect immigrants and organizations to the long history of immigration, to the complex roles of philanthropy and pluralism, and the particular politics of each community.

In chapter 4 I examined how in these three contexts immigrant-serving nonprofits adopt and evolve an identity that is a reflection of the immigrants they represent. These organizations cannot be understood simply as rational actors, as some interest group scholars have argued. These organizations also cannot be understood as any other type of nonprofit, since voting and electoral participation are so much more integral to the identity of immigrants than they are to other individuals served by different nonprofits. Since most immigrant-serving nonprofits are established for nonpolitical reasons, and since the people they serve are defined by their civic status, how these organizations participate in electoral politics works in slightly different ways. The process of institutional identity formation should be understood to be unique to each immigrant-serving organization, and thus each may transition to become a hybrid organization, and later an interest group, as it reflects the relative and changing political efficacy and political attitudes of immigrant constituents. This is why the two organizations presented at the very start of the book, ACCESS and NICE, adopted such different electoral strategies. And why the MinKwon Center and KCCP, similar in certain ways, approach elections in entirely different ways.

The statistical evidence presented in chapter 5 further illustrated these cases and supports the larger theory. To answer research question 2, I found that immigrant-serving nonprofits do not simply respond to external factors, such as a particularly heated political campaign; rather, what seems most consistently important are factors related to mission and identity. Those nonprofits that most resemble interest groups—the ones with an aspect of their mission that is focused on politics—were consistently the most likely to participate in electoral activities. This is much as we would expect, and it supports using theories from interest group studies to help explain the behaviors of nonprofits. Other findings were more surprising. Immigrant-serving nonprofits were also not driven solely by capacity, as some previous research has argued. Resources mattered, though participating in electoral activities and certain strategies was much more connected to the orientation of the mission toward politics, the range of issues the organization addresses, and the characteristics of those the organization serves. Chapter 2 suggested that many immigrant-serving nonprofits have adopted an identity that precludes electoral politics because of the long history in the United

States of discouraging nonprofits from participating in politics. Evidence from chapter 5 showed that a majority (60 percent) of immigrant-serving nonprofits employ no electoral tactics at all. Federal regulations have codified this perception through the 501(c)(3) nonprofit status, but federal regulations actually forbid only a few electoral tactics. Immigrant-serving nonprofits often incorrectly pin a decision not to participate in elections on their protected IRS status. That decision also reflects the deeply ambiguous nature of politics for most immigrants. Immigrant-serving organizations sometimes opt to remain far from electoral politics because those they serve are not eligible to vote, are fearful of voting, or are uninterested in a political system that does not reflect who they are.

On the contrary, other organizations serve constituents who are thirsty for political representation and eager for the organization to voice their concerns with candidates. These organizations reflect that high level of political efficacy with an identity that is tied to politics and a set of electoral tactics that best represents their constituents. The statistical analysis demonstrated this by comparing Hispanic American, Asian American, and Middle-Eastern American organizations, but in actuality there are organizations within each of these broad immigrant categories that adopt aggressive electoral strategies or no strategy at all, based on the identity of their constituents. I hope future research can further disaggregate these umbrella immigrant categories to better compare how different organizations within the Hispanic American community participate and how that compares to different organizations within the Asian American community. This fine-grained analysis will require large-scale and longitudinal data collection but promises to better explain the identities adopted by immigrant-serving organizations.

The analysis presented earlier in the book did not find that immigrant-serving nonprofits were entirely insulated from the external political context. In response to research question 3, respondents to the survey, and also interviewees, indicated that the passage of a new law in Florida greatly altered electoral strategy, leading many to opt out of registering and mobilizing voters, the voter-focused strategy I captured in chapter 5. And the findings showed that when a local campaign, such as the Democratic primary race in New Jersey, is closely contested, immigrant-serving nonprofits seem to respond by employing a larger array of electoral tactics.

Moreover, and to further answer research question 3, immigrant-serving nonprofits seem to respond to dramatic political events. Immigrants have been subject to abhorrent hate crimes, and immigrant-serving nonprofits seem to adjust their electoral strategies accordingly. When a hate crime occurs, immigrant organizations target those running in local elections, such as Congressman Walsh outside Chicago, potentially the official with the most direct responsibility for addressing these crimes. This finding suggests that those organizations that are willing to participate in elections do so with a keen eye toward strategy.

Other external factors also drive electoral venue choice. Organizations operating in traditionalistic states are much less likely to move beyond their locality and target statewide electoral venues, such as a race for governor. Given that state political culture is unlikely to change anytime soon, this is a potentially worrisome finding, since it suggests organizations in certain states will be less likely to provide a voice in state affairs. And since these states, including North Carolina, Georgia, and Tennessee, are also where much of the growth in immigration is occurring, increasing numbers of immigrants may be without proper institutional representation in state and national policy making. Future research should pay much more attention to these new gateways for immigrants. I hope future scholars will build on the analysis of this book to compare the ways that political context in these new locations, in places such as Nashville and Charlotte, differs from that of traditional centers of immigration like New York and Chicago. This approach will help the field better understand new trends in immigrant politics, and also help organizations operating in unfamiliar terrain deal with sometimes hostile new communities.

Many of the findings of this book are drawn from statistical analysis, but through dozens of interviews I have also provided answers to the research questions using qualitative methods. For example, through interviews with nonprofit leaders, I can answer research question 1 in so far as organizations that opt *not* to participate in electoral politics do not always do so out of ignorance, but rather they often make thoughtful judgments about organizational identity. In Virginia, the board of the Greater Richmond Bengali Association (GRBA) met to consider a request from a political candidate. The board weighed the implications of sharing information about the candidate with the organization's members. In the end, the board realized that even this minimal foray into electoral politics might put off members who did not share the candidate's partisan persuasion, and a majority voted not to share the candidate's information. GRBA decided to remain a primarily service-oriented organization and not begin the transition to a hybrid organization or interest group. To decide otherwise would risk losing the support and trust of members and to sacrifice the authenticity of the organization's identity.

Conversely, other organizations have deliberated on electoral participation and sought out ways to transition to the hybrid type of organization. In Michigan, the six groups that made up the Consortium of Hispanic Agencies grew frustrated with the limitations of their advocacy agenda. The groups in the consortium agreed that greater participation in elections would enhance their effectiveness, but they believed that they had too few free resources to adopt new electoral tactics. The consortium turned to major philanthropic foundations to expand capacity, which provided new financial resources and access to voter databases. A collaborative approach within Detroit—as well as with external institutional financial patrons—enabled the consortium to better represent Hispanic American immigrants in the area. Given what we learned in chapter 2 about the history and patterns of support from foundations, the success of this approach should not be a surprise.

In other parts of the country, interviews showed the growing sophistication of elaborate electoral strategies. Leaders of the MinKwon Center in New York described how the organization expanded from serving just the social needs of Korean Americans to providing a multistep process of electoral engagement. MinKwon remains a small organization, but leaders saw the violence done to the Korean American community in the 1980s and1990s and decided to integrate technology and volunteers in the 2000s to change the organization's identity. Now it is a major player in mobilizing voters and giving a voice to a community that had been silent in the past. MinKwon has made the transition to become a hybrid organization, no longer oriented purely toward providing social services. Not only does the case of MinKwon support the research findings of this book; it also serves as a practical example for other immigrant-serving nonprofits. I hope that its history here offers lessons for nonprofit leaders who perceive similar circumstances and are looking to change their organizations.

The reliance on technology is appropriate for some organizations but not all. Chapter 5 showed the disparities in how Hispanic, Asian, and Middle-Eastern American organizations adopted social media. Hispanic American organizations have been the fastest to use Twitter and Facebook, in part because of the characteristics of those they serve. The interviews I drew from also explained aspects of how technology can be used. Voto Latino, for example, targeted younger Hispanic American citizens with a technology-focused electoral strategy because of the growth of that demographic group and its familiarity with social media. Familiarity with social media can be crucial to organizations as well. If Voto Latino had opted, for instance, to use Facebook rather than Twitter to mobilize younger Hispanic voters, it would have been rejected as inauthentic, since Facebook is viewed as the technology of older voters and not aligned with the authentic identity of the voters the organization served. On the contrary, many of the Asian American nonprofit leaders I interviewed believed that the older demographic profile of their constituents made technology ineffective. Leaders of Desi Vote, for example, said that a more traditional electoral strategy, based on knocking on doors and phone reminders in an appropriate language, would mobilize a larger portion of the Asian American immigrant community. These appear to be sound strategies, but they do portend an institutional digital divide that may separate organizations that do and do not adopt technology. For scholars of digital politics, I hope these findings provide a direction for future research to better explore the differences and the inequities in how organizations use technology.

The qualitative interviews provided throughout the book also show how organizational leaders interpret the identity of those they serve and then seek to reflect that identity with the operations of the organization. This process of reflection involves decisions whether or not to participate in electoral politics, as well as about electoral strategy. The evidence from the analysis shows that certain organizations opt for a very public electoral strategy while others focus exclusively on voters. Some organizations work mainly with providing information to candidates in the form of policy reports, while others pursue private electoral strategies that may never be known outside the walls of the organization's office. Immigrant-serving nonprofit organizations pick and choose tactics in the electoral toolbox to reflect their identity. And some decide to do nothing at all, leaving electoral work to other organizations.

Overall, my hope is that these findings inform future research on various aspects of the immigrant political experience, and not just among those who study interest groups and nonprofits. At the start of the book, I argued that much of the research on immigrants has been done by political behaviorists interested in the individual voting and nonvoting decisions of immigrants. I have regularly drawn from that work and aimed to complement it with a more institutional focus on immigrants. My hope is that my findings can now be used by political behavior researchers. For example, the research by Janelle Wong and colleagues (2005) found that when Asian Americans affiliate with organizations, their propensity to participate in politics increases. Unfortunately it may be that organizational opportunities for immigrants are not equally distributed across communities. The findings from this book suggest that there is a good deal of variety in the types of organizations different immigrants can join. Some immigrants may have no organizations in their community that take part in politics or elections, thus decreasing the likelihood that they will join, and also decreasing the chance they will participate in politics. I hope my findings can influence how political behaviorists analyze the participation of immigrants by integrating more organizational factors into theoretical models.

In chapter 1, I referenced the excellent work by Lisa García Bedolla and Melissa Michelson (2012) on the effective get-out-the-vote activities of certain immigrant-serving organizations. Using experimental methods, they found organizations can increase turnout among low-propensity voters from ethnic communities. Those findings were necessarily drawn from some of the most politically oriented organizations; but given my findings that a large number of organizations never do get-out-the-vote, I hope future research integrates a wider range of organizations in understanding how voter mobilization works. There are exciting opportunities to do experimental studies with less politically oriented nonprofits and those organizations that employ just one or two electoral tactics. Can a limited electoral strategy work to increase turnout? If not, what is the threshold above which we can start to expect positive gains in immigrant voting and political participation? These are questions that collaborations between research behaviorists and institutionalists could answer.

These findings also suggest the desirability of continued investigations of the robustness of the system of pluralism in the United States. Scholars and practitioners have long worried about the unequal system of representation that favors the wealthy over the poor (Schattschneider 1960). As Jeffrey Berry has argued, nonprofit participation in politics offers to overturn these historic norms and represent those who have rarely had a voice. The findings here suggest some reason for hope, as well as other reasons for deep concern. If immigrants in general are only sporadically represented by nonprofits during elections, this raises questions as to how effectively the system of pluralism is working. Perhaps more problematic, if certain specific immigrant communities are even more rarely represented by nonprofits, as the evidence presented in the book suggests, there are even deeper questions about intra-immigrant inequities. The system of pluralistic representation seems to be working decently for Hispanic Americans, who appear to have nonprofits working on their behalf; but for other immigrants, electoral representation is less common. These findings raise questions for future research to investigate how well the system of pluralism is working in the United States.

The evidence from the book, therefore, is a mixed bag for understanding the plight of immigrants in the United States. There are hopes as well as concerns. The democracy is growing and maturing, but it is far from fully evolved, and many gaps remain. Fortunately, there are opportunities to address concerns in the future through the various political institutions that care, or purport to care, about immigrants. I hope the conclusions from this book advance not just scholarship on these issues, but also the practices of policy makers, political leaders, and nonprofits that possess the power to change. Below are some recommendations for what a few of these institutions can do.

What Can Political Parties Do?

Shortly after the election, the two major political parties grappled with what it meant to each of their futures: What would changing national demographics mean to future apportionment and control of the House of Representatives?

What would a larger nonwhite electorate mean to long-standing political traditions, policy, and strategy? And what could be done to advance Republican and Democratic candidates in the future?

Republican leaders—gasping for air after their second consecutive presidential defeat—quickly met to commiserate in an electoral postmortem. Their candidate, Mitt Romney, acknowledged that communication with minorities was a weakness of his campaign (Sides and Vavreck 2013). With this in mind, the Republican National Committee drafted a game plan focused on communication to curry favor with immigrant and ethnic voters, dubbed "The Growth and Opportunity Project."[5] The RNC called attention to the fact that

> if Hispanic Americans perceive that a GOP nominee or candidate does not want them in the United States (i.e. self-deportation), they will not pay attention to our next sentence. It does not matter what we say about education, jobs or the economy; if Hispanics think we do not want them here, they will close their ears to our policies. In the last election, Governor Romney received just 27 percent of the Hispanic vote. Other minority communities, including Asian and Pacific Islander Americans, also view the Party as unwelcoming. (8)

The report's authors wrote: "If we want ethnic minority voters to support Republicans, we have to engage them and show our sincerity" (7). They called on the party to embrace comprehensive reform, to form a new council and hire field staff charged with building grassroots support and educating Republican candidates about "particular culture, aspirations, positions on issues, contributions to the country, etc., of the demographic group they are trying to reach." They pleaded with the party to embrace early voting, something that many immigrant-serving nonprofits had adopted as a core part of their electoral strategies. They called for consultants and strategists to adopt more bilingual polling and to increase advertisement in Hispanic media outlets.

Republicans also began to create the data infrastructure that Democrats had such a head start on in 2012. New for-profit and nonprofit organizations formed that promised to link Republican candidates and organizations to the micro-level data used by Democrats and progressive organizations in 2012. Whether these new organizations, and the infrastructure they sought to build, would result in greater mobilization of immigrant voters remained to be seen as of the writing of this book.

Republican hand-wringing about the party's "immigrant problem" was assuaged by the pool of presidential hopefuls looking ahead to 2016. Two prominent Hispanic officials, Senators Marco Rubio and Ted Cruz, and the Indian

American governor of Louisiana, Bobby Jindal, who had starred at the 2012 Republican National Convention, provided hope for the party that the all-white tradition at the top of the ticket would soon change. Potential female candidates with strong ethnic ties, such as Susana Martinez and Nikki Haley, further reinforced a potential paradox of the upcoming presidential elections. The Republicans, not the Democrats, might run the first Hispanic American for the nation's top office, and that person might be joined by the first Indian American on a national ticket.

Nonetheless, the failure to win many Hispanic, Asian, and other ethnic minority votes was more than just a messaging and targeting problem. John Sides and Lynn Vavreck (2013) demonstrated that there is scant evidence that "micro-targeting" works, and the party's difficulties with Hispanic voters existed long in advance of the nomination of Mitt Romney. For the party to make gains among nonwhite voters, it needed a comprehensive plan based on an appealing policy agenda that addressed immigration but also the variety of other policy priorities of Hispanic, Asian, and other immigrant voters.

The Democratic Party may have had more success with candidates, but it still struggled to reach many groups of voters. In fact, several of the same reforms recommended by Republicans may in fact be applicable to their partisan opposition. For both parties, immigrants appear to remain a mystery.

What Can Immigrant-Serving Nonprofits Do?

It would be foolish for immigrant-serving nonprofits to simply believe the postelection rhetoric from Republicans and Democrats that each would embrace immigrants in the future. Rather, it seems clear that leaders in immigrant communities across the country who hope for a future with immigrants and ethnic minorities at the center of local, state, and federal politics must initiate more aggressive electoral programs. In doing so, leaders of nonprofits have to grapple with their various organizations' identities. In shifting from a purely service-oriented nonprofit to what I called a hybrid organization, these leaders have many difficult decisions to make. The transition should be informed by internal discussions among key stakeholders, including those in the community. These discussions need not simply replicate those of the past. Instead, organizations can find ways to stimulate a discussion of the future and of what the community sees for the next generation. In doing so, organizational leaders can initiate positive change in the political attitudes and levels of efficacy of local immigrants. The status quo need not be binding, even if attitudes may not be easy to change. Organizational officials will be fulfilling their role as leaders if they can

TABLE C.1 Themes for immigrant-serving nonprofit electoral participation

Embrace technology	Learn to use social media (Twitter and Facebook) and databases of voter information (Voter Activation Network).
Dedicate staffing	Create a new electoral engagement position or dedicate a portion of an existing position's time to election activities.
Institutionalize tactics	Build electoral activities into regular budgeting and planning for the future.
Adopt a continuous strategy	View elections as one aspect of a year-round array of civic activities including mobilizing the community to address local planning, state budgeting, and federal policy making.
Establish and join coalitions	Use the shared resources and expertise of existing electoral coalitions or form new coalitions with other immigrant nonprofits.
Understand new gateways	New gateway cities and communities provide new opportunities but must be understood as unique and different from traditional centers of immigrants.
Emphasize authenticity	Make decisions about elections based on what the community desires, and adopt electoral tactics that the community can respond to and with which it is most comfortable.

encourage immigrant communities to embrace a role in the civic life of cities and counties. In doing so, nonprofits will have helped immigrants find their voice, a truly noble outcome.

In the end, it may not be the case that every immigrant-serving nonprofit needs to become a hybrid organization and participate in elections. But if the right strategic decisions are made, a sufficient number will participate in an array of electoral tactics, and persistent concerns about low registration, voting, and other forms of political participation may be reduced. In order to do this, these organizations can draw on some of the evidence presented in this book (table C.1).

Technology

Immigrant-serving nonprofits can take advantage of the declining cost of electoral technology. The cost associated with data management is coming down every day. Off-the-shelf database software has the capacity that only expensive customized programs promised in the past. Many social media platforms are nearly cost-free to use (Selee 2013). And new political databases, such as that offered by NationBuilder, rent for less than $50 a month and lack the partisan leanings of the VAN (Kroll 2013). It is reasonable to presume that many of these costs will continue to decrease, though which platform remains in vogue will likely change. Nonprofits that want to engage in elections can look to incorporating technology into their activities but must routinely and regularly update technology choices.

Staffing

While technology costs may be decreasing, staff salaries and benefits are not. Even technologies that appear simple to use require some level of dedicated staffing. Not every immigrant-serving nonprofit can afford to hire a full-time social media director or coordinator of voter engagement; in fact, many organizations are run entirely by unpaid volunteers. For those with a paid staff, decisions must be made. Such staffing decisions will likely come at the cost of some other dimension of the organization's mission. Philanthropic foundations offer one short-term solution to this problem, providing the chance to earn grants to defray the cost of hiring temporary electoral staff or reward student volunteers; but grants are typically for a limited duration. Other, more reliable revenue sources must be found to build new electoral services into ongoing budget planning.

Institutionalization

As was demonstrated in chapter 5, the more institutionalized nonprofits were significantly more likely to engage in various electoral strategies. If an immigrant-serving nonprofit wants to dedicate staffing, use technology to disseminate electoral information, or employ a database to inform local voters of polling locations, then it needs to figure out how to institutionalize these tactics. That will likely mean convincing the community of the value of these services and then relying on its generosity to support new hiring. If the immigrant community is uncertain or ambivalent toward politics, this may be a difficult sell.

Continuous Strategy

One way for nonprofits to persuade the community is to conceptualize electoral engagement as part of a broader and continuous strategy of civic engagement. Elections occur on occasion, but there are regular opportunities to share the community's views on state policy, local planning, and on other government services. Nonprofits can explain to the community that electoral engagement is part of a continuous strategy of public and civic engagement. Bill Vandenberg of the Open Society Foundations stressed this perspective—what he called the "civic engagement continuum." This type of approach may be particularly useful for nonprofits that provide services to undocumented immigrants or noncitizens, for whom voting and elections are not readily available alternatives.[6] It is also a useful approach in anticipating unforeseen circumstances. Hate crimes, for example, frequently target immigrants, and given the increases in immigration in parts of the country that are unfamiliar with immigrants, this is likely a tragic trend that will persist. A continuous strategy of civic engagement permits nonprofits to respond to sudden and unexpected events. If the community remains engaged and mobilized throughout the year, not just in the lead-up to an election, nonprofits can respond more quickly to hate crimes. If a rally must be held, a community petition signed, or volunteers found to organize an event, a continuous strategy of civic engagement will permit quick responses, such as the response by the Sikh community in Wisconsin and the Hispanic American community on Long Island, New York.

Coalitions

Even for nonprofits that are unwilling to engage in electoral politics or adopt a continuous plan of civic engagement, they need to be certain there are other nonprofits in their community that will. Coalitions or networks of nonprofits provide one way to ensure this is the case. The New York Immigration Coalition or the Illinois Coalition for Immigrant and Refugee Rights are two successful examples. Each has developed the infrastructure, expertise, and experience to help local nonprofits. Coalitions also can link small nonprofits to national foundations to receive financial support for new activities. Where coalitions are absent, nonprofits should seek to form them, and where coalitions are weak, nonprofits should support them.

New Gateways

Coalitions are likely to be active and institutionalized in historic centers of immigration such as New York City and Chicago. In new gateways for immigrants, such as Charlotte, Nashville, and Las Vegas, even more concerted efforts are needed to build coalitions. These cities may have substantial undocumented populations, further complicating the task of organizing and promoting immigrant interests during elections. Notwithstanding that dilemma, the future for immigrants and immigration appears bright in places far from New York, Chicago, and Los Angeles. Nonprofits in these new gateway cities can borrow from other parts of the country but must adjust tactics and strategy to their unique socioeconomic and geographic circumstances. Failing to make these adjustments will likely result in inauthentic appeals for more political participation and the choice of ineffective tactics that will not galvanize the community. Immigrant-serving nonprofits must reflect the actual identity of the community they serve in the electoral realm, even amid continual efforts to shape and change that identity. This seems to be one of the central tensions faced by immigrant-serving nonprofits: how to promote a mission in an authentic and culturally appropriate way while at the same time inspiring members of the community to thrive and integrate into their new homes.

Authenticity

New gateway cities also raise questions about how each immigrant community can maintain its uniqueness, individuality, and authenticity. Coalitions have tended to favor pan-ethnic organizing, either explicitly or implicitly, even when certain communities have very different priorities and interests. Houston, for example, has a long history of Hispanic American residents, and they are well incorporated into city politics. But the growing population of Vietnamese Americans in the city poses serious challenges for the future. Vietnamese American nonprofits must promote the political and policy interests of those in their community and join in common cause with Hispanic Americans when issues overlap. For a model, that community might look to the success of the MinKwon Center in New York, an organization that has promoted the interests of the relatively new Korean American community in the city. MinKwon has over time embraced pan-Asian mobilization but still remains committed to its core Korean American constituency. This is a difficult balancing act, to be sure.

These seven concerns—technology, staffing, institutionalization, continuous strategy, coalitions, new gateways, and authenticity—offer opportunities, but new tactics should not be adopted automatically or haphazardly. Rather, these seven areas offer multiple considerations for immigrant-serving nonprofit staff, leaders, and community stakeholders to debate. An active debate may lead some nonprofits to remain at the periphery during election time, yet an active decision-making process will always trump passive decisions based on a lack of information, habit, or simple risk aversion.

For those organizations that opt to dip or plunge into electoral politics for the first time, either with a single toe or a full swan dive, there are hazards along with new opportunities. Anti-immigrant beliefs are alive in many parts of the country. Major factions of the Tea Party express virulently anti-immigrant and anti-immigration sentiments. Efforts to tighten voting laws have targeted organizations as well as voters. In Florida, Michigan, and elsewhere, the architects of new "third party" regulations knew that nonprofit organizations mattered during elections. It was nonprofit staff and volunteers that policy makers targeted when they enacted the new fines and potential prison time for violating election laws.

Nevertheless, opportunities also abound. The success stories mentioned throughout the book show what can be gained when immigrant-serving nonprofits fully participate in elections. Larger numbers of newly registered immigrants, increasing numbers of immigrant voters, and candidates that listen to immigrants in their own community are all the spoils of electioneering. While the evidence is not all clear, there are also reasons to believe that greater nonprofit engagement in elections can transform a community. Political efficacy and attitudes toward politics are not prone to change, but there are increasing signs that mobilization by community organizations can change voting behavior (García Bedolla and Michelson 2012) and that organizational leaders can elevate the political efficacy of rank-and-file members (Ahlquist and Levi 2013). Part of this may involve shifting from a view that Hahrie Han (2014) calls "mobilizer" focused to one that is "organizer" focused. Han suggests that an organizer-focused approach aims not just at turning out a community to vote or to show up at a public meeting, but at preparing community leaders through training and education. Immigrant communities will be transformed and elevated by nonprofits if new leaders emerge with the skills to participate in politics, including mobilizing the community, as well as running for office. Immigrant-serving nonprofit leaders play important roles in their community, and they should recognize that their power can transform political attitudes and beliefs. Continuing to rely on political parties or organizations from outside the community will likely result in unfulfilled hopes and sacrificed opportunities for expressing the authentic political voice of those being served.

Moreover, the theory of reflective electoral representation presented in this book suggests that nonprofits act as a mirror of the community and that an organization's mission serves as the best illustration of this reflection. But a mission statement should not be a static document, left unchanged and unedited for generations. Immigrant-serving nonprofits can use the revision of a mission statement as a mechanism to invite an active discussion about new directions and what the community actually desires. Through this dialogue, nonprofit leaders can stimulate the community to recognize what authentic political participation and representation means (Jacobson 2011). An active and regular process of revising an organization's mission statement, vision, and goals will ensure that organizations continue to reflect what the community wants, while at the same time promoting a spirit of change and growth.

Relevance for Other Nonprofits?

Immigrants are not the only groups that have an array of nonprofits providing services. Youth, the elderly, women, various faith communities, as well as lesbian/gay/bisexual/transgender Americans also receive services from nonprofit organizations. The lessons from this research about the ways immigrant-serving nonprofits engage in reflective electoral engagement can inform how other nonprofits participate in politics and elections. Nonprofits that serve these other communities must also work to best reflect the identity, beliefs, and desires of their constituents. While these communities may not look to the act of voting with the same reverence—the citizenship status of women, Christians, and the LGBT community, for instance, are rarely in doubt—elections are about more than just voting for candidates. State ballot initiatives have routinely placed gay marriage up for a popular vote. More spending on education or reduced spending on prenatal options for pregnant women, for instance, are frequently at stake in elections. Such issues often embody core interests and reflect the identity of a community. Elections may not always represent a policy choice, but representative nonprofits can look to elections, voting, and political participation as a way to advance community interests.

Immigrant-serving nonprofits also provide opportunities for cross-community partnerships and coalitions. For example, voting rights and recent efforts to change voting laws pose serious threats not just to immigrants. Fewer pre-election voting days may affect seniors with few transportation options; the elimination of Sunday voting or "souls to the polls" may threaten faith-based groups; and changes to in-state voting rules could limit voting opportunities for college students. Voting rights may be an area where a variety of communities that share few other interests can come together to lobby policy makers and collaborate during election season.

Looking Ahead to Future Elections

The 2012 election saw a host of political firsts and emerging awareness of immigrants as an important group of voters. But the issues confronted by immigrant and immigrant-serving nonprofits are not new. The immigrant story is truly the American story: complex and fraught with contradictions, yet offering great possibilities.

Immigrants have been subjected to the fickle push-and-pull of politics since the founding of the country. When immigrants served the political ambitions of urban machines, parties exchanged government services, jobs, and patronage for votes. When political times changed and reformers demonized political machines, new waves of immigrants were no longer the source of political strength and became a target of condemnation. New forces in U.S. society, philanthropic foundations in particular, sought to assimilate immigrants, strip them of their foreign ways, and add them to the American melting pot. Foundations have worked in partnership with nonprofit organizations ever since to provide services to immigrants in order to integrate newcomers into U.S. society. Voting remains one of the central tenets of this century-old plan to promote the value of a harmonious, singular vision of U.S. citizenship.

In the South, anti-immigrant animosities have long had a particularly violent and antidemocratic side. For the first half of the twentieth century, opposition to immigrants took the form of lynching and adoption of policies to restrict voting rights. Today, anti-immigrant hostilities are just as visible in the platform of Tea Party organizations and in the views of many Tea Party members. Hate crimes are on the rise, particularly against Hispanic Americans. And voting rights have again been the target of policy change by groups concerned about immigration and voter fraud. Many state legislatures have adopted measures to curtail the registration of new voters by nonprofit organizations and to erect new barriers to voting.

Elections in 2016 and beyond must be understood in the context of these historical precedents. But viewing the future as simply a replay of the past ignores or underestimates the potential for change. Demographic change continues to shape what states and localities look and sound like. To be sure, the impacts of dramatic increases in immigration over the last twenty years are barely understood. As new gateways for immigrants across the South and Midwest see large numbers of undocumented residents and first-generation immigrants give way to second- and third-generation citizens, political norms may begin to change. Elazar's simple formulation of which states are "traditionalistic" may need adjustment as states like North Carolina, Georgia, and Tennessee become centers of Hispanic, Asian, and Muslim Americans.

Change, though, will not happen solely through individual voters casting their ballot once every four years. New political institutions, nonprofit organizations, and coalitions of immigrants hold the promise of a common, collective, and powerful voice. If these new nonprofit organizations participate in future elections in the limited way they did in 2012, it is unlikely that the political environment of gateway communities will change. Elected officials will not shift their views of immigrants or consider the influence of immigrant voters when making policy. This is most harmful when those policies directly affect the lives of immigrants; but immigrants have an interest in nearly every policy decision made by local and state officials. Local zoning and development, school curriculum, and public health decisions are all immigrant issues, and each immigrant community will likely have a slightly different perspective on what should or should not be done. Policy makers who are not compelled to consider the variety of these new perspectives will never formulate policies sensitive to the needs of immigrants.

If, however, nonprofit organizations find authentic, appropriate, and responsive ways to participate in elections and policy debates, there is a much greater potential that policy makers will consider the perspective of immigrants. Policy makers may be less apt to adopt new policies like those in Arizona or Florida, which have explicitly and implicitly harmed immigrants. In doing so, the country will realize the goal of a democratic political system that reflects and represents the views of all citizens. And immigrants will find their voice.

TECHNICAL APPENDIX

The population of immigrant-serving nonprofits was established through a multi-stage process using the Urban Institute database made available by the National Center for Charitable Statistics (see http://nccs.urban.org/). The database contains the universe of nonprofit organizations that file annual taxes with the IRS. Organizations that earn below a threshold of $50,000 do not file the same tax forms and are excluded from this database. I selected all the 501(c)(3) nonprofits in the six states and downloaded organizational information including financial and nonfinancial variables (separate interviews were conducted with 501(c)(3) as well as other types of nonprofits). I then coded each organization for whether it provided services to immigrants, broadly defined. Akin to Cortés (1998) and Gleeson and Bloemraad (2012), I used keyword searches with the names of the 196 foreign countries in the world to identify a first set of groups. I then included pan-ethnic keywords such as "Hispanic," "Asian," "Caribbean," and "Arab." Finally, I coded for immigrant groups in general using keywords such as "immigrant," "immigration," and "newcomer." That process gave me an upper-bound list of organizations, but it included some false positives. I went through the list and eliminated groups that represented localities with country names, such as the Association of Paris (Illinois) or the Society of London (Michigan), as well as other obvious linguistic coincidences that falsely labeled an organization as immigrant serving. I investigated other organizations that had an ambiguous name or uncertain mission to clarify whether they belonged in the survey population. This process resulted in a count of 1,149 immigrant-serving nonprofit organizations.

Following common practices in the field, the survey consisted of a six-item questionnaire (see figure A.1) that was sent by standard mail and e-mail[1] to the executive director (or equivalent) of each organization on October 11, 2012. The survey instrument and other research protocols were approved by the

Please answer each item. Choose "skip" if you do not have information or choose not to respond to the item.

Organization Name (optional):

_____

Section I: About Your Organization

Question 1. Does your organization <u>devote substantial resources</u> to providing any of the following services to the community: (choose all that apply)

Skip ☐

☐ educational services
☐ health services
☐ food/nutritional services
☐ housing services
☐ arts/cultural/recreation services
☐ religious services
☐ business or financial services
☐ advisory services with government planning or policy committees

☐ political advocacy services with local, state, or national elected officials
☐ financial aid sent to the home country or region
☐ non-financial aid (supplies, books, medicine) sent to the home country or region
☐ other, briefly describe:

_____
_____
_____

Question 2. In general, is your organization focused on? (choose one)

Skip ☐

☐ local or community issues
☐ state-wide issues
☐ nation-wide issues

☐ international issues related to the home country or region

Question 3. On average, how many individuals do you serve each year? (choose one)

Skip ☐

☐ between 0 and 100
☐ between 100 and 500
☐ between 500 and 1,000

☐ between 1,000 and 5,000
☐ more than 5,000
☐ we do not serve individuals

FIGURE A.1.   Survey questionnaire

Section II: About the 2012 Election

Question 4. <u>Community Activities</u>. In respect to the 2012 election, is your organization or do you plan to be active in: (choose all that apply)

Skip ☐

☐ monitoring the news about the campaign, candidates, and/or the election
☐ voter registration activities (i.e. registering new voters prior to Election Day)
☐ voter mobilization activities (i.e. Get Out the Vote (GOTV) on Election Day)
☐ translating voter or campaign material from English into another language
☐ providing information to the community or public education about political candidates or issues
☐ joining a coalition of organizations focused on the election

Question 5. <u>Policy Activities</u>. In respect to the 2012 election, is your organization or do you plan to be active in: (choose all that apply)

Skip ☐

☐ providing issue or policy briefs on local or domestic issues to political candidates
☐ providing issue or policy briefs on foreign policy or international issues to political candidates
☐ creating a section of your web-site or social media page dedicated to the campaign
☐ forming a Political Action Committee (PAC) to give campaign donations to political candidates
☐ participating with a national organization focused on the 2012 election
☐ other, please describe briefly: _____

_____

Question 6. If you chose at least one of the activities from question 4 or 5, are these activities focused mainly at the: (choose one)

Skip ☐

☐ local-level elections: town, city, county, or mayor
☐ state-level elections: State Senate, State House of Representatives, State Attorney General, or Governor
☐ national-level elections: US House of Representatives, US Senate, or Presidential election
☐ a combination, please describe briefly: _____

_____

If you have any additional thoughts that you would like to share about your organization and the 2012 election, please do so here:

FIGURE A.1. Continued

Institutional Review Board of Seton Hall University, where I was employed at the time. Respondents to the survey were promised anonymity, and all research findings from the survey are presented in aggregated tables. Phone call and in-person interviews were conducted separate from the survey. The date for releasing the survey was chosen because it was far enough into the election for groups to have committed to whatever activity they would or would not do in the 2012 election, but early enough so that an organization would not forget or neglect to mention activities if I surveyed it far after the election (Lin and Van Ryzin 2012). Approximately half of the surveys were sent to organizations with the name of the executive director (or other senior official); the rest were sent attention "Executive Director." Follow-up e-mails were sent at two-week intervals, and then phone calls were made until the middle of December to ensure an appropriate response rate. Approximately thirty-five surveys were returned repeatedly by the U.S. Postal Service, and no phone contact could be made with these organizations. I concluded that they were not in operation, and I dropped them from the survey population. This resulted in 1,114 total organizations in the active survey pool.

Survey Response Rate

Twenty-two percent of the surveys that were sent out were successfully returned, a small response rate for survey research of individuals, but an acceptable response rate for surveys of nonprofit organizations, particularly when this was a solely voluntary survey. In a meta-analysis of mail surveys of nonprofits, Hager et al. (2003) showed that, with the exception of studies that can require nonprofit responses to surveys because of contractual or grant obligations, published research has ranged from as low as 10 percent (Olson 2000), 15 percent (Baldauf, Reisinger, and Moncrief 1999), and 16 percent (Sheehan 1996), though response rates between 25 and 45 percent are more typical (Cordes et al. 1999). Research suggests that the standard response rate for individual surveys, above 50 percent, is not necessarily appropriate for surveys of nonprofits, in part because response bias has been shown to be less of a concern (J. Smith 1997). In order to verify this, I compared respondents to nonrespondents. Because each nonprofit in the survey population has reported various organizational characteristics on an annual basis to the IRS, I can report several descriptive statistics to compare respondents and nonrespondents.[2] Respondents had on average $473,813 in annual revenue, had been operating in 2012 for just under seventeen years on average, and had on average 5.5 employees. The mean revenue of nonrespondents was $683,935, the mean number of employees was 7.49, and the mean organizational age of nonrespondents was eighteen years, all somewhat more than for respondents.

TABLE A.1   Survey response by state

	PERCENT IN SURVEY POPULATION	PERCENT OF SURVEY RESPONDENTS
New York	12.39	15.89
New Jersey	21.10	23.83
Illinois	26.12	21.96
Florida	23.61	16.36
Michigan	12.84	13.55
North Carolina	7.09	8.88

These differences do not appear to pose a serious problem to the analysis, however, because it is expected that since resources and age will be positively related to electoral activity, the findings from the respondents may be a slight underestimate of overall electoral activities. The findings should then be interpreted with this caveat in mind.

The response rate by state was also generally acceptable (see table A.1). In the full survey population, 24 percent of surveys were sent to nonprofits in Florida, 26 percent to nonprofits in Illinois, 13 percent to Michigan, 12 percent to New York, 21 percent to New Jersey, and 7 percent to North Carolina. Of those that responded to the survey, 16 percent were from Florida, 22 percent from Illinois, 13 percent from Michigan, 24 percent from New Jersey, 16 percent from New York, and 9 percent from North Carolina. This suggests that the response rate was lower than the norm for Florida and higher than the norm for Michigan, but about the same for the other three states.

In general, though nonrespondents and respondents were not identical and the response rate differed slightly by state, the fielding of the survey resulted in an unbiased set of organizations to analyze.

Comparing Survey Findings to Benchmarks

One of the first questions one must answer about survey data is whether the findings are reasonable and reliable: Do they comport with what one would expect in general, based on previous research? Table A.2 shows the range of policy interests for responding immigrant-serving nonprofits. Most were focused on social service–oriented issues, especially education, while a relatively small percentage addressed politics specifically, or government more generally. Because there is little systematic analysis of the electoral activities of nonprofits, particularly immigrant-serving nonprofits, it is difficult to establish a clear benchmark to compare the survey results or even know what expectations should be. The

TABLE A.2 Priority areas of survey respondent's missions

	PERCENT OF SURVEY RESPONDENTS
Education	62.2
Health	28.6
Food	16.2
Housing	14.1
Arts, culture, recreation	37.3
Religious	6.2
Business	7.9
Government advisory	5.4
Politics	8.3
Financial aid sent to home country	12.9
Nonfinancial aid sent to home country	14.1
Complex mission (group mentioned multiple policy areas)	54.4

study by Berry and Arons (2003) of nearly three thousand nonprofits across different policy areas is the most obvious, though the focus of that research was not on electoral activities but more generally on politics. Berry asked nonprofits about the extent of their engagement in various political tactics (giving testimony, lobbying legislators, etc.) and then presented data on those that described their organization as engaged at a "high level of activity." Berry found that 26 percent of respondents were working with a government advisory panel, 20 percent encouraged their members to send letters to policy makers, 12 percent of respondents were highly active in lobbying, and 6.9 percent in testifying before hearings. Berry's finding suggested that more nonprofits were *inactive* than active in politics, a conclusion that others have corroborated (Child and Grønbjerg 2007). The initial findings from this survey on immigrant-serving nonprofits suggest largely the same thing: a majority, nearly 60 percent of survey respondents, did not engage in any of the electoral tactics, and fewer than half that did engage used a single tactic.

Jennifer Mosley's (2011) more recent work on human-service nonprofits provides another comparison. She found that of the 321 organizations in her study, 84 percent participated in a coalition focused on public policy, 60 percent worked on regulations, 58 percent provided policy-related information to the public, and 45 percent had given testimony. The smallest percentages, 21 and 13 percent respectively, issued policy reports or participated in boycotts/demonstrations. In comparison to those findings, a smaller portion of immigrant-serving nonprofits in this research project used each of the available tactics. In particular, only 10 percent of respondents joined a coalition related to the election, a small fraction of what Mosley found for human-service nonprofits. However, Mosley's finding was drawn from coalition-joining in general, not bound by any temporal event such as a specific election. Another related study, by Kelly LeRoux (2011), examined social service nonprofits in sixteen metropolitan areas. She found that around a third (29 percent) of nonprofits surveyed in 2008 were involved in some way with registering voters. That finding is remarkably similar to the findings from this survey of immigrant-serving nonprofits four years later.

One of the closest comparisons that can be drawn is to Kristi Andersen's study (2010) of the missions of seventy-eight immigrant-serving community organizations in six cities. She found that only 13 percent (ten organizations in the study) "appear to include voter registration, voting, or other forms of participation as even a secondary part of their mission" (77). That study, though, was focused on the mission of the organization, so some portion of those organizations may have engaged in electoral work but did not have it explicitly incorporated into their official mission statement.

Finally, survey research was also done specifically on advocacy-based nonprofits in 2010. Funders Committee for Civic Participation (described in chapter 2) worked with the New Organizing Institute (NOI) Education Fund to conduct a survey of 501(c)(3) organizations that had a civic engagement program and that did individual get-out-the-vote.[3] Their findings thus are of a select group of the most active organizations. FCCP/NOI found that half (50 percent) of respondents planned to do voter registration during the 2010 election cycle. Half of those utilized the VAN to keep and organize voter registration data; nearly the same percentage (47 percent) used an off-the-shelf product such as Microsoft Excel or Access, rather than a sophisticated database system. These are fascinating comparative findings. While a much larger portion of these respondents were engaged in voter registration than in this survey, recall that their survey population was just advocacy organizations. This suggests that the evidence provided by the survey conducted for this book in 2012, which included the full population of immigrant-serving nonprofits, not just advocacy oriented, is consistent with patterns found elsewhere. It is also very interesting that so many of their respondents were using the low-tech options, rather than the widely heralded VAN. This finding speaks to the reality of how civic organizing and voter engagement works for most organizations, not just those who are afforded access to the advanced technology by foundations and other major funders.

Operationalizing Contextual Factors for Chapters 5 and 6

I relied upon several ways to operationalize the contextual variables for the analysis in chapters 5 and 6 (see table A.3). Consistent with Mosley (2011) and

TABLE A.3 Descriptive statistics

	PERCENT OF SURVEY RESPONDENTS	MEAN	MINIMUM	MAXIMUM
Total revenue		$473,813	0	$14,716,153
Age of organization in years		16.7	1	89
Number of employees		5.5	0	176
Hispanic Americans	22.0			
Asian Americans	35.3			
Middle-Eastern Americans	12.1			
Florida	14.5			
Illinois	19.5			
Michigan	12.0			
New Jersey	21.2			
New York	14.1			
North Carolina	7.9			
Political mission	9.5			
Institutionalized	18.5			
Multifaceted mission	54.5			

TABLE A.4 Publicly focused and privately focused strategy, logistic regression

	VARIABLE	PUBLICLY FOCUSED STRATEGY ODDS RATIO (STANDARD ERROR)	PRIVATELY FOCUSED STRATEGY ODDS RATIO (STANDARD ERROR)
Mission	Serve pan-immigrant community (compared to other)	.24 (.18)	2.17* (.90)
	Hispanic American (compared to other)	2.54* (1.22)	1.12 (.52)
	Middle-Eastern American (compared to other)	1.80 (1.19)	.90 (.57)
	Asian American (compared to other)	1.74 (.73)	1.32 (.58)
	Multifaceted (compared to single-issue)	1.75 (.68)	3.72*** (1.42)
	Politically oriented (compared to other)	5.80*** (3.43)	3.09* (1.72)
	Locally focused (compared to state or nationally focused)	1.38 (.51)	.77 (.26)
Organizational context	Revenue (log)	.91 (.11)	.91 (.10)
	Institutionalized (dichotomous based on number of employees)	3.46** (1.89)	2.09 (1.10)
	Age (log of years since formed)	1.03 (.23)	1.02 (.21)
Demographic context	Percent foreign-born in county (log)	1.59 (.51)	1.21 (.35)
Campaign and political context	Based in Florida (compared to not based in Florida)	.34* (.20)	1.16 (.54)

VARIABLE	PUBLICLY FOCUSED STRATEGY ODDS RATIO (STANDARD ERROR)	PRIVATELY FOCUSED STRATEGY ODDS RATIO (STANDARD ERROR)
Competitive campaign county (compared to not competitive)	1.77 (.73)	1.40 (.54)
Constant	.08 (.13)	.16 (.25)
Pseudo-R^2	.19	.14
N	215	215
LR chi^2	49.64	37.09

* p value < .10
** < .05
*** < .01

TABLE A.5 Voter- and issue-focused strategy, logistic regression

	VARIABLE	VOTER-FOCUSED STRATEGY ODDS RATIO (STANDARD ERROR)	ISSUE-FOCUSED STRATEGY ODDS RATIO (STANDARD ERROR)
Mission	Serve pan-immigrant community (compared to other)	1.45 (.69)	1.96* (.80)
	Hispanic American (compared to other)	2.89* (1.59)	.74 (.34)
	Middle-Eastern American (compared to other)	1.55 (1.12)	1.25 (.76)
	Asian American (compared to other)	2.37* (1.24)	1.32 (.57)
	Multifaceted (compared to single-issue)	2.11* (.89)	2.94*** (1.09)
	Politically oriented (compared to other)	6.18*** (3.84)	2.62* (1.56)
	Locally focused (compared to state or nationally focused)	1.23 (.48)	.74 (.25)
Organizational context	Revenue (log)	.78* (.09)	1.08 (.13)
	Institutionalized (based on number of employees)	8.39*** (4.87)	1.52 (.80)
	Age (log of years since formed)	.79 (.18)	1.02 (.21)
Demographic context	Percent foreign-born in county (log)	1.55 (.56)	1.08 (.30)
Campaign and political context	Based in Florida (compared to not based in Florida)	.31* (.19)	1.25 (.58)
	Competitive campaign county (compared to not competitive)	2.01* (.88)	1.31 (.49)
	Constant	.49 (.83)	.04 (.06)
Pseudo-R^2		.24	.11
N		215	215
LR chi^2		60.83	28.55

* p value < .10
** < .05
*** < .01

Grossmann (2012), I included a measure of the degree of institutionalization based on the number of professional staff employed by the organization. Those with more than the mean number of employees were coded as institutionalized, 1, and less than the mean coded as zero. Staff size, and the controls added for revenue and age in years of the organization came from IRS data from the Urban Institute. I controlled for whether the organization was pan-immigrant, coded as 1, versus focused on a single immigrant group, coded as zero. I included a measure of the focus of the group's mission ("local" versus "state" or beyond) as a control based on survey response. A final control was included, measured for the county in which each respondent nonprofit was located, equal to the percentage of the county population that were naturalized citizens, based on 2010 census data. The size of the foreign-born population may create a political environment in a city or county that encourages nonprofits to engage in elections.[4] Finally, I coded each respondent based on the competitiveness of the 2012 presidential race for its county. Since the president ultimately won 51 percent of the vote nationally, I coded the county that the nonprofit was located in as "competitive" if the president's vote tally in that county was within 5 percentage points (46 percent to 56 percent), and "uncompetitive" if the president's vote tally in that county was greater than 56 percent or less than 46 percent. Twenty-eight percent of respondents were located in "competitive" electoral counties using this approach.

Notes

INTRODUCTION: POLITICAL VARIETY AND ELECTORAL EFFICACY OF IMMIGRANT NONPROFIT ORGANIZATIONS

1. Based on an interview with Julia Chung, September 28, 2015.
2. I explain the origins and significance of Catalist/VAN in greater detail in chapter 2.
3. For the full history of ACCESS see http://www.wilsoncenter.org/sites/default/files/DUSS_Arab_America.pdf.
4. Based on an interview with Helen Samhan, July 25, 2012.
5. For a full history of the formation of NICE see http://www.queenstribune.com/archives/featurearchive/feature99/38/index.html.
6. Based on an interview with Valeria Treves, September 26, 2012.
7. See the Brennan Center report, http://www.brennancenter.org/sites/default/files/legacy/Democracy/VRE/Brennan_Voting_Law_V10.pdf.
8. Based on an interview with Young Lee, October 18, 2012.
9. To be sure, not every group that provides services to immigrants does so as a nonprofit organization, and therefore those types of groups are not the focus of this book. For example, for-profit companies operate in every large community and deliver a variety of services to recent immigrants, often including legal aid, language training, and private loans. The motivation of these for-profit entities, though, is not charitable or community service, but profit (either for individuals or shareholders); therefore they are not best understood as institutional representatives and are excluded from this book. Also, informal organizations abound in immigrant communities (Gleeson 2011). In addition, although ad hoc groups coalesce in countless communities to provide occasional services to immigrants, the informality of these groups greatly limits their ability to represent interests in most spheres of politics and during elections. These informal groups are also very difficult to contact, because their small size and lack of legal incorporation means they often lack a formal institutional status. Therefore, though these groups are important, they too are not a focus here. Moreover, immigrants are served and represented by nonprofit organizations that are not dedicated solely to their needs. Labor unions, health organizations, and women's groups are all linked in some communities with immigrants, but for each of those other nonprofits, immigrants are not the main object of their mission, therefore they do not usually act as representatives of immigrants. They are important in the broader study of immigrants, but not in a focused examination of immigrant-serving nonprofit organizations.

1. THE PRECARIOUS POSITION OF IMMIGRANTS

1. Based on an interview with Maria Teresa Kumar, June 12, 2012.
2. T-Mobile aggressively sought out a presence in Hispanic neighborhoods, including bilingual signage and staff. For more information see http://retailtrafficmag.com/management/siteoptimizer/t-mobile_drive_for_growth_06162010/.
3. The identification of this figure comes from questions 5 and 6 of the 2010 U.S. Census questionnaire, which asks separate questions about "origin" and "race." Those of Hispanic or "Latino" origin ("Mexican," "Puerto Rican," "Cuban," etc.) can then be of any race ("white," "black," "American Indian").

4. For more information see http://www.census.gov/prod/cen2010/briefs/c2010br-02.pdf.

5. For more information see http://www.migrationinformation.org/datahub/FB_maps/StateRankingsACS_2010_NFB_Growth_1990.pdf.

6. Louisiana, Missouri, and Iowa also lost seats based on decreases in population between 2000 and 2010. Washington State gained a seat.

2. FOUNDATIONS AND FUNDING

1. Sections of this chapter were published in a 2013 article, "Immigrant-Serving Nonprofits and Philanthropic Foundations," in *Nonprofit Policy Forum*.

2. According to the National Center for Charitable Statistics there were 1.5 million nonprofits in the United States in 2015, of which 1.07 million were 501(c)(3)s. See http://nccs.urban.org/statistics/quickfacts.cfm.

3. For more on the IRS regulations see http://www.irs.gov/irm/part7/irm_07-027-019.html#d0e599.

4. For more information see http://www.justice.gov/crt/combating-post-911-discriminatory-backlash-6.

5. Based on an interview with Hasan Jaber, February 25, 2013.

6. For more information see http://www.fordfoundation.org/issues/human-rights/protecting-immigrant-and-migrant-rights.

7. For more information see http://www.fordfoundation.org/grants/search.

8. For more information see https://www.carnegie.org/media/filer_public/b1/e2/b1e21cb6-80cf-4f6d-87ec-2271a6eb7b88/ccny_creview_2009_electoral.pdf.

9. For more information the President's Report from 2000 can be accessed via the Carnegie Corporation of New York archive at Columbia University at http://www.columbia.edu/cu/lweb/eresources/archives/rbml/Carnegie/index.html.

10. For more information see the annual report at http://www.issuelab.org/resource/carnegie_corporation_of_new_york_20042005_annual_report.

11. For more information see https://www.carnegie.org/media/filer_public/36/c5/36c501f9-ff2b-421f-9f90-e8b851f741c9/ccny_creporter_2008_vol5no1.pdf.

12. Based on an interview with Deb Ross, February 14, 2013.

13. Based on an interview with Felicia Bartow and e-mails with Daranee Pestod, June 21, 2013.

14. For more information see https://www.carnegie.org/media/filer_public/7c/74/7c744b4f-101f-4f4f-893e-3698675a62ad/ccny_cresults_2008_fourfreedoms.pdf.

15. For more information see http://www.statevoices.org/about-us/our-story/.

16. Ibid.

17. The company later merged with NGP Software in 2011.

18. For more information see https://www.accesscommunity.org/about/annual-reports.

19. Based on a phone interview with Nadia Tonova, March 26, 2013.

20. Based on a phone interview with Norman Bent, February 18, 2013.

21. Ibid.

22. For more information see http://chadetroit.org/assets/Consortium%20of%20Hispanic%20Agencies_WKKF%20grant%20announcement%20011212%20FINAL.pdf.

23. Based on a conversation with Ted Wang of Unbound Philanthropy.

24. Interestingly, some evidence suggests that there was no significant relationship between the size of the Hispanic population in a state and the introduction of voter ID laws (McKee et al. 2013).

25. For more information see http://www.bradleyfdn.org/program_interests.asp.

26. For more information see http://www.bradleyfdn.org/pdfs/Reports2010/2010Annual Report.pdf.

27. For more information see http://www.jsonline.com/blogs/news/176675811.html.

28. For more information see http://www.cis.org/About.

29. For more information see https://secure.freedomworks.org/site/SPageServer?page name=designated_1001_help.

30. For more information see http://www.freedomworks.org/about/about-freedom works.

31. For more information see http://www.thelibreinitiative.com/about-us#sthash.fzg wkQgj.dpuf.

32. See http://www.brennancenter.org/analysis/election-2012-voting-laws-roundup.

33. Based on an interview with Nadia Tonova, March 26, 2013.

34. Based on a phone interview with Ted Wang, March 29, 2013.

35. Based on an interview with Amardeep Singh, February 26, 2013.

36. Based on a phone interview with John Albert, May 31, 2013.

3. "YOU DON'T VOTE, YOU DON'T COUNT"

1. See poll results at http://www.bloomberg.com/news/2012-06-19/obama-immigration-policy-favored-2-to-1-by-likely-voters.html and also at http://www.latinodecisions.com/blog/2012/06/17/new-poll-latino-voters-enthusiastic-about-obama-dream-announcement-oppose-romney-policy-of-self-deport/.

2. Rather than continue to wait on Congress to legislate on the DREAM Act, in June the president announced an executive order (Deferred Action for Childhood Arrivals, or DACA) that would permit younger undocumented residents, those who came to the country before their sixteenth birthday and were less than thirty years old, to be given a temporary work visa, rather than be deported. DACA relied on "prosecutorial discretion" given to Department of Homeland Security officials to grant "deferred action" to those who sought the temporary visa. The decision was estimated to allow up to eight hundred thousand young immigrants the chance to remain in the country with the legal protections of a temporary, and renewable, work visa. While the move was not as ambitious as discussions of immigration reform in Congress, the president used his somewhat limited executive authority to make the change.

3. Based on a phone interview with Emily Manna, June 2012.

4. Based on an interview with Hoda Elshishtawy, June 2012.

5. For the full results see http://www.gallup.com/poll/116260/muslim-americans-exemplify-diversity-potential.aspx.

6. Based on an interview with Salah Mustafa, December 2012.

7. Data drawn from publicly available information on the website of the Center for Responsive Politics, opensecrets.org, in July 2012.

8. From the campaign website http://rothmanfornewjersey.com, which was discontinued prior to the publication of this book.

9. The campaign posted a link to an article, http://www.jta.org/2012/01/10/news-opinion/politics/in-n-j-pro-israel-stalwart-rothman-faces-a-primary-battle.

10. See data from the Center for Responsive Politics, http://www.opensecrets.org/industries/recips.php?Ind=Q05&cycle=2012&recipdetail=H&Mem=Y&sortorder=U.

11. To read the information see http://www.investigativeproject.org/3546/islamist-fellow-traveler-rep-bill-pascrell.

12. To read the I Vote Israel information see http://www.northjersey.com/news/more-progressive-than-pascrell-rothman-tells-editorial-board-1.1213946.

13. For the full bill see http://www.legislature.mi.gov/%28S%28npf03ervitqtju4ncqfu psqy%29%29/mileg.aspx?page=getobject&objectname=2011-SB-0754.

14. For more information and to read the testimony see http://www.demos.org/sites/default/files/publications/Testimony_SB754_751_803_Michigan_Demos.pdf.

15. Based on a phone interview with Doua Thor, July 31, 2012.

16. See the campaign website for Duckworth for Congress.

17. For more information on the Lead Foundation see http://www.leadcolorado.org/foundation-history/.

18. See the campaign website for Walsh for Congress, https://web.archive.org/web/20121012195756/http://walshforcongress.com/issues/foreign-affairs.

19. Based on an interview with Gerald Hankerson, April 4, 2013.

20. For the transcript of the speech see http://www.npr.org/2012/09/04/160574895/transcript-julian-castros-dnc-keynote-address.

4. A MODEL OF IMMIGRANT-SERVING ENGAGEMENT

1. Based on an interview with Steve Choi (who subsequently was hired as the executive director at the New York Immigrant Coalition), August 4, 2012.

2. Based on an interview with James Hong, August 23, 2012.

3. See the full KCCP mission statement at http://www.kccprinceton.org/about/mission-statement/.

4. Based on an interview with Young Lee, October 18, 2012.

5. See IRCO's mission statement at https://www.portlandoregon.gov/oni/60298.

6. See the CHIRLA website at http://www.chirla.org/.

7. Based on an interview with John Albert, May 31, 2013.

8. Based on an interview with Navdeep Singh, July 18, 2012.

9. Based on an interview with Kathleen Fermicola, February 14, 2013.

10. Based on an interview with Chi-Ser Tran, June 7, 2012.

11. Based on an interview with AABOA board members, May 30, 2014.

12. Based on an interview with Alan Kaplan, October 17, 2012.

13. Based on an interview with Leticia De La Vara, July 3, 2012.

14. Based on an interview with Hasan Jaber, February 25, 2013.

15. Based on an interview with Jerry Clarito, September 5, 2012.

16. Based on an interview with Helen Samhan, July 25, 2012.

17. Based on an interview with Tasha Moro and Jazmin Garcia, June 4, 2012.

18. See https://www.justice.gov/crt/minority-language-citizens.

19. Based on an interview with Priya Murthy, July 26, 2012.

20. Based on an interview with Navdeep Singh, July 18, 2012.

21. Based on an interview with Taz Ahmed, July 26, 2012.

22. Based on an e-mail from Ami Gandhi, January 29, 2013.

23. Based on an interview with Ali Najmi, August 2, 2012.

24. Based on a phone interview with Ami Gandhi, August 7, 2012.

25. Based on a phone interview with David Castillo, July 17, 2012.

26. Based on an interview with Hoda Elshishtawy, June 26, 2012.

27. Based on an interview with Jazmin Garcia, June 4, 2012.

28. Based on an interview with Amrita Singh, July 11, 2012.

29. Based on a phone interview with Gregory Cendana, June 12, 2012.

30. Based on an interview with Carolina McCready, September 6, 2012.

31. Based on a phone interview with Abby Mills, September 5, 2013.

32. Based on an interview with Alan Kaplan, October 17, 2012.

33. Based on a phone interview with Dave Heinan, March 8, 2013.

34. Based on an interview with Nadia Tonova, March 26, 2013.

5. FROM MISSION TO ELECTORAL STRATEGY

1. Based on an e-mail exchange with Dale Asis, September 6, 2012. The organization ended its operations in 2014.

2. Based on an interview with Chaitali Roy, October 18, 2013.

3. But a question remains as to whether these electoral tactics can actually be conceived as a single index. Do they group together along a single reliable measure, or are there in fact multiple indices of electoral work? In order to test this, I used factor analysis with varimax rotated factors to tease out whether the nine individual tactics align along one or more dimensions. The factor analysis revealed that there was one dominant dimension (eigenvalue of 3.41) and two secondary dimensions (eigenvalues of .68 and .44) along which these dimensions align. Because the eigenvalues were so low for the other two dimensions, they cannot be treated as important dimensions and were disregarded. The single, dominant factor, electoral engagement, suggests that the simple electoral index is the continuum along which immigrant-serving electoral work aligns.

4. As a result, that eight-item measure had a low mean of .96 and a standard deviation of 1.62. Though there is a leftward skew in the data toward no tactics, there is evidence of a range of tactical choices from weakly engaged to strongly engaged.

5. To measure publicly focused, I coded (voter registration, voter mobilization, joining a coalition, providing information to community, and issuing policy briefs on domestic issues / issuing policy briefs on foreign policy issues). To measure private focused, I coded (monitoring campaign news, translating voter information, and website). Each measure then is a dichotomous variable equal to 1 if the respondent engaged in at least one of these tactics and zero otherwise.

6. To measure voter focused, I coded (voter registration, voter mobilization, translating, providing information to the community, and website). To measure issue focused, I coded (monitoring the news, issuing policy briefs on domestic issues, and issuing policy briefs on foreign policy issues). Each measure then is a dichotomous variable equal to 1 if the respondent engaged in at least one of these tactics and zero otherwise.

7. There was also the possibility that resources might interact with organizational characteristics, which then lead to the choice of electoral tactics. It may be the case that an organization chooses a very narrow, single-issue mission because of limited resources, and that the narrow mission then leads to predictable choices of only a small number of electoral tactics. In fact, though, the survey respondents suggest that this complication does not bear out in reality. Respondents with a more multifaceted mission had statistically the same amount of resources as those with a single-issue mission, though there are small differences at the tails: a larger portion of high-revenue nonprofits had a multifaceted mission (31.1 percent) than did low-revenue nonprofits (18.9 percent). Similarly, organizational age measured in years was no different between multifaceted and single-issue respondents. This suggests that the varied nature of the nonprofit's mission, revenue, and age are each generally independent factors in relation to electioneering.

8. The coding scheme focused on the initial "splash" page for each organization. If the organization's splash page contained a link, mention, icon, or other reference to Facebook or Twitter, it was coded as 1. If Facebook or Twitter had no mention, it was coded as zero. The same procedure was used for 2012, 2011, and 2010, using the archives available at archive.org. If the organization's website was not available or not included in the archive, the organization was dropped as missing. I thank Noah Ginter for his assistance with this aspect of the project. Sections of this analysis appeared in a 2015 article titled "The Institutional Digital Divide: Immigrant-Serving Nonprofit Organization Adoptions of Social Media," in *Social Science Computer Review*.

9. Based on a phone interview with Juan Alfaro, January 17, 2013.

10. Based on a phone interview with Lindolfo Carballo, October 19, 2013.

11. Based on a phone interview with Diana Mejia, March 28, 2014, and Ana Bonilla Martinez, April 4, 2014.

12. Interview with Dr. Joy Cherian, July 9, 2012.

13. Based on a phone interview with Remziya Suleyman, July 17, 2012.

14. To read the ACO mission see http://acotn.org/about-us/missionobjectives/.

15. Based on an interview with Joy Bruce, September 18, 2013.

6. CHOOSING WHERE TO FOCUS

1. See http://www.pewresearch.org/2012/08/06/ask-the-expert-how-many-us-sikhs/.

2. See http://archive.adl.org/learn/ext_us/volksfront/crime.asp?LEARN_SubCat= Extremism_in_America&xpicked=3&item=volksfront.

3. According to the U.S. Department of Justice, "A hate crime can be generally defined as a crime which in whole or part is motivated by the offender's bias toward the victim's status. . . . Hate crimes are intended to hurt and intimidate individuals, because they are perceived to be different with respect to their race, color, religion, national origin, sexual orientation, gender or disability. The purveyors of hate use physical violence, verbal threats of violence, vandalism, and in some cases weapons, explosives, and arson, to instill fear in their victims, leaving them vulnerable to subsequent attacks and feeling alienated, helpless, suspicious and fearful." See http://www.justice.gov/archive/crs/pubs/ university92003.htm#21.

4. See press release at http://sikhcoalition.org/advisories/2013/victory-10-months- after-oak-creek-fbi-group-votes-to-track-sikh-hate-crimes.

5. For more information about CAIR-Chicago see http://www.cairchicago.org/ about-us/.

6. Based on an interview with John Albert, May 31, 2013.

7. Based on an interview with Ved Chaudhary, July 16, 2012.

8. Based on an e-mail from Jumana Judeh, June 9, 2013.

9. Based on an interview with Remziya Suleyman, July 19, 2012.

10. See http://www.maketheroad.org/article.php?ID=1981.

11. See http://www.maketheroad.org/article.php?ID=1981.

12. See http://www.licivicengagement.org/advisory_10_26_2011.

13. Based on an interview with Dr. M. Zaher Sahloul, November 14, 2012.

14. Based on an interview with Jazmin Garcia, June 4, 2012.

15. Based on an interview with Abdelnasser Rashid, April 25, 2013.

16. Based on an interview with Ami Gandhi, August 7, 2012.

17. An earlier version of this analysis was presented at the "Violence and the City" workshop at the City University of New York, Murphy Institute, May 8, 2015.

18. There are more sophisticated analytical approaches that adjust for multistage decision making. Because of the relatively small sample size, those approaches were not feasible here. Also, because those respondents that did not engage in any tactics did not face a second-stage choice of venue, including them in a more sophisticated model did not fit.

19. New York, New Jersey, and Illinois are "individualistic," and Michigan is "moralistic."

20. Because of concerns about multicollinearity between the variable for traditionalistic states and the dummy variable for Florida, I chose to use the former and drop the later in the analysis.

21. The variable ranges from .49 percent to 25 percent, with a mean of 11.05 percent (standard deviation of 6.24). Because of this large skew, there are only a small number with very large percentages of naturalized citizens; I converted this variable to its log form in order to avoid violating the statistical assumption of linearity of independent variables.

22. Based on an interview with Juan Alfaro, January 17, 2013.

23. Based on an e-mail from Ami Gandhi, January 29, 2013.

24. The pseudo-R^2 values of .27 and .22 suggest models that reasonably fit the data.

CONCLUSION: BOLDLY REPRESENTING IMMIGRANTS IN TOUGH TIMES

1. To read the full court ruling see http://www.courts.wa.gov/index.cfm?fa=controller.managefiles&filePath=Opinions&fileName=860211.pdf.

2. For the full survey results see http://www.naasurvey.com/resources/Presentations/2012-aapipes-national.pdf.

3. To see the data go to http://www.census.gov/prod/2013pubs/p20–568.pdf and http://www.pewresearch.org/fact-tank/2013/05/08/six-take-aways-from-the-census-bureaus-voting-report/.

4. For the full Supreme Court decision see http://www.supremecourt.gov/opinions/12pdf/12–96_6k47.pdf.

5. For the full report see http://growthopp.gop.com/rnc_growth_opportunity_book_2013.pdf.

6. Based on an interview with Bill Vandenberg, October 22, 2012.

TECHNICAL APPENDIX

1. I had graduate assistants search the name of each organization to identify an e-mail contact for each organization. Approximately one-third of the organizations had no available e-mail address and were thus contacted solely by traditional mail.

2. Twenty-seven organizations responded to the survey but did not include the name of their organizations, which was permitted in the instructions to the survey. These responses could not be matched to any organizational characteristics and are not included in the comparative analysis, nor in the bivariate and multivariate analysis to come later.

3. See their full report at http://neworganizing.com/wp-content/uploads/2010/11/NOI-FCCP-Tech-Survey-2009.pdf.

4. I tested each model with a full set of dummy variables for state effects. The state variables were not significant in any of the models and did not change the sign or significance of any of the other variables. For that reason, I present the results with only the Florida dummy compared to other.

Works Cited

Ahlquist, J., and M. Levi. 2013. *In the Interests of Others: Organizations and Social Activism*. Princeton, NJ: Princeton University Press.

Allen, M., and J. Vandehei. 2013. "The Koch Brothers' Secret Bank." *Politico,* September 11. http://www.politico.com/story/2013/09/behind-the-curtain-exclusive-the-koch-brothers-secret-bank-096669#ixzz2es3AQ8ei.

Ambinder, M. 2009. "How Democrats Won the Data War in 2008." *Atlantic,* October 5. http://www.theatlantic.com/politics/archive/2009/10/exclusive-how-democrats-won-the-data-war-in-2008/27647/.

Andersen, K. 2010. *New Immigrant Communities: Finding a Place in Local Politics*. Boulder, CO: Lynne Reiner.

Anderson, E. 2008. "Experts, Ideas, and Policy Change: The Russell Sage Foundation and Small Loan Reform, 1900–1941." *Theory & Society* 37 (3): 271–310.

Arnsberger, P., M. Ludlum, M. Riley, and M. Stanton. 2008. "A History of the Tax-Exempt Sector: An SOI Perspective," 105–35. Washington, DC: Internal Revenue Service.

Assaf, A. 2012a. "Congressman Pascrell Is Best for New Jersey." NJ.com, May 28. http://blog.nj.com/dr_aref_assaf/2012/05/congressman_pascrell_is_best_for_new_jersey.html.

———. 2012b. "Rothman Is Israel's Man in District 9." NJ.com, February 19. http://blog.nj.com/dr_aref_assaf/2012/02/rothman_is_israels_man_in_district_9_pascrell_is_the_peoples_choice.html.

Audebert, C. 2009. "Residential Patterns and Political Empowerment among Jamaicans and Haitians in the U.S. Metropolis: The Role of Ethnicity in New York and South Florida." *Human Architecture: Journal of the Sociology of Self-Knowledge* 7 (4): 53–68.

Avery, M., and D. McLaughlin. 2013. *The Federalist Society: How Conservatives Took the Law Back from the Liberals*. Nashville, TN: Vanderbilt University Press.

Baldauf, A., H. Reisinger, and W. Moncrief. 1999. "Examining Motivations to Refuse in Industrial Mail Surveys." *Journal of Market Research Society* 41 (3): 345–53.

Barreto, M. A. 2005. "Latino Immigrants at the Polls: Foreign-Born Voter Turnout in the 2002 Election." *Political Research Quarterly* 58 (1): 79–86.

Barreto, M. A., and J. Muñoz. 2003. "Reexamining the 'Politics of In-Between': Political Participation among Mexican Immigrants in the United States." *Hispanic Journal of Behavioral Sciences* 25 (November): 427–47.

Baumgartner, F. R., and B. D. Jones. 1993. *Agendas and Instability in American Politics*. Chicago: University of Chicago Press.

Beltran, C. 2010. *The Trouble with Unity: Latino Politics and the Creation of Identity*. New York: Oxford University Press.

Bernhardt, A., R. Milkman, N. Theodore, D. Heckathorn, M. Auer, J. DeFillipis, A. Gonzalez, V. Narro, J. Perelshten, D. Polson, and M. Spiller. 2009. "Broken Laws: Unprotected Workers: Violations of Employment and Labor Laws in American Cities." National Employment Law Project. http://www.unprotectedworkers.org/index.php/broken_laws/index.

Berry, J. M. 1999. *The New Liberalism: The Rising Power of Citizen Groups*. Washington, DC: Brookings Institution Press.

Berry, J. M., with D. Arons. 2003. *A Voice for Nonprofits.* Washington, DC: Brookings Institution Press.

Birkland, T. A. 1997. *After Disaster: Agenda Setting, Public Policy, and Focusing Events.* Washington, DC: Georgetown University Press.

Bloemraad, I., and E. de Graauw. 2011. "Immigrant Integration and Policy in the United States: A Loosely Stitched Patchwork." Institute for Research on Labor and Employment, Working Paper Series.

Bloemraad, I., and C. Trost. 2008. "It's a Family Affair: Intergenerational Mobilization in the Spring 2006 Protests." *American Behavioral Scientist* 52 (4): 507–32.

Bob, C. 2012. *The Global Right Wing and the Clash of World Politics.* New York: Cambridge University Press.

Boehmke, F. J., S. Gailmard, and J. Patty. 2013. "Business as Usual: Interest Group Access and Representation across Policy-Making Venues." *Journal of Public Policy* 33 (01): 3–33.

Borchers, C., and A. Wirzbicki. 2012. "Asian Americans Voted More Heavily for Barack Obama." *Boston Globe*, November 9. https://www.bostonglobe.com/news/politics/2012/11/09/asian-americans-voted-more-heavily-for-barack-obama-than/gdcKynV3Hq3OgSeOlNEhHM/story.html.

Boris, E. 2006. "Introduction—Nonprofit Organizations in a Democracy: Varied Roles and Responsibilities." In *Nonprofits and Government: Collaboration and Conflict*, 2nd ed., edited by E. Boris and E. Steurele, 1–36. Washington, DC: Urban Institute Press.

Boushey, G., and A. Luedtke. 2011. "Immigrants across the U.S. Federal Laboratory: Explaining State-Level Innovation in Immigration Policy." *State Politics & Policy Quarterly* 11 (4): 390–414.

Bravender, R. 2012. "Kraft Abandons Conservative Group." *Politico*, April 4. http://www.politico.com/story/2012/04/kraft-flees-group-over-stand-your-ground-074893.

Brown, H. 2015. *Tea Party Divided: The Hidden Diversity of a Maturing Movement.* Santa Barbara, CA: Praeger.

Buenavista, T. 2010. "Issues Affecting US Filipino Student Access to Post-secondary Education: A Critical Race Theory Perspective." *Journal of Education for Students Placed at Risk* 15:114–26.

Burghart, D. 2012. "View from the Top: A Report on Six National Tea Party Organizations." In *Steep: The Precipitous Rise of the Tea Party*, edited by L. Rosenthal and C. Trost, 67–97. Berkeley: University of California Press.

Caldeira, G. A., M. Hojnacki, and J. Wright. 2000. "The Lobbying Activities of Organized Interests in Federal Judicial Nominations." *Journal of Politics* 62 (1): 51–69.

Campbell, C. 2012a. "ABC Hosts NY-6 Candidate Forum." *New York Observer*, May 5. http://observer.com/2012/05/abc-hosts-ny-6-candidate-forum-video/.

———. 2012b. "Meng Touts Support from Latino Pols." *New York Observer*, May 5. http://observer.com/2012/04/meng-touts-support-from-latino-pols/.

Carrigan, W. D., and C. Webb. 2003. "The Lynching of Persons of Mexican Origin or Descent in the United States: 1948–1928." *Journal of Social History* 37 (2): 411–38.

Chan, S. 2012. "Grace Meng Counting on Asian Immigrant Voters in Her Bid for Congress." Feet in Two Worlds, June 25. http://fi2w.org/2012/06/25/grace-meng-counting-on-asian-immigrant-voters-in-her-bid-for-congress/.

Chen, D. W. 2012. "A Breakthrough Candidate and Potential Star." *New York Times*, June 27. http://www.nytimes.com/2012/06/28/nyregion/grace-meng-is-rising-star-for-asian-new-yorkers.html?pagewanted=all.

Cheng, C. I.-F. 2013. *Citizens of Asian America: Democracy and Race during the Cold War.* New York: NYU Press.

Child, C. D., and K. A. Gr<ø>nbjerg. 2007. "Nonprofit Advocacy Organizations: Their Characteristics and Activities." *Social Science Quarterly* 88 (1): 259–81.

Cho, W. T. 1999. "Naturalization, Socialization, Participation: Immigrants and (non) Voting." *Journal of Politics* 61 (4): 1140–55.

Cho, W. K. T., J. G. Gimpel, and T. Wu. 2006. "Clarifying the Role of SES in Political Participation: Policy Threat and Arab Mobilization." *Journal of Politics* 68 (4): 977–91.

Christian, L., S. Keeter, K. Purcell, and A. Smith. 2010. "Assessing the Cell Phone Challenge." Pew Research Center, May 20. http://www.pewresearch.org/2010/05/20/assessing-the-cell-phone-challenge/.

Cobb, R. W., and C. Elder. 1983. *Participation in American Politics: The Dynamics of Agenda-Building.* Boston: Allyn & Bacon.

Cooper, M. 2013. "After Ruling, States Rush to Enact Voting Laws." *New York Times*, July 5. http://www.nytimes.com/2013/07/06/us/politics/after-Supreme-Court-ruling-states-rush-to-enact-voting-laws.html?pagewanted=all.

Cordero-Guzmán, H. 2005. "Community-Based Organisations and Migration in New York City." *Journal of Ethnic and Migration Studies* 31 (5): 889–909.

Cordero-Guzmán, H., N. Martin, V. Quiroz-Becerra, and N. Theodore. 2008. "Voting with Their Feet: Nonprofit Organizations and Immigrant Mobilization." *American Behavioral Scientist* 52 (4): 598–617.

Cordes, J. J., J. R. Henig, E. Twombly, and J. Saunders. 1999. "The Effects of Expanded Donor Choice in United Way Campaigns on Nonprofit Human Service Providers in the Washington, D.C., Metropolitan Area." *Nonprofit and Voluntary Sector Quarterly* 28 (2): 127–51.

Costain, A. N. 1981. "Representing Women: The Transition from Social Movement to Interest Group." *Western Political Quarterly* 34 (1): 100–113.

Crenshaw, K. 1991. "Mapping the Margins: Intersectionality, Identity Politics, and Violence against Women of Color." *Stanford Law Review* 43:1241–99.

Dahl, R. A. 1961. *Who Governs?* New Haven, CT: Yale University Press.

de Castro, A., G. C. Gee, and D. Takeuchi. 2008. "Job-Related Stress and Chronic Health Conditions among Filipino Immigrants." *Journal of Immigrant and Minority Health* 10 (6): 551–58.

de Graauw, E. 2008. Nonprofit Organizations: Agents of Immigrant Political Incorporation in Urban America. In *Civic Hopes and Political Realities: Immigrants, Community Organizations, and Political Engagement*, edited by S. K. Ramakrishnan and I. Bloemraad, 323–50. New York: Russell Sage Foundation Press.

de Graauw, E., S. Gleeson, and I. Bloemraad. 2012. "Funding Immigrant Organizations: Suburban Free-Riding and Local Civic Presence." New York: Center for Nonprofit Strategy and Management—Working Paper Series.

de Leon, E., M. Maronick, C. De Vita, and E. Boris. 2009. "Community-Based Organizations and Immigrant Integration in the Washington, D.C., Metropolitan Area." Washington, DC: Urban Institute.

DeSipio, L. 1996. "Making Citizens or Good Citizens? Naturalization as a Predictor of Organizational and Electoral Behavior among Latino Immigrants." *Hispanic Journal of Behavioral Sciences* 18 (2): 194–213.

——. 2002. "Immigrant Organizing, Civic Outcomes: Civic Engagement, Political Activity, National Attachment, and Identify in Latino Immigrant Communities." Irvine, CA: Center for the Study of Democracy.

——. 2006. "Latino Civic and Political Participation." In *Hispanics and the Future of America*, edited by M. Tienda, 447–80. Washington, DC: National Academies Press.

Disch, L. 2012. "The Tea Party: A 'White Citizenship' Movement?" In *Steep: The Precipitous Rise of the Tea Party*, edited by L. Rosenthal and C. Trost, 133–51. Berkeley: University of California Press.

Dye, T. 2001. *Top Down Policymaking*. Ann Arbor: University of Michigan Press.

Dye, T., H. Ziegler, and L. Schubert. 2012. *The Irony of Democracy*. Boston: Wadsworth.

Eastman, C. L. S. 2012. *Shaping the Immigration Debate: Contending Civic Societies on the US-Mexico Border*. Boulder, CO: First Forum Press / Lynne Rienner.

Ecklund, E. H., and J. Z. Park. 2005. "Asian American Community Participation and Religion: Civic Model Minorities." *Journal of Asian American Studies* 6 (1): 1–22.

Elazar, D. 1966. *American Federalism: A View from the South*. New York: Crowell.

Elazar, D., V. Gray, and W. Spano. 1999. *Minnesota Politics and Government*. Lincoln: University of Nebraska Press.

Ennis, S., M. Ríos-Vargas, and N. Albert. 2011. "The Hispanic Population." *2012 Census Briefs*. Washington, DC: U.S. Census Bureau.

Erickson, R., G. C. Wright, and J. McIver. 1993. *Statehouse Democracy*. Cambridge: Cambridge University Press.

Esterling, K. M. 2007. "Buying Expertise: Campaign Contributions and Attention to Policy Analysis in Congressional Committees." *American Political Science Review* 101 (1): 93–109.

Fallin, A., R. Grana, and S. Glantz. 2013. "'To Quarterback behind the Scenes,' Third-Party Efforts: The Tobacco Industry and the Tea Party." *Tobacco Control* 0:1–10. http://tobaccocontrol.bmj.com/content/23/4/322. full?sid=73db454a-b664-4c6c-83d3-e98e90cd4262.

Farrell, J. 2012. "New Jersey Ninth District Primary Quickly 'Headed into the Toilet.'" Philly.com, May 31, 2012. http://articles.philly.com/2012-05-31/news/31923660_1_democratic-delegation-national-democratic-party-paterson.

Feldman, G. 2013. *The Irony of the Solid South: Democrats, Republicans, and Race, 1865–1944*. Birmingham: University of Alabama Press.

Ferris, J. M., and H. J. Harmssen. 2009. "Foundation Practices for Public Policy Engagement." Los Angeles: Center on Philanthropy and Public Policy, USC.

Fisher, P., and T. Pratt. 2006. "Political Culture and the Death Penalty." *Criminal Justice Policy Review* 1 (March): 46–60.

Fox News Latino. 2012. "Florida Puerto Ricans Draw Unprecedented Attention from Both Presidential Campaigns." Fox News, August 2. http://latino.foxnews.com/latino/politics/2012/08/02/florida-puerto-ricans-emerge-as-crucial-voting-bloc-for-romney-and-obama/.

Fraga, L. R. 2009. "Building through Exclusion: Anti-Immigrant Politics in the United States." In *Brining Outsiders In: Transatlantic Perspectives on Immigrant Political Incorporation*, edited by J. Hochschild and J. Mollenkopf, 176–92. Ithaca, NY: Cornell University Press.

Franz, M. 2008. *Choices and Changes: Interest Groups in the Electoral Process*. Philadelphia: Temple University Press.

García Bedolla, L., and M. Michelson. 2012. *Mobilizing Inclusion: Transforming the Electorate through Get-Out-the-Vote Campaigns*. New Haven, CT: Yale University Press.

Garrett, S. 1978. "Eastern European Ethnic Groups and American Foreign Policy." *Political Science Quarterly* 93 (2): 301–21.

Gioia, D. A., K. N. Price, A. Hamilton, and J. Thomas. 2010. "Forging an Identity: An Insider-Outsider Study of Processes Involved in the Formation of Organizational Identity." *Administrative Science Quarterly* 55 (1): 1–46.

Gleeson, S. 2011. "Where Are All the Immigrant Organizations? Reassessing the Scope of Civil Society for Immigrant Communities." Berkeley, CA: Institute for Research on Labor and Employment UC Berkeley.

———. 2012. *Conflicting Commitments: The Politics of Enforcing Immigrant Worker Rights in San Jose and Houston.* Ithaca, NY: Cornell University Press.

Gleeson, S., and I. Bloemraad. 2012. "Assessing the Scope of Immigrant Organizations: Official Undercounts and Actual Underrepresentation." *Nonprofit and Voluntary Sector Quarterly* 42 (2): 346–70.

Golway, T. 2014. *Machine Made: Tammany Hall and the Creation of Modern American Politics.* New York: Liveright.

Goss, K. 2013. *The Paradox of Gender Equality: How American Women's Groups Gained and Lost Their Public Voice.* Ann Arbor: University of Michigan Press.

Green, D., and A. Gerber. 2008. *Get Out the Vote: How to Increase Voter Turnout.* 2nd ed. Washington, DC: Brookings Institution Press.

Greer, C. 2013. *Black Ethnics: Race, Immigration, and the Pursuit of the American Dream.* New York: Oxford University Press.

Grossman, A. 2012. "Asians Starts Flexing Political Muscle." *Wall Street Journal,* July 5. http://www.wsj.com/articles/SB10001424052702304550004577509082609460166.

Grossmann, M. 2011. "Just Another Interest Group?" In *The Expanding Boundaries of Black Politics,* edited by G. Persons, 291–308. Piscataway, NJ: Transaction.

———. 2012. *The Not-So-Special Interests: Interest Groups, Public Representation, and American Governance.* Stanford, CA: Stanford University Press.

Gur, H. R. 2012. "King of Queens: An Unconventional Republican." *Times of Israel,* August 21. http://www.timesofisrael.com/king-of-queens-an-unconventional-republican/.

Hager, M. A., S. Wilson, T. Pollak, and P. M. Rooney. 2003. "Response Rates for Mail Surveys of Nonprofit Organizations: A Review and Empirical Test." *Nonprofit and Voluntary Sector Quarterly* 32 (2): 252–67.

Haider-Markel, D. P. 2006. "Acting as Fire Alarms with Law Enforcement? Interest Groups and Bureaucratic Activity on Hate Crime." *American Politics Research* 34 (1): 95–130.

Hajnal, Z., and T. Lee. 2011. *Why Americans Don't Join the Party: Race, Immigration, and the Failure (of Political Parties) to Engage the Electorate.* Princeton, NJ: Princeton University Press.

Hajnal, Z., and J. Trounstine. 2005. "Where Turnout Matters: The Consequences of Uneven Turnout in City Politics." *Journal of Politics* 67 (2): 515–35.

Hall, R. L., and A. V. Deardorff. 2006. "Lobbying as Legislative Subsidy." *American Political Science Review* 100 (1): 69–84.

Halpin, D. 2014. *The Organization of Political Interest Groups.* London: Routledge.

Han, H. 2014. *How Organizations Develop Activists: Civic Associations and Leadership in the 21st Century.* New York: Oxford University Press.

Hero, R., and C. Tolbert. 1996. "A Racial/Ethnic Diversity Interpretation of Politics and Policy in the States of the U.S." *American Journal of Political Science* 40 (3): 851–71.

———. 2004. "Minority Attitudes and Citizen Attitudes about Government Responsiveness in the American States: Do Social and Institutional Context Matter?" *British Journal of Political Science* 34 (1): 109–21.

Hochschild, J., and J. Mollenkopf, eds. 2009. *Bringing Outsiders In: Transatlantic Perspectives on Immigrant Political Incorporation.* Ithaca, NY: Cornell University Press.

———. 2010. "Immigrant Political Incorporation: Comparing Success in the United States and Western Europe." *Ethnic and Racial Studies* 33 (1): 19–38.

Hoffman, G. 2012. "NJ Race Figures in Israel 'Get-out-the-Vote' Drive." *New Jersey Jewish News,* July 2. http://njjewishnews.com/article/9924/nj-race-figures-in-israel-get-out-the-vote-drive#.Vm7pgEorKM8.

Hoffman, J. 2013. "Take Control of the Message through a Media Frame: A Case Study in Cooperating Recasting." *Nonprofit Quarterly.* January.

Hofstadter, R. 1965. *The Paranoid Style in American Politics*. New York: Random House / Vintage.

Hojnacki, M., and D. C. Kimball. 1998. "Organized Interests and the Decision of Whom to Lobby in Congress." *American Political Science Review* 92 (4): 775–90.

Holyoke, T. T. 2003. "Choosing Battlegrounds: Interest Group Lobbying across Multiple Venues." *Political Research Quarterly* 56 (3): 325–36.

Holyoke, T. T., H. Brown, and J. Henig. 2012. "Shopping in the Political Arena: Strategic State and Local Venue Selection by Advocates." *State and Local Government Review* 44 (1): 9–20.

Horwitz, R. 2013. *America's Right: Anti-establishment Conservatism from Goldwater to the Tea Party*. Malden, MA: Polity.

Howell, S., and A. Shryock. 2003. "Cracking Down on Diaspora: Arab Detroit and America's 'War on Terror.'" *Anthropological Quarterly* 76 (3): 443–62.

Hsiao, A. 2001. "Chinatown in Limbo." *Village Voice*, May 29. http://www.villagevoice.com/news/chinatown-in-limbo-6415721.

Hu, W. 2013. "South Asians in Queens to Get Ballots in Bengali." *New York Times*, July 2. http://www.nytimes.com/2013/07/03/nyregion/south-asians-in-queens-to-get-ballots-in-bengali.html?_r=0.

Hung, C.-K. R. 2007. "Immigrant Nonprofit Organizations in U.S. Metropolitan Areas." *Nonprofit and Voluntary Sector Quarterly* 36 (4): 707–29.

Hung, C.-K. R., and P. Ong. 2012. "Sustainability of Asian-American Nonprofit Organizations in U.S. Metropolitan Areas." *Nonprofit and Voluntary Sector Quarterly* 41 (6): 1136–52.

Innis-Jiménez, M. 2013. *Steel Barrio: The Great Mexican Migration to South Chicago, 1915–1940*. New York: NYU Press.

Issenberg, S. 2012. *The Victory Lab: The Secret Science of Winning Campaigns*. New York: Crown.

Jacobson, R. D. 2011. "The Politics of Belonging: Interest Group Identity and Agenda Setting on Immigration." *American Politics Research* 39 (6): 993–1018.

Jamal, A. 2005. "The Political Participation and Engagement of Muslim Americans: Mosque Involvement and Group Consciousness." *American Politics Research* 33 (4): 521–44.

Jamal, A., and N. C. Naber. 2008. *Race and Arab Americans before and after 9/11: From Invisible Citizens to Visible Subjects*. Syracuse, NY: Syracuse University Press.

Junn, J. 1999. "Participation in Liberal Democracy: The Political Assimilation of Immigrants and Ethnic Minorities in the US." *American Behavioral Scientist* (June/July): 1416–37.

——. 2012. "Mobilizing Group Consciousness." In *Transforming Politics, Transforming America: The Political and Civic Incorporation of Immigrants in the United States*, edited by T. Lee, S. K. Ramakrishnan, and R. Ramírez, 32–50. Charlottesville: University of Virginia Press.

Kaplan, T. 2012. "Date Blamed for Low Vote in Primaries." *New York Times*, June 27. http://www.nytimes.com/2012/06/28/nyregion/ny-congressional-primaries-drew-few-voters.html.

Kaplowitz, C. A. 2005. *LULAC, Mexican Americans, and National Policy*. College Station: Texas A&M University Press.

Karch, A. 2013. *Early Start: Preschool Politics in the United States*. Ann Arbor: University of Michigan Press.

Karpathakis, A. 1999. "Home Society Politics and Immigrant Political Incorporation: The Case of Greek Immigrants in New York City." *International Migration Review* 33:55–78.

Kasdan, D. 2012. "States Restrictions on Voter Registration Drives." Brennan Center for Justice.

Kingdon, J. W. 1995. *Agendas, Alternatives, and Public Policies*. Boston: Little, Brown & Co.

Kroll, A. 2013. "The Evangelist." *American Prospect*, October 9. http://prospect.org/article/evangelist.

Kurien, P. 2001. "Constructing 'Indianness' in Southern California: The Role of Hindu and Muslim Indian Immigrants." In *Asian and Latino Immigrants in a Restructuring Economy: The Metamorphosis of Southern California*, edited by M. López-Garza and D. R. Diaz, 289–312. Stanford, CA: Stanford University Press.

Lee, T. 2000. "The Backdoor and the Backlash: Campaign Finance and the Politicization of Chinese Americans." *Asian American Policy Review* 9:30–55.

———. 2008. "Civic Engagement as a Pathway to Partisanship Acquisition for Asian Americans." In *The State of Asian America: Trajectory of Civic and Political Engagement*, edited by P. Ong, 207–40. Los Angeles: LEAP.

LeRoux, K. 2011. "Examining Implementation of the National Voter Registration Act by Nonprofit Organizations: An Institutional Explanation." *Policy Studies Journal* 39 (4): 565–89.

LeRoux, K., and K. Krawczyk. 2013. "Can Nonprofit Organizations Increase Voter Turnout? Findings from an Agency-Based Voter Mobilization Experiment." *Nonprofit and Voluntary Sector Quarterly* 43 (2): 272–92.

Lester, K., and E. Peterson. 2012. "New Indian SuperPAC Jumps into Duckworth-Walsh Race." *Daily Herald*, October 31. http://www.dailyherald.com/article/20121031/news/710319609/.

Lien, P.-t. 2001. *Making of Asian America through Political Participation*. Philadelphia: Temple University Press.

———. 2004. "Asian Americans and Voting Participation: Comparing Racial and Ethnic Differences in Recent U.S. Elections." *International Migration Review* 38 (2): 493–517.

Lien, P.-t., M. Conway, and J. Wong. 2004. *The Politics of Asian Americans: Diversity and Community*. New York: Routledge.

Lienas, B. 2012. "Obama Win Fueled by Latino Voter Muscle, Fox Exit Polls Show." Fox News Latino, November 8. http://latino.foxnews.com/latino/politics/2012/11/08/obama-win-fueled-by-latino-voter-muscle-fox-exit-polls-show/#ixzz2eJzP11Tn.

Lieske, J. 2010. "The Changing Regional Subcultures of the American States and the Utility of a New Cultural Measure." *Political Research Quarterly* 63:538–52.

Lim, E. T. 2013. "The Anti-Federalist Strand in Progressive Politics and Political Thought." *Political Research Quarterly* 66 (1): 32–45.

Lopez, M. H., and D. Dockterman. 2011. "U.S. Hispanic Country of Origin Counts for Nation, Top 30 Metropolitan Areas." Washington, DC: Pew Hispanic Research Center.

MacLean, N. 1994. *Behind the Mask of Chivalry: The Making of the Second Ku Klux Klan*. New York: Oxford University Press.

Mahoney, C. 2008. *Brussels versus the Beltway: Advocacy in the United States and the European Union*. Washington, DC: Georgetown University Press.

Mandeville, J. 2007. "Public Policy Grant Making: Building Organizational Capacity among Nonprofit Grantees." *Nonprofit and Voluntary Sector Quarterly* 36 (2): 282–98.

Márquez, B. 2014. *Democratizing Texas Politics: Race, Identity, and Mexican American Empowerment, 1954–2002*. Austin: University of Texas Press.

Martin, I. W. 2013. *The Rich People's Movements: Grassroots Campaigns to Untax the One Percent*. New York: Oxford University Press.

Martinez, G. 2008. "Latinos Push for Cabinet Posts." *Politico*, November 7. http://www.politico.com/story/2008/11/latinos-push-for-cabinet-posts-015375.

Masuoka, N., and J. Junn. 2013. *The Politics of Belonging: Race, Public Opinion, and Immigration*. Chicago: University of Chicago Press.

McAdam, D., and S. Tarrow. 2010. "Ballots and Barricades: On the Reciprocal Relationship between Elections and Social Movements." *Perspectives on Politics* 8 (2): 529–42.

McCarthy, J., and M. Zald. 2001. "The Enduring Vitality of the Resource Mobilization Theory of Social Movements." In *Handbook of Sociological Theory*, edited by J. Turner, 533–66. New York: Springer.

McIlwain, C., and S. Caliendo. 2012. *Race Appeal: How Candidates Invoke Race in US Political Campaigns*. Philadelphia: Temple University Press.

McKay, A. 2011. "The Decision to Lobby Bureaucrats." *Public Choice* 147 (1–2): 123–38.

McKee, S. C., D. A. Smith, W. D. Hicks, and M. Sellers. 2013. "Evolution of an Issue: Voter ID Laws in the American States." Paper presented at APSA 2013 Annual Meeting, Chicago. http://ssrn.com/abstract=2300630.

McMahon, S. H. 1999. *Social Control and Public Intellect: The Legacy of Edward A. Ross*. New Brunswick, NJ: Transaction.

McNutt, J. G., and K. M. Boland. 1999. "Electronic Advocacy by Nonprofit Organizations in Social Welfare Policy." *Nonprofit and Voluntary Sector Quarterly* 28 (4): 432–51.

McQuade, A. 2011. "Why LWV Florida Can't Register Voters." League of Women Voters, December 8. http://lwv.org/blog/why-lwv-florida-cant-register-voters.

Merry, M. K. 2010. "Emotional Appeals in Environmental Group Communications." *American Politics Research* 38 (5): 862–89.

Meyer, D. S. 1993. "Protest Cycles and Political Process: American Peace Movements in the Nuclear Age." *Political Research Quarterly* 46 (3): 451–79.

Meyer, S. 1980. "Adapting the Immigrant to the Line: Americanization in the Ford Factory, 1914–1921." *Journal of Social History* 14 (1): 67–82.

Michelson, M. 2003. "Political Efficacy among California Latinos." *Latino Research Review* 5 (2–3): 5–15.

Mintrom, M. 2000. *Policy Entrepreneurs and School Choice*. Washington, DC: Georgetown University Press.

Mireles, G. F. 2013. *Continuing La Causa: Organizing Labor in California's Strawberry Fields*. Boulder, CO: Lynne Rienner.

Monogan, J. E. 2013. "The Politics of Immigrant Policy in the 50 US States, 2005–2011." *Journal of Public Policy* 33 (01): 35–64.

Montalto, N. V. 2012. "A History and Analysis of Recent Immigrant Integration Initiatives in Five States." Cranford, NJ: Diversity Dynamics.

Montalvo, I. 2012. "Baja fuego Alan Grayson por comercial de la 'pava.'" *La Prensa*, August 7. http://www.laprensafl.com/Bajo_fuego_Alan_Grayson_por_comercial_de_la_pava.

Mosley, J. E. 2011. "Institutionalization, Privatization, and Political Opportunity: What Tactical Choices Reveal about the Policy Advocacy of Human Service Nonprofits." *Nonprofit and Voluntary Sector Quarterly* 40 (3): 435–57.

——. 2014. "From Skid Row to the Statehouse: How Nonprofit Homeless Service Providers Overcome Barriers to Policy Advocacy Involvement." In *Nonprofits and Advocacy: Engaging Community and Government in an Era of Retrenchment*, edited by R. Pekkanen, S. Smith, and Y. Tsujinaka, 107–35. Baltimore: Johns Hopkins University Press.

Mossakowski, K. 2007. "Are Immigrants Healthier? The Case of Depression among Filipino Americans." *Social Psychology Quarterly* 70 (3): 290–304.

Nicholson-Crotty, J. 2009. "The Stages and Strategies of Advocacy among Nonprofit Reproductive Health Providers." *Nonprofit and Voluntary Sector Quarterly* 38 (6): 1044–53.

Olson, M. 1971. *The Logic of Collective Action: Public Goods and the Theory of Groups.* Cambridge, MA: Harvard University Press.

Parker, C., and M. A. Barreto. 2013. *Change They Can't Believe In: The Tea Party and Reactionary Politics in America.* Princeton, NJ: Princeton University Press.

Parmar, I. 2012. *Foundations of the American Century: The Ford, Carnegie, and Rockefeller Foundations in the Rise of American Power.* New York: Columbia University Press.

Pekkanen, R., and S. R. Smith. 2014. "Nonprofit Advocacy in Seattle and Washington, DC." In *Nonprofits and Advocacy: Engaging Community and Government in an Era of Retrenchment*, edited by R. Pekkanen, S. R. Smith, and Y. Tsujinaka, 47–65. Baltimore: Johns Hopkins University Press.

Peters, J. 2010. "Planned Switch to G.O.P. Stirs New York Governor Race." *New York Times*, March 18. http://www.nytimes.com/2010/03/18/nyregion/18levy. html?pagewanted=all&_r=1.

Pew Research Center. 2012. "The Rise of Asian Americans." Washington, DC. http://www.pewsocialtrends.org/2012/06/19/the-rise-of-asian-americans/.

Portes, A., C. Escobar, and R. Arana. 2008. "Bridging the Gap: Transnational and Ethnic Organizations in the Political Incorporation of Immigrants in the United States." *Ethnic and Racial Studies* 31 (6): 1056–90.

Postel, C. 2012. "The Tea Parties in Historical Perspective: A Conservative Response to a Crisis of Political Economy." In *Steep: The Precipitous Rise of the Tea Party*, edited by L. Rosenthal and C. Trost, 35–46. Berkeley: University of California Press.

Powers, S. 2012. "Congressional Race Could Pit Political vs. Ethnic Identity." *Orlando Sentinel*, March 29. http://articles.orlandosentinel.com/2012-03-29/news/os-grayson-quinones-distrit-9-2-20120326_1_hispanic-republicans-hispanic-voters-hispanic-community.

Pralle, S. 2006. "The 'Mouse That Roared': Agenda Setting in Canadian Pesticides Politics." *Policy Studies Journal* 34 (2): 171–94.

——. 2009. Shopping Around: Environmental Organizations and the Search for Policy Venues. In *Rethinking Advocacy Organizations*, edited by A. Prakash and M. K. Gugerty, 177–200. Ann Arbor: University of Michigan Press.

Putnam, R. D. 2000. *Bowling Alone: The Collapse and Revival of American Community.* New York: Simon & Schuster.

Ramakrishnan, S. K., and I. Bloemraad, eds. 2008. *Civic Hopes and Political Realities: Immigrants, Community Organizations, and Political Engagement.* New York: Russell Sage Foundation Press.

Ramakrishnan, S. K., and T. J. Espenshade. 2001. "Immigrant Incorporation and Political Participation in the United States." *International Migration Review* 35 (3): 870–909.

Ramakrishnan, S. K., and C. Viramontes. 2006. "Civic Inequalities: Immigrant Volunteerism and Community Organizations in California." San Francisco: Public Policy Institute of California.

——. 2010. "Civic Spaces: Mexican Hometown Associations and Immigrant Participation." *Journal of Social Issues* 66 (1): 155–73.

Ramírez, R., and J. Wong. 2012. "Nonpartisan Latino and Asian American Contactability." In *Transforming Politics, Transforming America: The Political and Civic Incorporation of Immigrants in the United States* (Race, Ethnicity, and Politics), edited by T. Lee, S. K. Ramakrishnan, and R. Ramírez, 151–74. Charlottesville: University of Virginia Press.

Reckhow, S. 2012. *Follow the Money: How Foundation Dollars Change Public School Politics*. New York: Oxford University Press.

Rhodes, J. 2012. *An Education in Politics: The Origins and Evolution of No Child Left Behind*. Ithaca, NY: Cornell University Press.

Rignall, K. 1997. "Building an Arab-American Community in Dearborn." *Journal of the International Institute* 5 (1). http://hdl.handle.net/2027/spo.4750978.0005.106.

Robbins, S. M. 2010. "Play Nice or Pick a Fight? Cooperation as an Interest Group Strategy at Implementation." *Policy Studies Journal* 38 (3): 515–36.

Roelofs, J. 2003. *Foundations and Public Policy: The Mask of Pluralism*. Albany: SUNY Press.

——. 2007. "Foundations and Collaboration." *Critical Sociology* 33 (3): 479–504.

Rogers, R. R. 2006. *Afro-Caribbean Immigrants and the Politics of Incorporation: Ethnicity, Exception, or Exit*. Cambridge: Cambridge University Press.

Ross, E. A. 1913. "American and Immigrant Blood: A Study of the Social Effects of Immigration." *Century Magazine*, December, 225–32.

Rouse, S. M. 2013. *Latinos in the Legislative Process: Interests and Influence*. New York: Cambridge University Press.

Rubenzer, T. 2008. "Ethnic Minority Interest Group Attributes and US Foreign Policy." *Foreign Policy Analysis* 4 (2): 169–86.

Sandfort, J. 2008. "Using Lessons from Public Affairs to Inform Strategic Philanthropy." *Nonprofit and Voluntary Sector Quarterly* 37 (3): 537–52.

Sandoval, C. 2010. "Civic and Political Activism: Understanding Immigrants in Civil Society." University of Chicago, Mobilization, Political Change, and Civic Engagement.

San Miguel, G., Jr. 2013. *Those Who Dared: Ethnic Mexican Struggles for Education in the Southwest since the 1960s*. College Station: Texas A&M University Press.

Saul, S. 2012. "Looking, Very Closely, for Voter Fraud." *New York Times*, September 16, A1.

Schattschneider, E. 1960. *The Semi-Sovereign People*. New York: Holt, Reinhart, and Winston.

Schlozman, K. L., and J. Tierney. 1986. *Organized Interests and American Democracy*. New York: Harper & Row.

Schmidt, R., Y. M. Alex-Assensoh, A. Aoki, and R. Hero. 2013. *Newcomers, Outsiders, and Insiders: Immigrants and American Racial Politics in the Early Twenty-First Century*. Ann Arbor: University of Michigan Press.

Schneier, M. 2012. "Why American Jews and Muslims Backed Obama by Huge Margins." On Faith, November 9. http://www.washingtonpost.com/blogs/guest-voices/post/why-american-jews-and-muslims-backed-obama-by-huge-margins/2012/11/09/70a671c6-2ac0-11e2-bab2-eda299503684_blog.html.

Selee, A. 2013. *What Should Think Tanks Do? A Strategic Guide to Policy Impact*. Stanford, CA: Stanford University Press.

Sheehan, R. M. 1996. "Mission Accomplishment as Philanthropic Organization Effectiveness: Key Findings from the Excellence in Philanthropy Project." *Nonprofit and Voluntary Sector Quarterly* 25 (1): 110–24

Sherman, J. 2012. "Bachmann Finds Friends Back Home." *Politico*, July 23. http://www.politico.com/news/stories/0712/78830.html.

Sides, J., and L. Vavreck. 2013. *The Gamble: Choice and Chance in the 2012 Presidential Election*. Princeton, NJ: Princeton University Press.

Silver, M. 2012. "Unique Billboard Voter Registration Campaign in Georgia." *Epoch Times*, September 25, 1.

Skocpol, T. 1999. "Associations without Members." *American Prospect*, December 19. http://www.prospect.org/cs/articles?article=associations_without_members.

Skocpol, T., M. Ganz, and Z. Munson. 2000. "A Nation of Organizers: The Institutional Origins of Civic Voluntarism in the United States." *American Political Science Review* 94 (3): 527–46.

Skocpol, T., and V. Williamson. 2012. *The Tea Party and the Remaking of Republican Conservatism.* New York: Oxford University Press.

Smith, A. C. 2012. "Alan Grayson Trying to Knock Out John Quinones." *Tampa Bay Times*, August 7. http://www.tampabay.com/blogs/the-buzz-florida-politics/content/alan-grayson-trying-knock-out-john-quinones.

Smith, J. 1997. "Nonresponse Bias in Organizational Surveys: Evidence from a Survey of Groups and Organizations Working for Peace." *Nonprofit and Voluntary Sector Quarterly* 26 (3): 359–68.

Sommerhauser, M. 2012. "Bachmann Accuses Muslim House Member of Brotherhood Ties." *USA Today*, July 20. http://usatoday30.usatoday.com/news/politics/story/2012-07-20/bachmann-brotherhood-comments/56370300/1.

Star-Ledger Editorial Board. "Bill Pascrell, Not Steve Rothman, Should Get Ninth District Congressional Seat." *Star-Ledger* (New Jersey), May 27. http://blog.nj.com/njv_editorial_page/2012/05/bill_pascrell_not_steve_roth.html.

Steil, J. P., and I. B. Vasi. 2014. "The New Immigration Contestation: Social Movements and Local Immigration Policy Making in the United States, 2000–2011." *American Journal of Sociology* 119 (4): 1104–55.

Stevens, D., and B. Bishin. 2011. "Getting Out the Vote: Minority Mobilization in a Presidential Election." *Political Behavior* 33:113–38.

Strolovitch, D. 2006. "Do Interest Groups Represent the Disadvantaged? Advocacy at the Intersection of Race, Class, and Gender." *Journal of Politics* 68 (4): 893–908.

Su, R. 2012. "Urban Politics and the Assimilation of Urban Immigrant Voters." *William and Mary Bill of Rights Journal* 21 (2): 653–89.

Suárez, D. F. 2009. "Nonprofit Advocacy and Civic Engagement on the Internet." *Administration & Society* 41 (3): 267–89.

Swasko, M., and T. Gregory. 2011. "Naperville Not Putting Out Welcome Mat for Islamic Religious Center." *Chicago Tribune*, October 7. http://articles.chicagotribune.com/2011-10-07/news/ct-met-naperville-mosque-20111007_1_islamic-center-naperville-s-planning-naperville-planning.

Tafoya, B. 2012. "Rep. Walsh's Comments Infuriate Muslims." CBS Chicago, August 10. http://chicago.cbslocal.com/2012/08/10/rep-walshs-comments-infuriate-muslims/.

Taylor, P., M. H. Lopez, J. Martínez, and G. Velasco. 2012. "When Labels Don't Fit: Hispanics and Their Views of Identity." Pew Research Center, April 4. http://www.pewhispanic.org/2012/04/04/v-politics-values-and-religion/.

Teles, S. M. 2009. *The Rise of the Conservative Legal Movement.* Princeton, NJ: Princeton University Press.

Thompson, F. 1920. "Schooling of the Immigrant." New York: Carnegie Corporation of New York.

Toqueville, A. 1898. *Democracy in America.* New York: Century Co.

Truman, D. 1951. *The Governmental Process: Political Interests and Public Opinion.* New York: Alfred A. Knopf.

Uhlaner, C., B. Cain, and D. R. Kiewiet. 1989. "Political Participation of Ethnic Minorities in the 1980s." *Political Behavior* 11 (3): 195–213.

Vanderkooy, P., and S. J. Nawyn. 2011. "Identifying the Battle Lines: Local-National Tensions in Organizing for Comprehensive Immigration Reform." *American Behavioral Scientist* 55 (9): 1267–86.

Varsanyi, M. W. 2006. "'Getting Out the Vote' in Los Angeles: The Mobilization of Undocumented Migrants in Electoral Politics." In *Latinos and Citizenship: The Dilemma of Belonging*, edited by S. Oboler, 219–46. New York: Palgrave Macmillan.

Vaughn, S. K., and S. Arsneault. 2014. *Managing Nonprofit Organizations in a Policy World*. Washington, DC: CQ Press / Sage.

Verba, S., K. L. Schlozman, and H. Brady. 1995. *Voice and Equality: Civic Voluntarism in American Politics*. Cambridge, MA: Harvard University Press.

Vieldmetti, B. 2013. "Milwaukee Man Gets Jail Time for Voting Twice in Presidential Election." *Milwaukee-Wisconsin Journal Sentinel*, October 17. http://www.jsonline.com/news/crime/milwaukee-man-is-sentenced-to-jail-term-in-voter-fraud-case-b99122337z1-228189351.html.

Wald, K. 2008. "Homeland Interests and Hostland Politics: Politicized Ethnic Identity among Middle Eastern Heritage Groups in the United States." *International Migration Review* 42 (2): 273–301.

Walker, J. L., Jr. 1991. *Mobilizing Interest Groups in America: Patrons, Professionals, and Social Movements*. Ann Arbor: University of Michigan Press.

Webb, C. 2002. "The Lynching of Sicilian Immigrants in the American South, 1886–1910." *American Nineteenth Century History* 3 (1): 45–76.

Weidenbaum, M. 2009. *The Competition of Ideas*. New Brunswick, NJ: Transaction.

Weissert, C. S., and J. H. Knott. 1995. "Foundations' Impact on Policy Making: Results from a Pilot Study." *Health Affairs* 14 (4): 275–86.

Weldon, S. L. 2012. *When Protest Makes Policy: How Social Movements Represent Disadvantaged Groups*. Ann Arbor: University of Michigan Press.

Wells, C. 2015. *The Civic Organization and the Digital Citizen: Communicating Engagement in a Networked Age*. New York: Oxford University Press.

Wilson, C. 2011. "Immigrant Nonprofit Organizations and the Fight for Comprehensive Immigration Reform." *Nonprofit Policy Forum* 2 (2): 25.

Wilson, S. 2011. *Melting Pot Modernism*. Ithaca, NY: Cornell University Press.

Wirt, F. M. 1991. "'Soft' Concepts and 'Hard' Data: A Research Review of Elazar's Political Culture." *Publius* 21 (2): 1–13.

Wong, J. 2006. *Democracy's Promise: Immigrants and American Civic Institutions*. Ann Arbor: University of Michigan Press.

Wong, J., P.-t. Lien, and M. Conway. 2005. "Group-Based Resources and Political Participation among Asian Americans." *American Politics Research* 33 (4): 545–76.

Wong, J., S. K. Ramakrishnan, T. Lee, and J. Junn. 2011. *Asian American Political Participation: Emerging Constituents and Their Political Identities*. New York: Russell Sage Foundation.

Wright, J. R. 1996. *Interest Groups and Congress: Lobbying, Contributions, and Influence*. New York: Addison Wesley.

Wyszomiriski, M. J. 1998. "Lobbying Reform and Nonprofit Organizations: Policy Images and Constituent Policy." *Policy Studies Journal* 26 (3): 512–25.

Zia, H. 2001. *Asian American Dreams: The Emergence of an American People*. New York: Farrar, Straus and Giroux.

Zunz, O. 2014. *Philanthropy in America: A History*. Princeton, NJ: Princeton University Press.

Index

Note: *c* indicates material by chapter; *f* indicates material in figures; *n* indicates material in notes; *t* indicates material in tables.

CPSIA information can be obtained at www.ICGtesting.com
Printed in the USA
BVOW02s2343110916

461717BV00003B/25/P